Wonderful walks

from
dog-friendly campsites

on a budget!

Anna Chelmicka

Hubble & Hattie

Anna Chelmicka
1948–2024
Unstoppable adventurer

www.hubbleandhattie.com

First published 2025 by Hubble & Hattie, an imprint of David and Charles Ltd, c/o Veloce office: 2 Poundbury Business Centre, Middle Farm Way, Poundbury, Dorchester, DT1 3WA England.
Tel 01305 260068/e-mail info@veloce.co.uk.
ISBN: 9781787119444 © Anna Chelmicka & David and Charles Ltd 2025.

Contents

Introduction

I love to travel about the UK and Europe in my motorhome with my dogs, finding interesting walks and exploring the countryside. The first dog that accompanied me on my travels was Ruby, and later her daughter Amber joined us.

For the walks in the second book of this series, *More Wonderful Walks from Dog-friendly Campsites near Pubs* I was accompanied by Pearl. She is a very special dog because she is the direct descendent, the great granddaughter, of my wonderful dog Ruby, and the granddaughter of Amber.

It was Ruby who helped me recover from a life changing illness and adjust to the changed circumstances in which I found myself. As I slowly adapted to my new situation, Ruby was always there, supporting and encouraging me. She was such a special dog and had a profound effect on my life. My first book, entitled *My Friend Ruby*, is about her. When Ruby had her second litter I kept the darkest bitch, She was a rich golden colour so it seemed appropriate to call her Amber.

For several years the three of us, Ruby, Amber and I, had a wonderful time travelling in my motorhome all over Europe: Switzerland, Italy, Poland, Germany, as well as France and Luxembourg. We also travelled extensively throughout the UK tramping all over the countryside.

Pearl exploring the countryside.

Ruby and Amber in Italy.

Pearl and I carried on the tradition of travelling about in my motorhome exploring the UK and Europe, finding walks and enjoying the countryside, especially whilst researching my three *Wonderful Walks ...* books. Recently, Pearl and I have been accompanied by her son Pippin. He too loves going out and about in the motorhome.

We have discovered some amazing places. It made me realise just how special the British countryside is and how fortunate we are to be able to access so much of it.

Anna Chelmicka

Motorhoming and walking

Over the past few years public interest in motorhomes has increased enormously. There was a notable spike in 2020 and 2021 due to the Covid pandemic when the trend was for 'staycations' while there were restrictions on foreign travel. This resulted in a shortage of motorhomes at the time, as demand outstripped supply. Consequently there was a steep rise in the cost of motorhomes. This trickled down to the second hand market, where prices have also increased significantly.

Though the worst of the pandemic is now, thankfully, a memory, many people have indicated they will continue to take their holidays in Britain. This has resulted in a continued interest in caravans and motorhomes, so prices are still quite high and stocks are still low, which has surprised industry experts. Many of those who have ordered a new motorhome have had to wait several months for delivery. Hopefully this will not always be the case.

There are several reasons for the increase in popularity of motorhomes. The often quoted ones are:

- The freedom it allows you to go anywhere, any time
- You can take your pets
- It is quick and easy to set up and pack up
- Frequently used items can be left in the vehicle when not in use
- Packing is easier as it is bigger than a suitcase!
- As the name implies, it is a 'home'; familiar, with favourite and comfortable possessions all around
- It even has all the necessary facilities that make it self-sufficient, allowing you to camp off grid

A common activity for many motorhomers is to tour around visiting various places and to wild camp en-route. At the time of writing, the most popular tour in the UK is the N500. This scenic 516 mile (830km) route zigzags around the north coast of Scotland, starting and finishing at Inverness Castle. It is not an easy drive as many of the roads meander about and are very narrow.

The route was only created in 2015 as a marketing strategy by the Tourism Project Board of the North Highland Initiative (NHI). The aim was to consolidate tourist provision and support local businesses in the less popular areas of Scotland, namely

Caithness, Sutherland & Ross-shire. It has proved to be enormously successful, as it seems to be on every motorhomer's wish list.

The marketing strategy achieved its aims, in raising the profile of the less visited areas of Scotland. In fact it was so successful it has acquired an iconic status almost equivalent to that of Route 66 across the United States. It became a 'MUST DO' expedition. The growth in motorhome hire has allowed many people to cross this off their 'to do' list, as it was an easier and cheaper option than some of the more exotic foreign destinations. Then, when the pandemic restricted overseas travel, more people became interested in this new home-grown tourist attraction. Its popularity has increased to such an extent there are concerns as to its continued viability.

The increase in the number of visitors has resulted in an economic upturn in the region, but this has mostly been confined to the larger cities and towns rather than the rural areas. In fact, in some instances it has had a detrimental effect. Instead of people renting a holiday home and spending a few days in the vicinity motorhomers whizz through, sometimes stopping over for just one day.

Of course there has been a significant increase in traffic on the roads, which has had a huge impact. Journeys now take longer, especially in the summer, which irritates the local population. Because the country roads that form much of the N500 were not made to cope with such an increase in the volume of traffic, frustrations are evident in the rise in incidences of bad and even dangerous driving. In fact there has been an alarming increase in the number of accidents and deaths on these roads.

Then there is the environmental impact; not just on the air quality due to the fumes from so many more vehicles, but also damage to the environment. Tyre marks have ruined various places and, to my mind even worse, some visitors have emptied their waste where they have wild camped. Motorhomes may be self-sufficient, but every few days the water needs to be replenished; the waste water disposed of and the toilet cassette cleaned out. This should be done at a campsite or designated area, not in a public place. Ugh!

This is one of the reasons why I, personally, rarely wild camp. More crucially for me as a solo traveller I feel vulnerable pitching up in some remote location. Should anything happen I have no one with me to help. Secondly, the driving is totally my responsibility. Being able to appreciate the scenery as I pass is impracticable as I have to concentrate on the road, especially as it will be unfamiliar. Looking for somewhere to pull over and park up is an additional stress for me I can do without. My preference is to drive directly to a campsite, then I can chill out beside the motorhome (drink in hand), wander along country paths with a four-legged companion, and leisurely explore the local surroundings with my dogs (as seen on Channel 5 *Million Pound Motorhomes* S4 E2).

I decided to get a motorhome so I could take my wonderful dog Ruby with me when travelling about. Camping with a motorhome seemed the perfect solution as she could come too. Ruby has long gone, but I still go out with my dogs; her great-granddaughter Pearl, and her great-great grandson Pippin. What facilities there are for dogs is therefore still a significant factor in ascertaining a good campsite.

The quest to find suitable campsites is still as difficult now as when I first acquired my motorhome, even with the colossal amount of information now available on the internet.

Wonderful walks from dog-friendly campsites on a budget

Yes, there are many references to dogs. However, these are mostly only with regard to them being welcome. Occasionally in the small print, mention is made of a dog exercise area, but rarely is any other information offered.

But off I go to research. It is very hit and miss. Sometimes there is nothing specific for dogs; it is just that the campsite allows dogs on site. On other occasions dog exercise areas are provided. These are as equally unpredictable. Some are just the size of a postage stamp, other sites have small wooded areas or large grassed fields with plenty of space for dogs of all sizes to walk and chase balls. Then again others have nothing specifically designated for dogs, but are near fields or parks where dogs can be exercised.

There are even some campsites that provide washing facilities for dogs so they can be cleaned up before entering the living space. Personally, I rarely use such a facility, but I can see this as being useful especially if the ground is wet and muddy. If my dogs are dirty I put some water in a bucket, wash them with a sponge, then rub them down with a towel. Labradors are easy to clean as they are what I call 'Teflon' dogs: with their short coats the dirt and wet easily rubs off.

Unfortunately, it isn't until I arrive and book into a campsite that I know if the dogs are going to be as well catered for as I am. Generally I only book a site for a couple of days a short time before setting off. If the dogs and I find it unsuitable we then move on, if, however it exceeds our expectations we extend our stay.

Having a dog, especially one as active as a Labrador, necessitates lots of walking. I do not want to break camp and prepare the motorhome for a journey to find suitable, interesting walks for the dogs and then afterwards drive back and re-pitch. This rather spoils an outing. So over time I have added the close proximity of footpaths to my wish list of campsite requirements.

Looking closely at OS Maps I noticed some campsites were very close to footpaths and bridleways and quite long walks seemed possible. The problems I encountered trying to find really good sites for dogs were replicated trying to find sites close to walking trails. Unfortunately, yet again, there was little information and few instructions about any walks in the locality of the campsites, even though in the intervening years the internet has improved enormously. Again, while walks were sometimes mentioned, more detailed information was rarely forthcoming until registering at a campsite. But by then of course this information, though useful, was too late.

Once I had found a campsite that suited the dogs I put the location into the OS Maps search box to bring up the appropriate map. From this I could see what footpaths, bridleways and trails were nearby. It was really useful in helping me make an informed decision, but it was very time consuming and convoluted. Even then sometimes the choice proved to be unsuitable. Footpaths might be so overgrown that they were unusable or they had simply disappeared. At other times the trail was on a minor road which was very busy and made for unpleasant walking. Occasionally there were no stiles or gates and accessing the route required scrambling over walls and fences. Every now and then the campsite was further away from the footpaths than appeared on the map. Even so, I did find some excellent sites and lovely walks of varying lengths. I also discovered parts of the country that were totally new to me.

I have travelled about in the motorhome with my dogs having a marvellous time researching for my previous two walking books, "Wonderful Walks from Dog-friendly Campsites throughout the UK" and "*More* Wonderful Walks from Dog-friendly Campsites throughout the UK near Pubs". It has taken a considerable amount of time and effort but has provided me with the opportunity to discover some remarkable places in the UK, which are not on the tourist trail, to appreciate the diverse environments to be found in Britain and to meet some incredible people.

Seeing my work in print has been exhilarating and exciting. Hearing that people have enjoyed my books and found them useful is extremely satisfying. This third volume was researched and written at the request of some of my readers, who wanted to enjoy the same camping and walking experiences, with their canine companions, on a limited budget.

I hope you enjoy this book as much as the others, find it useful, agree that they are indeed 'Wonderful Walks', and have as much fun as I have had with all my dogs, Ruby, Amber, Pearl and Pippin.

Happy walking!

Respecting the countryside

In this country we are very lucky to have access to so much of the countryside. This is a consequence of the 1949 National Parks and Access to the Countryside Act. Many, many people were involved in ensuring this legislation was ratified. Its objectives were to protect the countryside and to ensure that it was free for all to enjoy. This was to be achieved with the establishment of National Parks and other agencies such as nature reserves.

As times have changed and circumstances altered, so over the years the Act has been modified. Nevertheless the basic principles have remained the same.

So, as stipulated by the UK Government's guidelines regarding 'Rights of Way and Accessing Land' (see www.gov.uk), walkers have the right to:

- Access some land for walking
- Use public roads and pavements or public right of ways such as footpaths or bridleways
- Use the 'right to roam' on open access land such as mountains and moors, etc
- Access private land if the landowner gives permission
- Access private land if there is a local tradition or right of access

The 'Rights of Way and Accessing Land' information on the UK government website gives more detail as to the exact entitlements and restrictions for walkers, horse-riders or outdoor users. See Appendix i.

In Scotland the Outdoor Access Code is slightly different.

The Land Reform (Scotland) Act came into force in 2003. This established a statutory right of responsible access over most areas of land and inland water.

The main messages from the Scottish Outdoors Access Code (SOAC) are:

- Take responsibility for your own actions
- Respect the interests of other people
- Care for the environment.

Essentially there are very few restrictions as to where you can walk, ride a bicycle, swim, canoe, kayak or wild camp in Scotland's countryside. The Scottish law leaves it for individuals to use the countryside as they wish, while respecting their surroundings, the land, people and, most importantly, leaving it in perfect condition for others to also use. See Appendix i for details.

These extensive and, to my mind, amazing and unique rights over our land carry with it huge responsibilities. These are set out in the Country Code.

Shortly after the 1949 act was passed it was decided that officially formulated guidance was needed for those accessing the land, even though common sense mostly sufficed. So in 1950 a Country Code was devised, with the most recent modification being in 2012.

So, when walking please do observe the Country Code, which states:

RESPECT OTHER PEOPLE
- Consider the local community and other people enjoying the outdoors
- Leave gates and property as you find them and always try to follow paths and trails.

PROTECT THE NATURAL ENVIRONMENT
- Leave no trace of your visit, and take your litter home
- Keep dogs under effective control

ENJOY THE OUTDOORS
- Plan ahead and be prepared
- Follow advice and local signs

See Appendix i for the full and detailed Country Code.

So, enjoy the right we have to explore our wonderful, diverse countryside and appreciate it, but do remember your responsibilities and adhere to the Country Code.

You also have the responsibility to keep yourself safe. Though we do not have any dangerous animals in the UK, such as wolves (yet) or bears, there are dangers. The weather, for example, can, in an instant, change a pleasant outing into an emergency, especially if walking in the hills and more remote parts of the country. Also, accidents can happen. It is advisable to follow the motto of the Scouts and Guides and "be prepared".

The walks in this book are not especially challenging so it is easy to be prepared and stay safe. My suggestions are not definitive or applicable to all situations, and they will certainly not prevent accidents, but they will help and hopefully allow you to enjoy the walks more.

Maps

The maps of each walk in the book are not very detailed as they use the copyright free OS Open Data maps. It is absolutely essential that you have the relevant Ordnance Survey Map preferably OS Explorer Map. (Google Maps is not detailed enough). This can be either a paper map or a digital one. To keep myself safe I carry both.

In today's digital age there are many other ways of accessing OS maps. I personally still buy and use the paper version. As I have been walking all over the UK I have a shelf full of Explorer maps, many of which have become quite tatty with use.

Paper maps should be used for several reasons:

Wonderful walks from dog-friendly campsites on a budget

- The walk can be seen in context of the surrounding locality.
- If the view is extensive it is possible to identify distant landmarks with a map of a larger area.
- It is possible to turn a paper map in the direction of the walk. Digital devices usually automatically turn the maps back to a North South orientation when the device is turned around.
- With a paper version there are no worries of the battery running out.
- Also, having a signal is not a necessity. In more remote areas the lack of a signal is a fairly regular occurrence.

Nowadays, OS maps supply not only paper maps but also digital maps. It provides a range of products and services to suit various devices. This is THE go to place for mapping needs..

To access OS Landranger and Explorer maps digitally an annual subscription is necessary. This also entitles OS maps to be downloaded onto other devices via the OS Map App. This is brilliant; a SatNav for walkers. The OS Map App itself is free but some of the features such as Explorer and Landranger Maps need to be purchased. Also available to purchase are dedicated GPS units with Landranger or Explorer maps of the whole of the UK together with a variety of accessories. More information about Ordnance Survey maps and the services they provide can be found on their website.

Surprisingly, Ordnance Survey maps have a long history. The department was first set up as part of the Board of Ordnance way back in the 1700s during the reign of George lll, and its task was to provide detailed maps to the military that would be useful in times of war. There was a very real threat of invasion by Napoleon in the late 1700s. The defending forces needed very detailed information of the south coast area of England.

It was in 1801 that the first 1 inch to the mile map was produced. This was of the county of Kent. Thus began the mapping of the country using the effective Principle of Triangulation which has resulted in the trig points on the top of so many of the hills. It took many, many years and a veritable army of people to produce the maps. Over time other people and organizations discovered just how useful the maps were. Eventually, in the 1900s maps were produced for the leisure market and general public. These became extremely popular especially with walkers, and as early as the 1970s Ordnance Survey began producing leisure metric maps.

Today, Ordnance Survey Maps, or OS Maps as it has recently been rebranded, produce two kinds of detailed maps for outdoor enthusiasts: the Landranger Series and the Explorer maps. The one with the purple cover is the Landranger with a scale of 1:50,000 which means that every 1cm on the map represents 500m on the ground. The series with the orange cover is the Explorer Map with a scale of 1: 25,000. This means every 1cm on the map is 250m on the ground. These Explorer Maps are by far the best for walking as they show more detail, including field boundaries.

The service the Ordnance Survey offers is unique. It continues to embrace new technology to improve the products it is able to offer the general public. Therefore it is important that we support OS Maps so it can continue with the work it does.

Mobile phone

Nowadays mobile phones greatly reduce risks if used properly, especially for walkers. As a lone walker it is a vital piece of equipment. When setting out make sure your phone is fully charged. Be aware, that some places have no signal or only a weak one. If you use apps on the phone, such as mapping or fitness monitoring, you need to be especially watchful of the battery usage. There are various options to ensure your battery lasts. For example, you can carry a powerbank. Some will allow you to re-charge your phone two or even more times whilst on the go. If excursions are inclined to be long the weight and physical size of the powerbank is a significant factor. Alternatively you can take a dedicated phone with a pay-as-you-go sim card just for calls and texts.

So keep safe. Take a mobile phone with you which has enough battery charge to last for your excursion irrespective of the length of the outing and the size of the group.

Clothing

Although expensive specialist attire is not necessary for general walking it is essential to wear sensible clothing. Trousers are a better option than shorts even if it is hot for protection against prickly plants and stinging nettles. They need to be comfortable and if possible of a light material so that, unlike denim, if they get wet they will not become too heavy and so dry quickly. It is best to wear several layers of thinner garments as this is easier to adjust for a sudden spell of warm weather. I find it useful to take a wool hat, scarf and gloves in case the temperature suddenly drops. It is surprising how much this helps. Of course rain gear is nearly always a requirement as there are often rain clouds just over the horizon. The one item that is vital is appropriate footwear. Designated walking boots or shoes are essential. They support the foot and have a good grip crucial for muddy and uneven surfaces. Most outdoor shops sell a range of specialized walking footwear from the incredibly expensive to the reasonably priced.

Check weather

Some people proclaim "the UK doesn't have climate only weather". This is because conditions change so much, not just from day to day but from hour to hour. Even though walking in this country is generally an everyday humdrum pastime, it can on occasion turn into an extremely unpleasant or even dangerous activity, if the weather should become inclement. I do not like walking in the rain and mist. I do too much of this type of walking on a regular basis with the dog. I much prefer it to be clear, and if possible, sunny when I can see more and really appreciate the variety and beauty of the countryside.

Nowadays, with access to a variety of weather forecast apps and programs in various devices, it is much easier to ascertain the weather hour by hour as opposed to the usual daily forecasts. Also as technology has enabled the gathering of more data and made the tracking of weather patterns easier so the forecasts have become more accurate.

So, before setting out, check the weather!

Too often people venture out unprepared, and the Mountain Rescue Teams or Coastguards have to be called out. On two occasions when I have stayed at Glen Nevis Campsite at the foot of Ben Nevis I have witnessed possible emergency incidents. One even involved a helicopter which hovered dangerously close to the mountain side. I have to confess to it being thrilling to watch, like a film. I did not discover the outcome on either occasion. I assume all was well.

If you stay at Glen Nevis Campsite do go down the road to the Ben Nevis visitors' centre. It is unlike any other visitors' centre. It is extremely interesting and informative with the emphasis on being safe outdoors. There is a section on maps and navigating, the weather and also one on appropriate clothing. There is also a large section about the Mountain Rescue Teams. These are made up of volunteers who go out in all conditions to find those walkers who get into difficulties. I was astounded to discover how many times they are called out, not only to Ben Nevis but also generally. To avoid being a Mountain Rescue statistic assess the conditions before setting out. However, should you need assistance it is extremely helpful to all concerned if your precise location is known. This can easily be done if you have a smart phone with the OS Map App and the What3Words App which gives an accurate grid reference for the emergency services to use.

Control dogs

This country has another exceptional tradition, and that is to be allowed to take our dogs to so many places with so few restrictions. It is not like this in many other countries. It is therefore the responsibility of all dog owners to ensure they have control over their pets and do not annoy or upset others or in any way jeopardize our current freedom.

Owners need to help their dog be confident and relaxed with other strange dogs. At the very least they need to tolerate passing dogs. This is essential on campsites and narrow footpaths. Sometimes space is quite cramped and dogs have to pass quite close to each other. I find it distressing when dogs react aggressively, barking ferociously and snarling as Pearl and I pass by along the accepted route. On the other hand it is wonderful when Pearl finds a new companion to play with.

It is generally recognized as a necessity to have the dog on a lead at certain times; for example near livestock, especially sheep. When it comes to larger animals how the dog is managed depends on the circumstances. My present dog Pearl thinks horses are large dogs and wants to play with them so she becomes rather skittish which is not sensible behaviour. Ruby, however, was frightened of them as her first close encounter with a horse was beside an electric fence which she accidently touched. As a consequence she was wary of all horses and stayed well clear. I was happy to let her off a lead in a field of horses.

Again the situation with regard to cattle depends upon circumstances. I have been reassured many times that cattle are harmless except when cows have calves and one accidently gets between the mother and her offspring. Generally the presence of a dog merely arouses their curiosity. Unfortunately I have had some frightening experiences. Having ten or more cows crowding round is alarming. It is not unknown for walkers to be trampled to death by a herd of cows.

Advice is conflicting. On the occasions I have found myself in a field of high-spirited horses or cows I have quickly moved towards the edge of the field by a fence or hedge. The self-preservation instincts of animals causes most cows and horses to slow down so as not to injure themselves by charging into the hedge or fence. This usually gives some space and time to move rapidly to the exit. I have scrambled over many a gate and stile shoving the dog ahead of me. If the situation looks tense I let the dog off the lead as they can undoubtedly move much faster than me and can generally out-run or out-dodge the cattle. I am extremely cautious when I encounter livestock. I rarely take Pearl into a field with cows.

When out and about with your dog it is important to know them well. It is also extremely important to be able to control your dog both on and off lead. In my opinion the best way to really understand your dog and learn how best to control them is to train them.

Training dogs is not something done only when they are puppies, it should be a continual ongoing process. I took Ruby to classes every week for most of her life. She loved it. She really enjoyed doing all the exercises and learning new tricks even when she was quite old. Pearl is very young. She too likes attending her classes and like Ruby is clever, but she is a very different dog. She loves agility, especially running through the tunnels.

Because my dogs have all been so good and well behaved I feel confident taking them with me in the motorhome and exploring the countryside. I have travelled extensively over the UK and even been to several countries on mainland Europe.

Having a well trained dog that responds to commands makes outings more pleasurable for both you and your dog.

Another responsibility of dog owners, which I am happy to say is usually adhered to, is the removal and disposal of dog mess in an appropriate waste bin. Unfortunately, it has become commonplace for the bags of dog faeces to be either tossed into the hedges, hung on branches of trees or left on the side of tracks and footpaths. A disgusting and most objectionable habit. Firstly, it is an environmental act of vandalism. Not only does it spoil the countryside but it takes many years for the bag and its contents to decay, even if the bag is biodegradable. Secondly, it is extremely selfish and inconsiderate. There is no provision for these bags to be collected and properly disposed of, and quite rightly there are few volunteers for such an unpleasant task. This has become such an issue in recent months that MPs have joined the debate.

So as not to walk several miles carrying a bag of dog poo, which no one likes to do, the "stick and flick" method is recommended as an option by some organizations, including the National Trust. The idea is to find a stick and flick the mess out of the way into a verge or hedgerow. This is not an ideal remedy, but it is far better than bags of poo decorating the trees and hedges and littering the countryside.

With so many people taking their dogs with them when walking, the inclusion of the "Dog Walking Code of Conduct" is becoming more customary in public spaces. The Kennel Club has always offered such advice. (See Appendix i). Nowadays other organizations are reminding dog owners of their responsibilities. The most succinct and inclusive one I have come across is the one advocated by the Pembrokeshire Coast National Park in the events magazine *Coast to Coast*, as follows:

Wonderful walks from dog-friendly campsites on a budget

Pembrokeshire Coast National Park 'Dog Walking Code of Conduct'

LOOK AFTER YOUR DOG:
- Keep your dog close and in sight- on the lead if necessary and always if it won't recall immediately to you.
- Make sure your dog wears a collar, identification disc and is micro-chipped.
- Don't allow your dog near cliff edges, rough seas or strong tidal currents.
- Think of the weather – on hot days cars and beaches can be too hot for dogs.

LOOK AFTER OUR COAST AND COUNTRYSIDE:
- Always pick up your dog's mess; this is a legal requirement on beaches and places where people walk and play.
- Take your bagged dog waste home or put it in a litter bin.
- Ensure your dog is on a lead near farm animals and doesn't approach or chase birds or other wildlife.
- When cattle are present keep your dog on a lead unless you feel threatened – in which case let your dog go and make your way to safety.
- Follow signs and abide by byelaws such as dog restrictions on beaches.
- Keep your dog to the path when walking in the countryside.

BE CONSIDERATE OF OTHERS:
- Show respect for other people and their dogs.
- Keep your dog away from horse riders, cyclists and picnics.
- Don't allow your dog to bark excessively.

Remember that not everyone likes dogs, especially small children.

Having an obedient four-legged companion, for me, adds an extra dimension. It is really enjoyable discovering the many wonderful places in this country. Having been given so many rights in regard to exploring the countryside, we must all make sure we fully accept and fulfil our responsibilities.

Campsites

Just as each person is unique and yet part of the human race, so campsites come in all shapes and sizes, are distinctively different, and yet have a commonality. At one end of the spectrum are those sites which are just a flat field with maybe a tap, while at the other extreme are the all-singing, all-dancing campsites providing a whole range of amenities, sometimes even fitness centres and spa facilities, and which are more like holiday parks. However, most campsites are somewhere between these extremes.

There are two main organizations that cater specifically for anyone who likes camping. They are the Camping and Caravanning Club and the Caravan and Motorhome Club. Over the years these clubs have grown from very small beginnings to the large organizations they are today, offering a whole range of services to their members. Both clubs own and run a considerable number of campsites located throughout the country. These have a specific, easily recognized 'modus operandi', which has resulted in well-designed sites with premium facilities for showering, washing dishes and doing the laundry, etc, in a neatly kept and attractive setting. The wardens are always helpful and efficient. These campsites are usually the yardstick by which all others are judged, even though they rarely have additional facilities such as bars, cafés or swimming pools.

A number of smaller independently owned campsites are affiliated to these two main clubs. The Camping and Caravanning Club call them CS (Certificated Sites), the Caravan and Motorhome Club CL (Certified Locations). They are often located in secluded places, near beaches, on working farms or beside pubs. Again, just like larger more commercial campsites they vary enormously in the facilities they offer; some are very basic, offering little more than a tap and chemical disposal provision; others are more comprehensive offering electric hook-up, toilets and showers.

In order for these smaller campsites to be certified by either of the two clubs they have to fulfil a strict set of criteria. These include pitches being at least 20ft (6m) apart; a maximum stay of 28 days; no caravan should be unoccupied overnight; no more than five units on site at any one time, and all visitors must be a member of the appropriate club. Though these campsites are endorsed by the relevant club, the owners are responsible for the bookings and the prices charged. There are an enormous number of CS and CL sites to choose from all over the UK. Information about them can be found on the websites of the Camping and Caravanning Club and the Caravan and Motorhome Club.

As campsite requirements are particular to each individual site, reviews are not always helpful, whereas facts are. I have endeavoured to provide information about each campsite. Because I have two dogs the suitability of the site for them is of paramount importance. Also as we all like walking (especially my dogs) it is also vital there are footpaths close by to allow us to explore the countryside.

So, what I look for in a campsite:

- Dogs are welcome
- A flattish space for the motorhome. While I prefer it to be grass, in wet weather this can become so soft the motorhome becomes bogged down and stuck. This is not a pleasant experience!
- Nearby footpaths to explore the countryside
- Electric hook-up so I have the luxury of using my electrical appliances, especially the heater in the winter, and, of course, to charge various devices. As technology develops there is more and more demand for electricity. A solution for those who like wild camping is to have a solar panel. I prefer the ease of an existing electric supply.
- Toilet block so I don't have to empty my cassette so often
- Showers that are more spacious than mine in the van
- Wi-Fi or mobile signal, so I can listen to podcasts and plan the next stage of the trip

If I am lucky the following amenities will be on site or nearby, to increase the comfort quotient:

- A dog exercise area large enough to give the dog a stretch first thing in the morning and last thing at night, or to chase a ball or frisbee
- A shop where provisions can be replenished
- A café to indulge in delicious cakes, or a pub for a good pub meal
- A TV connection, which can be an enjoyable distraction on occasion

I rarely go to holiday parks, as they are generally too big. Because I am a solo traveller with dogs I am not able to use many of the additional services provided for entertainment. However, these parks may be preferable for young families, and might include some of the following facilities:

- Swimming pool
- Children's play area
- Fitness centre
- Spa facilities
- Horse riding outings
- Crazy golf
- Evening entertainment such as bingo or live shows
- Animal petting
- Bar and/or restaurant
- Clubhouse to host a range of entertainment activities

The combination of amenities and facilities to be found on campsites is vast, making each place quite distinctive. One of the pleasures of travelling about is seeing how a campsite description corresponds to reality, and discovering the special characteristics of each site.

I am happy with campsites that are well managed and maintained similar to the 'club' campsites. Not all the campsites I visited were of this standard, but they did all have electric hook-up, toilets and showers, while a few had other facilities, such as a shop. Similarly the facilities for dogs varied. These are appraised by Pearl in the 'Pearls of Wisdom' sections.

Fees for campsites are just as variable as the campsites themselves. How the fees are constructed also varies. Casually researching some campsites to visit I was startled to discover how expensive it can be for a night for a pitch; some were in excess of £50.00. Camping holidays are usually thought of as a cheap option, but not so at this price. I was intrigued, especially as there appeared to be a steep rise in campsite fees. This has been attributed to the pandemic and the high cost of energy. I thought more investigation of campsite fees was necessary.

When I found what appeared to be a suitable campsite to visit I checked out the charges. To get as accurate a picture as possible I selected several dates to include off season, a bank holiday and the summer months. This sounds quite straightforward but with so many different ways of charging for a pitch it has proved to be extremely convoluted and complicated. You need to be a whizz kid to make sense of the different charges and select the best deal for a particular time of the year. The situation is made even more difficult in that some campsites don't display the charges on their websites.

There seems to be four main ways campsites set their prices:

1. Flat rate. The simplest is a flat charge which includes the unit, two adults and electric hook-up (EHU). For Bank Holidays and the summer months this system is often good value.
2. Itemized. Another method is to itemize each element. This includes a separate charge for the pitch, adults, children, awnings, dogs, electric and any other facility available. This system favours solo travellers like me, but can be extremely expensive for families.
3. Seasonal. Many campsites also adjust their charges during the year. Some only have two variations; High Season/Low Season. Some have as many as four price variations; Low/Mid/High and Peak season.
4. Complicated. These different ways of calculating charges can be further adapted by:
    ◦ type of unit.
    ◦ type of pitch, grass, hardstanding, super or premium
    ◦ number of adults or children
    ◦ extras, eg dogs and awnings (sometimes electric is an extra)

All these different factors make it very difficult to establish the final charge.

The two Clubs and the National Trust use the third option (an individual charge for each element) as well as a different price band for a section of the year. As stated,

Wonderful walks from dog-friendly campsites on a budget

this benefits solo travellers, but becomes rather expensive over the bank holidays and during the summer months. Non-members can use Club sites, but they pay an additional premium which makes it even more expensive. A bonus is that there is no charge for dogs. Some other campsites do charge for having a dog. This can be anything from £1.00 to £5.00 a night for each dog.

There are no common factors to indicate which system campsites use when setting their fees. Usually, though, smaller campsites with fewer facilities charge a flat fee. Though this may be a bit expensive during the colder months it is often a cheaper option during Bank Holidays and the summer months. Sometimes the price varies slightly depending on the extras, eg awnings or dogs etc.

Larger campsites with extensive facilities are primarily catering for families, so they generally charge an all-inclusive rate, for example: unit+EHU+2 adults+2 children, with sometimes even a dog included. Usually this charge is significantly more during the school holidays. With this method solo travellers are disadvantaged, though occasionally it will be considerably cheaper out of season, as many of the facilities are closed down

Then for me, there is the issue of dogs. I cannot understand why there should be a fee for a dog and why some campsites charge so much. Then there may be a restriction on numbers of dogs campsites will accept. This too varies considerably. Many campsites have a limit of two dogs. Those with more than two dogs should phone ahead, as some campsites do occasionally make exceptions to this rule. Other sites have no restrictions at all. Again, check this when booking.

I have noticed a recent trend for what are usually referred to as 'super' or 'service' pitches. This is generally a hardstanding area with all the services supplied right to it. So on the perimeter of the hardstanding is a water tap, electric hook-up, TV connection, Wi-Fi signal and a waste drain. Again there is a surcharge for such pitches. As with campsites which provide swimming pools or bars etc, these additional provisions are an enjoyable luxury, but not ones I require. Frequently these pitches are charged at a premium rate.

It appears the increase in interest in caravans and motorhomes has resulted in raised expectations of both campsites and vehicles. Some motorhomes are very luxurious, and quite large and expensive. My own is modest and rather old. Although I prefer a simpler experience, I do like a bit of convenience or luxury with electric hook-up, toilets and showers.

For this book I looked for campsites that had suitable facilities for me and the dogs, are near footpaths with plenty of places to walk, and offer good value for money.

Because of all the different ways of calculating the cost of a pitch, I've set a benchmark against which to compare the various costs of a pitch. The actual charge of each individual campsite (at time of writing) can be found in Appendix ii at the back.

£:   excellent value for money
££:   very good value (my benchmark)
£££:   good value
££££:   fair
£££££: expensive, but by no means the dearest. These campsites are exceptional in some way, so worth a visit (although maybe just a short one).

Because of the various ways the cost of pitches is calculated, I have classified the pricing structure as follows:

1. Flat rate (no change throughout the year)
2. Flat rate/seasonal (flat rate changes according to time of year)
3. Itemized (a charge for each component; eg pitch, electric, per adult etc)
4. Itemized/seasonal (charges are itemized and change according to the time of year)
5. Complicated (difficult to establish how charges were calculated)

After the campsite report and 'Pearls of Wisdom' I've given each campsite:

- a value for money £ rating
- a pricing structure classification
- pros and cons summary

Of course, campsites change their fees from year to year, particularly if they have upgraded amenities. So the only way to be certain of the charges is to check on the website or phone the campsites directly beforehand, and to do this again at the time of booking.

Have fun camping and walking with your dog, and I hope the information given here helps you better understand the pricing system and how to get the best value for your money.

Finding the walks

The campsites in this book are located throughout the UK, which has been divided into seven regions; three or four areas from each region have been selected for exploration:

- **Wales**
Camarthenshire, Gwynedd, Monmouthshire

- **North East**
Lincolnshire, North Yorkshire, Northumberland

- **North West**
Cheshire, Cumbria, Lancashire

- **Central**
Herefordshire, Nottinghamshire, Oxfordshire

- **South East**
Bedfordshire, Berkshire, Suffolk

- **South West**
Cornwall, Devon, Dorset, Wiltshire

- **Scotland**
Fife, Lothian, Skye

Two extra campsites have been included for the South West, because they are particularly special. So, the book comprises 23 campsites with detailed instructions for 46 walks.

Each of the following chapters covers one of these regions. The campsites and the accompanying walks are in alphabetical order of the county.

To begin, there is a brief summary of the unique characteristics of the county followed by a description of the campsite. Then there is the most important section, 'Pearls of Wisdom' in which my dog Pearl shares what she thinks of the campsite and walks, giving a dog's eye view.

Following this are step-by-step instructions for the walks with a map for each. First is the short walk of between 4-6 miles (6-10km), and then the instructions for the longer walk, which is intended to take a whole day, between 8-11 miles (13-18km).

The final section in each chapter is a brief account of the activities and attractions in the immediate vicinity, within an approximate 10 mile (16km) radius of the campsite. It may be possible to walk to some of them though there is not always a convenient walking route.

The campsites and walks have been purposely selected to illustrate the huge variety and diversity to be found in the UK. There are campsites with just basic facilities as well as some with a range of services. Similarly the walks traverse a range of landscapes.

All these walks are possible with dogs, and if they are well behaved the jaunts are easier and more enjoyable. The dogs need to be agile to manage the stiles, fences and walls, and there is the very occasional sheep-proof stile which may require a helping haul and shove for them to get over if they are too big to lift.

These walks are not particularly challenging as most of the routes are along tracks and across fields. However, a reasonable degree of fitness is necessary and a moderate level of stamina as there are stiles and gates to climb over and some quite steep hills. Consequently these walks are not suitable for pushchairs or wheelchairs. As for children, parents need to decide which walks are appropriate for their child.

Bear in mind that although the walk descriptions were correct at time of writing, some changes to the route may have occurred since, such as updated signposts, changes to access, or newly created pathways. It is always sensible to carry an up-to-date map, or a mobile phone with GPS, and check up-to-date timetables for those routes that incorporate a bus or train journey.

This book can be used to plan your dog-friendly camping and walking adventures in various ways:

- For a weekend break, going to just one campsite and doing the walks from there
- For longer trips of about a week and exploring a specific region, visiting all three campsites and doing all nine walks
- For planning an extended expedition: visiting several regions and choosing a selection of campsites, walks and attractions from each area
- You could even combine your trips with some from the other two books in this series. All three books provide a range of ideas for camping, walking and exploring the UK.

Walks in Wales

(Camarthenshire, Gwynedd, Monmouthshire)

Carmarthenshire – A hidden gem

OS MAPS: EXPLORER 178 LLANELLI & AMMANFORD/RHYDAMAN

The county of Carmarthenshire in Wales is somewhat overlooked, being situated between the popular tourist areas of Pembrokeshire in the west and The Gower in West Glamorgan. With the motorway ending at its eastern border, many tourists either drop off southwards to the beaches of the Gower or power across it to the more popular seaside places on the western coast of Wales.

It cannot even boast an iconic mountain range. With only the foothills of the Cambrian Mountains slipping across the northern border and the famous Brecon Beacons spilling over the northeast border, Carmarthenshire has only gentle rolling hills instead of stunning peaks and views. In addition it is sandwiched between two rivers: the River Loughor with its long wide estuary that forms the border with Glamorgan to the east, and the River Teifi to the north which marks the border with Ceredigion. Also of note is the The River Tywi, special in that its entire course is in Wales, which flows through the middle of the county and out into Carmarthen Bay. The southern border of the county is a long tortuous coastline due to the two immense estuaries.

One of the amazing beaches of Pembrey in Camarthenshire.

However Carmarthenshire does have the distinction of being known as the 'Garden of Wales'. Precisely why is not clear, perhaps because it is the home of the National Botanical Gardens of Wales, or because it is a farming county and produces top quality food, or it just because the landscape is so green and luscious looking. Why is irrelevant, because the county has much to offer.

In addition to the National Botanical Gardens there are many other interesting gardens dotted all over the county. With agriculture being a mainstay there is plenty of green open space. There are the woods, ancient forests and amazing beaches, not forgetting the various historical buildings; so plenty to do and discover.

It was to Carmarthenshire that Wales' most famous poet and writer, Dylan Thomas, retreated to recuperate and write after his exploits and tours, even though he had been born in neighbouring Glamorgan and spent a considerable time elsewhere in the world. After his first visit at the age of 19, it was to Langharne, on the coast overlooking the estuary of the River Tar as it flows into Carmarthen Bay, that he returned, finding solace with his family and inspiration to continue writing. For the last four years of his life he lived with his wife in the Boathouse, along with the Writing Shed above, where he worked inspired by the views of the three estuaries. Access was along a footpath which ran parallel to the coast and down some steps.

The Boathouse is a simple place, so visits are usually short. The Writing Shed is not actually open, with the interior only visible through a glass door, but it is understandable how the amazing outlook fuelled Dylan's creativity. Today Langharne is as bustling and vibrant a place as it was in 1948 when Dylan moved there. Both he and his wife are buried in St Martin's cemetery.

The town of Carmarthen is the capital of the county, strategically located on the banks of the River Tywi as it meanders down to the sea. It is one of the oldest towns in Wales having been an important regional capital of the Romans, and the gateway to west Wales. The Welsh name of the town is Caerfyrddin which means 'Merlin's Fort', conjuring up images of Welsh mythology – wizards, dragons, heroes and heroines – yet also a vibrant, modern fascinating place. There is lots to discover and this can be done via the 13 walks suggested on the local council website, another hidden gem like the county it represents.

PEMBREY COUNTRY PARK CAMPSITE

This campsite is not to be confused with the Caravan and Motorhome Club site a mile to the east. The bonus for this site is that it is actually in the Country Park and so the Park amenities are to hand. At the entrance is a licensed restaurant which allows dogs, and various activities such as a miniature railway or crazy golf, all just a short stroll away.

This is a large campsite with 320 grass pitches of different kinds; some seasonal, some fully serviced, some with only electric hook-up, and others just a pitch; so it caters for a wide range of campers including tents. Obviously the charges vary according to the pitch type. The pitches are large so it does not feel too cramped, and because it is divided into sections it does not feel excessively large. The amenities block is near the entrance so is quite far from some of the pitches. It was adequate, but I imagine it might be stretched when the site is full. Similarly, it is a popular site with families because of all the activities

Wonderful walks from dog-friendly campsites on a budget

on offer, so during the school holidays it gets very busy. The bonus of this campsite is the easy access at the rear of the site into the woods which has miles of trails and the proximity of a fabulous sandy beach. Again, do check, as dogs are restricted from parts of the beach during July and August.

PEARLS OF WISDOM 🐕

Oh wag my tail; what a fab-u-lous place. Through a gate straight into the woods. On and on and on; so many different ways to go and so much to inspect. Then surprise, surprise there was the beach with clumps scattered about to have a good nose around. Running and trotting on this yellow stuff was odd; sometimes firm sometimes slipping away from my paws; all so exciting and being able to have the occasional swim was fantastic. The outing to the lighthouse was okay; too much hard black stuff not enough grass. Would love to go again and find more trails in the woods.

RATING: £££

PRICING STRUCTURE (SEE CHAPTER 3) – VARIABLE

PROS:
- Good location
- Café, restaurant and activities walking distance
- Adjacent to large woods
- Near beach
- Plenty of places nearby to walk dogs

CONS:
- Variable price according to pitch and season
- Amenities block some distance away
- No food shop
- Very busy during school holidays

The dogs loved the beach because there were lots of interesting clumps to sniff!

'HUNTING THROUGH THE WOODS FOR THE BEACH' ROUTE

SHORT WALK – HUNTING THROUGH THE WOODS FOR THE BEACH
Distance: 6mi (9.6km)
Duration: 3.5hr (Easy)
Terrain: Footpaths, tracks, sandy paths, woods, beach

Section 1: 1.5mi (2.4km)
- Exit campsite via the gate into the forest, situated at the opposite end of the campsite entrance access road, passing a play area on the left
- Turn right along path, passing campsite on right, then turning left opposite another entrance to campsite
- Follow path across junction into Pembrey Forest, by noticeboard, onto wide track
- Continue along path across next junction
- Turn left just after passing picnic tables on left, onto narrow path winding through the woods, under two bridges and out to wide track

Section 2: 1.5mi (2.4km)
- Turn right along track, then right again at next junction
- Turn left at next junction onto wide grass track
- Go straight ahead at next junction on wide, straight, long track with many hoof prints, passing orange post No 3 out to the road
- Turn left along road, then left again onto wide earth track, by orange post No 6
- Straight on at first junction (orange No 9) and second junction (orange No 13)
- Turn left at third junction (orange No 18), then sharp right on track winding through woods, up and down slope (sandy) out to stony track with road visible on right

We found a bear! Is there another one over there?

- Turn left passing orange No 21 on right
- Turn right at picnic table, then up the sandy track, bearing left (orange No 19)
- Go straight across stony track, passing orange No 23 on left, onto grass track, passing yellow No 28 on left, then up slope to T-junction (yellow No 29)

Section 3: 2mi (3.2km)
- Turn left along long straight sandy track, turning right at third junction and passing picnic tables
- Go straight on at bend, up steep very sandy slope, through woods, and over sand dunes to the beach
- Turn left along beach, turning left again at large red noticeboard (CE 58)

Section 4: 1mi (1.6km)
- Bear left up slope (across dunes), then turn right down to road
- Turn along road, then right by orange bins to T-junction
- Turn right along wide track, ignoring all paths off, passing adventure playground, and miniature railway on left
- Turn left along gravel path, close to wooden fence of railway on right
- Bear left across green to campsite entrance.

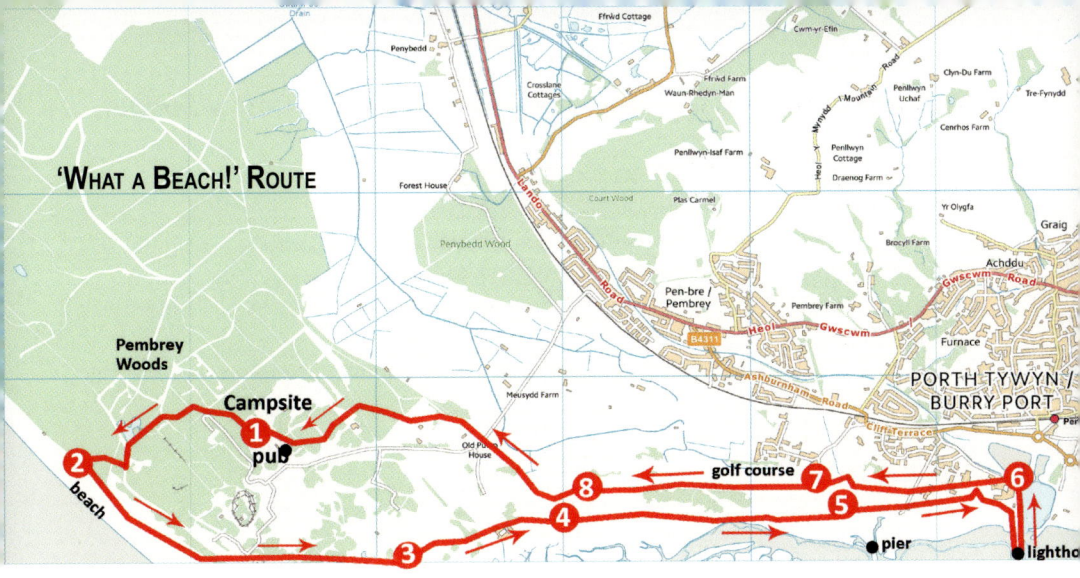

'WHAT A BEACH!' ROUTE

LONG WALK – WHAT A BEACH!
Distance: 7.5mi
Duration: 3.5hr (Easy)
Terrain: Tracks, woods, beach, cycle path, roads (quiet), golf course (balls)

Section 1: 0.75mi (1.2km)
- Exit campsite via the gate into the forest, at the opposite end of the entrance access road, passing a play area on the left
- Continue straight ahead along wide track to junction, turning left
- Go straight on across two junctions, bearing right at large wooden bear sculpture
- Turn left at next junction, signposted green No 8, keeping close to fence on right
- Turn left, then sharp right, signposted green arrow along wide earth track, passing fence on right, steps on left out to open space with noticeboard at foot of large mounds (sand dunes)
- Turn left from noticeboard along green track to another noticeboard on right
- Turn right onto sandy path, up and over sand dunes, taking left fork down steps to the beach

Section 2: 1mi (1.6km)
- Turn left along amazing beach to noticeboard CE53 (+ additional small sign 'no horses this way')
- Turn left uphill off of beach

Section 3: 0.75mi (1.2km)
- Go straight ahead along narrow sandy path to small car park
- Continue through car park along access road to left bend

Section 4: 1.25mi (2km)
- Bear right between two huge stone slabs onto wide gravel path – Wales Coastal Path
- Follow track with sea on right

- If feeling adventurous, drop down to beach at sea wall on right of huge boulders; bear right onto narrow path with sea on right
- Follow path parallel to coastal path, keeping close to sea wall, crossing inlet either via small stones or boulders of sea wall (if high tide this may not be possible)
- Turn left 50yd (45.7m) after last boulder onto narrow sand path going uphill onto coastal path turning right
- Continue along path across wide junction (detour along right path to Pembrey Harbour Pier)

Section 5: 1mi (1.6km)
- Continue along path through car park to path opposite, passing caravan park on left
- Take right fork down to beach
- Turn left along sand path close to dunes on left out to wide track
- Turn right passing lighthouse on right, out to promontory
- Retrace steps passing lighthouse, harbour walls, picnic area and Burry Port Yacht Clubhouse (possible refreshments) and boats, on left

Section 6: 0.75mi (1.2km)
- Turn left along Wales Coastal Path, left again at junction, then right, passing caravan park on right
- Cross car park onto coastal path opposite (Paths off to right lead to a pier, which is interesting to visit)

The leisure boats in Burry Port.

- Turn right at junction (leading to pier) onto tarmac path
- Turn left at next junction onto stony track
- At bend, continue straight onto grass path with white post on right, to cross golf course

Section 7: 1mi (1.6km)
- Take wide grass path bearing slightly left, as several times it crosses gravel path used by golfers (watch for flying balls) out to road
- Turn left along road

- ## Section 8: 1mi (1.6km)
- Turn immediately right along coastal path, along verge of road, up slope onto coastal path, signposted
- Bear left passing archery entrance on left and huge model bike on right
- Take right fork at junction along access road (be aware of traffic)
- Turn left at right bend down through barrier
- Follow road to large open space, bearing right to campsite entrance

IN THE VICINITY
CYCLING
There are plenty of trails in the forest, around the Country Park and along the Millennium Coastal Path. It is also possible to hire bicycles at the Ski & Activity Centre.

GOLF
On the outskirts of Burry Port just two miles away is Ashburnham Golf Club; a championship course. The club welcomes visitors during the week. For information see the club's website.

PEMBREY COUNTRY PARK
Spread across some 500 acres (200ha) of parkland, Pembrey Country Park has something for everyone and is a popular destination. In addition to the campsite there is a visitors' centre, a café, adventure play areas, which do not allow dogs, and a miniature railway. Because the campsite is located in the Park, there is easy access to the amenities, including:
Crazy Golf
The crazy golf course is near Pembrey Country Park and Beach car park 1
Pembrey Ski and Activity Centre
A short distance from the campsite is this dry ski slope where you can also go 'Tubing'
Pembrey Forest
This is one of the UK's rare dune forests, with pine trees planted on the sand dunes during 1929 and 1954 to replace the trees that were used for timber in the two world wars. Situated next to the Park and the campsite, this amazing forest has miles of tracks to follow, some leading to the golden sands of the beach. Besides the abundance of wildlife to be seen, there are also relics of the war: ammunition dumps, bunkers and pillboxes, as well as train lines.

Wonderful walks from dog-friendly campsites on a budget

BURRY PORT

Just three miles (4.8km) from the campsite is this coastal town, which, from 1948, was an important harbour. In 2000 it was upgraded to a marina, so now the fishing boats are outnumbered by leisure crafts. Jutting out from the town into Carmarthen Bay is the striking lighthouse, while on the other side of the marina is the RNLI station. Burry Port's claim to fame is the visit by Amelia Earhart in 1928. A memorial recording this is situated on Stepney Rd.

LLANELLI

This is the largest town in the county and is only five miles from Burry Port. At one time the major economy was steel and coal mining, and, although this has declined, there is still some steel fabrication industry, primarily for packaging. The surrounding rural areas are used for mostly sheep and dairy farming.

Gwynedd – The Welsh speakers' county
OS MAPS: EXPLORER OL 18 HARLECH PORTHMADOG & Y BALA

The unique feature of Gwynedd county is that it has the largest concentration of Welsh speakers: over 64%, so is considered the heartland of the language. This is probably due to its geography, being situated in the northwest corner of Wales, hemmed in by sea to the west and north. The mountainous range of Snowdonia sweeps from the southwest across the county to the northeast, where it tumbles down towards the sea, leaving just a fairly flat sliver of coastal strip. Thus this region is isolated from the rest of Wales.

Like many mountainous areas, Snowdonia's landscape has many peaks and valleys. Initially glaciers carved out the valleys, but these are now filled with burbling streams, plummeting waterfalls, and rivers plunging down to the coast. The area was considered so important that in October 1951 it was designated Snowdonia National Park, encompassing a staggering 827sq mi (2140sq km) of countryside. It was the first National Park in Wales, but the third in Britain, and is now one of 15. It is named after the highest peak, Snowdon, at 3560ft (1085m).

In February 2023 the names have been changed into Welsh so it is now Parc Cenedlaethol Eryri (Snowdonia National Park) and Yr Wyddfa (Mt Snowdon). A two year transition period has been agreed with English in brackets, but I think it will take longer than this for printed publications to fully adjust.

The name may have changed, but this has not altered the landscape. There are still nine mountain ranges, which include all of the 15 mountains of Wales (including, of course, Snowdon). A peak is classified as a mountain if it is at least 2000ft (600m) above sea level. The 1995 film *The Englishman Who Went up a Hill and Came Down a Mountain*, starring Hugh Grant and Colm Meaney, was based around this idea, although set in south Wales.

Snowdonia National Park (Parc Cenedlaethol Eryri) is also littered with lakes of various sizes, again due to the movement of glaciers across the landscape many millennia ago. Some of the lakes are so large they are used as reservoirs. Then there are pockets of woodland scattered about the region, many with native trees such as oak, ash and rowan. In

The mountains of Snowdonia sweep down towards the sea.

sharp contrast to this are the 74 miles of stupendous coastline with beaches and shores as striking as any hill or mountain. All of which contributes to the variety and diversity of the area and wildlife, not immediately evident at first, but also representative of the county itself.

History records Gwynedd as a significant territory of the Principality of Wales, maintaining its independence against all comers, including the Romans, until the late 13th century when King Edward I finally, by 1283, gained control of it, the last remaining Welsh principality, building castles at Caernarfon and Harlech. Even so, the local population was able to preserve the Welsh traditions and culture, partly due to the secluded environment. During the Industrial Revolution the problematic terrain did not impede the development of huge quarries for slate. But as far as agriculture was concerned, Snowdonia (Eryri) was really only suitable for the farming of hardy sheep.

Nowadays, though the slate industry is still important, it greatly reduced in size during the 20th century. Similarly with agriculture; small family farms are unsustainable so have merged into larger concerns that employ fewer people. However, just recently there has been an increase in the film and television industry, with offices relocating to the area.

Tourism is important here, as there are approximately four million visitors a year. This is understandable with so many outdoor activities available, especially in the National Park. In addition there is the rack-and-pinion railway which clambers up Snowdon. This was opened in 1896, and reaches a height of 2927ft (892m) – a much easier way to climb the mountain. Then there is the Mediterranean-style village of Portmeirion, designed by Sir Clough-Williams Ellis and used as the location for filming the 1960s TV series *The Prisoner*. Information about the village needs to be obtained beforehand, as there is a charge to visit, and dogs are prohibited. And of course there are the castles to visit.

Wonderful walks from dog-friendly campsites on a budget

So Gwynedd has plenty to offer the visitor, but because it is such a popular holiday destination the downside is that it can be rather expensive. The more reasonably priced alternatives quickly become fully booked.

LLECH CAMPSITE

The campsite is situated in Snowdonia National Park at the end of a narrow country lane, and the views of the mountains are incredible, although surprisingly the immediate surroundings are very flat. This is because it is on the banks of the River Dwyryd as it snakes across the huge estuary on its way to the sea, thus allowing easy access to an extensive coastal area. Beware, at high tide there is only a small strip of water-free land beside the access road. This makes for an unusual and fascinating daily happening that can be safely viewed from the benches near the entrance.

This is a small campsite with just 13 pitches. Stretched out along one side of the first field are seven pitches with electric hook-up. The remaining six pitches are around the perimeter of the adjoining field. Levelling blocks are useful, as the fields slope slightly. The amenities block has very recently been modernized, and the two unisex shower rooms are enormous. There is a dish-washing area and, most usefully, considering the proximity of the coastal plain, a dog wash area. It is a well organized and efficiently run campsite.

The campsite on the banks of the River Dwyryd surrounded by fields of sheep.

PEARLS OF WISDOM 🐾

It's that smell again, sort of tangy and salty – water. I hope it's swim time. Funny, we didn't swim, but there was a lot of water about in puddles and troughs and the ground was very squishy. It was fabulous dashing about, leaping over ditches and things, exploring with my son. We did get very wet and muddy, and I didn't like the dog wash! Next time we went out, how strange: there was water almost up to the road, but not really deep enough for swimming. There were lots of other interesting places to explore, but again I could have done without so many sheep. They seem so stupid, but not as frightening as cows.

RATING £££
PRICING STRUCTURE; (SEE CHAPTER 3) – FLAT RATE/VARIABLE
PROS:
- Simple easy pricing (two seasons. High July/Aug only)
- Excellent value during weekends
- Good location
- Shop on site
- Bus stop nearby
- Helpful staff

CONS:
- Levelling blocks useful
- Lots of sheep
- Popular site, booking essential

SHORT WALK – CHALK AND CHEESE
Distance: 4mi (6.4km)
Duration: 2hr (Moderate)
Terrain: (There is a possibility of sheep at any stage on this walk; be vigilant) Footpaths, dykes, fields, tracks, trees, gates, kissing gates, some steep climbs, roads (mostly quiet/one busy, take care)

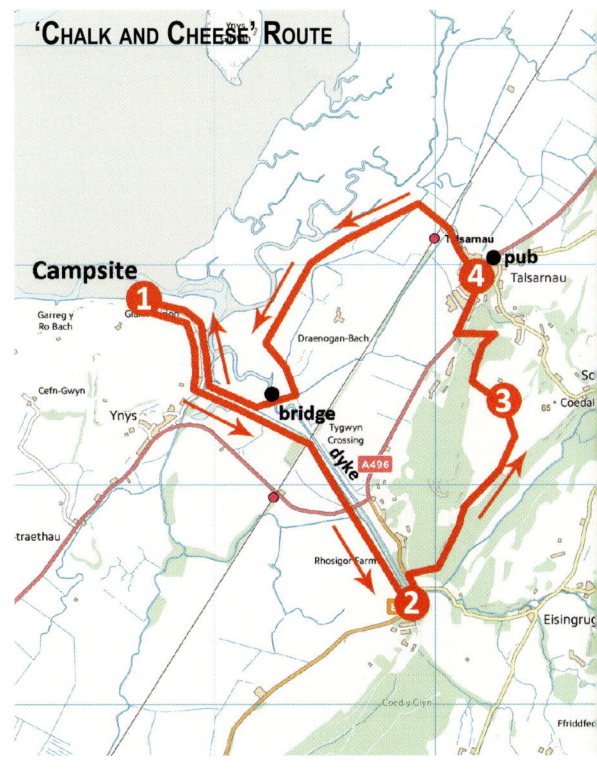

'CHALK AND CHEESE' ROUTE

Section 1: 1.25mi (2km)
- Exit campsite via entrance
- Follow road round right bend to house, passing footpath signpost on right
- Turn left immediately past house, signposted, through gate onto wide grass dyke (beware, possibly sheep) passing amazing bridge on left, through three wooden gates to cross rail-line
- Go straight on through gate, round pipeline on left, along grass dyke through kissing gate out to road

One of the wide grassy dykes in the valley of the River Dwyryd.

- Cross road, through kissing gate opposite, still on grass dyke, through second gate, cross track through third gate opposite, still on grass dyke, out to road

Section 2: 1mi (1.6km)
- Turn left across bridge, round left bend, through gate on right into field, signposted
- Bear right, uphill across field into trees, along stony path bearing right through broken gate
- Go straight on, still climbing, to derelict stone walls on right
- Turn right into space created by walls, then left along grass path, through gate into woods
- Bear left, zig-zagging uphill on to wide grass path, climbing steadily to top
- Turn left over boulders onto grass path
- Take left fork along narrow path (views)
- Continue along path downhill, go through gap in wall
- Bear right onto track beside wall on right, then left towards barns, through gap in wall into field
- Bear left through gap in wall on left, crossing field through gap ahead

Section 3: 0.75mi (1.2km)
- Bear right onto wide grass path through gate
- Cross track through second gate opposite, onto access road to junction
- Turn right uphill, then left onto narrow path, signposted, on to footpath

- Continue downhill along path to A496
- Turn right along road (pavement is narrow in places), towards pub (good place for refreshments if open)

Section 4: 1mi (1.6km)
- Turn sharp left immediately before pub, signposted railway station
- Follow winding road passing play area on left
- Continue straight ahead at bend to cross rail-line (take care) onto wide track
- Turn left immediately after stile (sheep proof) to dyke onto wide stony track (this was easier for us because of several sheep gathered around a difficult stile)
- Follow the path parallel to dyke on left, round left bend, up onto dyke by kissing gate on left
- Continue along grassy dyke, turning right down steps at stile
- Go straight on, over large wooden footbridge, up to top of dyke
- Turn right towards house, through kissing gate out to road
- Turn right along road to campsite entrance

LONG WALK – TO THE CASTLE
Distance: 8.5mi (13.6km)
Duration: 5hr (longer if visiting castle)
Moderate
Terrain: footpaths, fields, woods, tracks, steps, gates, kissing gates, stiles (lots of sheep proof stiles and gates in Section 5 & 6; some are problematic to cross), roads (mostly quiet), mostly flat

Section 1: 1.25mi (2km)
- Exit campsite via entrance along road towards house
- Turn right before house, through gate into field
- Bear left along edge of field with wall on left, go through gate on left into second field
- Bearing right, continue along edge of field with fence now on right, over large stone steps in right corner
- Continue along edge of field, keeping high stone wall ahead on right

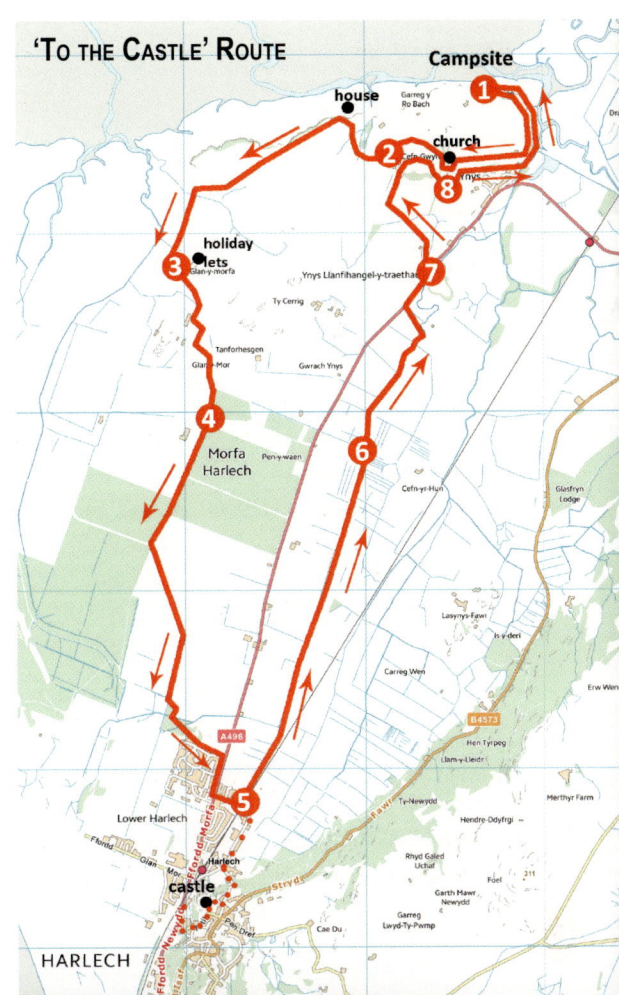

'TO THE CASTLE' ROUTE

- Follow wall round to left, through gate in wall and out to access road (St Michael's Church)
- Go straight on, passing church entrance on right, following wall round to right, and turning sharp left down steps to waymarker
- Turn sharp right, bearing left, to steep steps ahead through gate into field
- Bear right uphill to cross field, passing waymarker on left, to fence at corner on right
- Turn left at corner, keeping close to fence on left
- Turn left at next fence corner, still with fence on left
- Bear slightly right, passing house on left, downhill through gate to access road

Section 2: 1mi (1.6km)
- Bearing right, follow access road, taking left fork winding down towards house
- Turn left onto grass path immediately after crossing brook, with gully on left
- Bear right towards bushes, onto narrow footpath winding through bushes, then take path parallel to sea on right
- Follow path through kissing gate, past small hill on right, through kissing gate
- Continue ahead, passing small hill on left through second kissing gate
- Bearing right follow path, keeping hill on left, through kissing gate, and passing farm on left

Section 3: 1.mi (1.6km)
- Bear slightly right along stony track, passing holiday homes on left, through gate onto access road
- Continue along road, through gate on right after barns
- Turn immediate left through kissing gate into field
- Bear right across field, through gate, continue bearing right towards telegraph pole, through another kissing gate in left corner
- Go straight on along edge of field, passing buildings on right, through kissing gate
- Cross road, bearing right though barrier onto concrete track to junction

Section 4: 1mi (1.6km)
- Turn left through kissing gate into field; cross through kissing gate opposite
- Cross field through gate in left corner
- Cross field towards gate opposite, turning right along edge of field, with fence on left, over footbridge, through kissing gate and onto footpath between trees
- Follow path over footbridge through trees, passing houses on right, into lane leading to road
- Turn right along A496, crossing at pedestrian crossing
- Turn right then immediate left, along wide track towards rail-line
- Turn left before rail-line through gate into field

Although Harlech Castle is only 0.5mi (0.8km) along the A496, the entrance to it is up a very steep winding hill. Unusually, dogs on leads are allowed on the ground floor levels.

Harlech Castle dominates the surrounding countryside.

The beautiful sandy beaches of Harlech are 0.75mi (1.2km) from the A496, near the railway station along Ffordd Glan-Mor. There are also two places for refreshments: one in the castle, and the other, Caddy Café, is at the bottom of the steep climb to the castle. Most of the streets of Harlech, around the castle, are very narrow and very steep.

- From the castle car park, turn into Ffordd Pen Llech
- Follow road downhill to junction
- Turn right along Hwylfar Nant to T-junction, turning left to cross rail-line

Section 5: 1.5mi (2.4km)
- Turn immediately right through kissing gate into field
- Continue straight ahead, along edge of field with rail-line on right, to rail access gate
- Bear left across field, through gate ahead into field
- Continue straight ahead along edge of field, parallel to stream on left, through gate into another field
- Go straight on, keeping close to stream on left, along edge of next eight fields, out to track (Most of the stiles are sheep proof but only the odd one is a bit challenging. The gates are not well maintained and some are difficult to open)

Section 6: 1mi (1.6km)
- Cross track to field opposite, continue along path with stream on left, into second field
- Follow stream across next two fields, through gates or over stiles as necessary
- In fifth field, follow stream as it winds across field, crossing it via an earth bridge
- Go straight on through gate opposite, following stream now on right
- Turn sharp left at earth bridge, crossing field to kissing gate opposite, out to road (Take care, busy road)
- Turn right along road turning first left along cul-de-sac

Section 7: 0.75mi (1.2km)
- Follow road uphill through Gwyn Farm
- Turn right along stony track, through gate into field
- Bear right to fence corner, continuing straight ahead keeping close to fence on right to next corner
- Bear right down hill, through gate, down steps
- Turn right, then left, up steps

Section 8: 1mi (1.6km)
- Turn right keeping close to church wall on left, through gate round left bend into field
- Cross field to left corner, over stone steps
- Go straight on along edge of field, close to hedge on left, through gate along edge of next field onto track
- Follow track through gate to road
- Turn left along road to campsite entrance

IN THE VICINITY – HARLECH
FISHING
Fishing on the estuary is difficult because the water comes in at different times and heights. It is easier 7mi (11.2km) upstream near the village of Maentwrog but a permit might be necessary. Ask at campsite reception for details.

GOLF
One of the best golf courses is on the outskirts of Harlech Royal St David's Golf Club. Visitors come from all over the world to play on the famous greens. Go online to book a round.

PUBLIC TRANSPORT
There is a bus which runs from the village of Ynys on the A496 just 0.5mi (0.8km) away. The trains that run from Pwllheli to Machynlleth stop at Talsarnau Station just 1.5mi (2.4km) from the campsite along an easy pleasant footpath. Ask at reception for details.

FFESTINIOG RAILWAY

This heritage train starts at Porthmadog which can be easily reached from Talsarnau Station near the campsite. It is a rare narrow gauge railway, which, in the course of its 13.5mi (21.7km) journey, climbs over 700ft (213m) through some amazing landscape to the small town of Blaenau Ffestiniog.

ST MICHAEL, YNYS

This church is on a knoll behind the campsite on the route of the long walk. It is a most unusual church in an unusual place, and well worth a visit. When it was built it was surrounded by the sea at high tide. Since the 12th century the tide has receded and it is now inland. It has been refurbished several times and has several interesting graves: the builder's mother, a Lord Harlech, author Richard Hughes, alongside ordinary sailors and their families. The church is also the start of a 4.5mi (7.2km) pilgrimage trail to St Tecwyn's church, Llandecwyn.

HARLECH CASTLE

This was built by Edward I between 1282 and 1289. Over the centuries it played a significant role in various skirmishes until 1647 when the victorious armies attempted to destroy it. They were not very successful, leaving the impressive ruins that there are today and now managed by the Welsh government. It is a fascinating place to visit and dogs are allowed on the lower levels.

PORTMADOG

On the other side of the estuary is this relatively new town having been created from 1810-1811. It is one of the largest towns in Snowdonia with an interesting assortment of shops and is also the terminal for the Ffestiniog Railway.

LLANFAIR MINES

On the outskirts of Harlech just five miles (8km) away are these slate mines. Entry is through the main tunnel into various caverns, all of which were manmade over 100 years ago. Dogs are allowed.

PORTMEIRION

Also on the opposite shore of the estuary is this most unusual village, where a fee is charged for entry, but dogs are not allowed. This is because it is a folly, built as an experiment between 1925 and 1975. It is now a popular tourist attraction.

Monmouthshire: The Welsh Valleys

OS MAPS: EXPLORER OL13 BRECON BEACONS (EASTERN AREA)
EXPLORER 166 RHONDDA & MERTHYR TYDFIL

Monmouthshire's authenticity as a fully Welsh county has been uncertain for at least the last 400 years, partly because England is on its eastern border. The situation was exacerbated by Henry VIII's wish to fully integrate Wales into his domain. Despite being of Welsh descent he wanted to reduce the influence of the local Welsh gentry, hence his so called 'Acts of Union'. These divided Wales into seven counties with an English administrative system imposed upon them. To ensure conformity and unity he banned Welsh speakers from public office. Monmouthshire was one of these seven regions, and its proximity to England over the years has hugely diluted its 'Welshness', especially in those areas which were considered part of adjacent English counties.

This change of county boundaries and names was not unusual. It occurred again during the 20th century, apparently due to changing population patterns. Some residents were not happy with this, so as recently as the 1990s further alterations were established as a compromise. This has rather muddied the waters. Depending who you speak to and which maps are used as reference, towns and villages move about from county to county. This is so with parts of the South Wales Valleys, which at times have been considered part of Monmouthshire.

However the South Wales Valleys are designated, the landscape and countryside of the region is unique. It is a product of the geological history and structure of the underlying rocks due primarily to the rise and fall of the land many, many millennia ago. During a 'fall' period the coal forming rocks were laid down, and as the land continued to rise and fall so the coal seams were squeezed together. Then came the ice age which produced huge glaciers in the mountains of the Brecon Beacons. These gradually melted and spread southwards over the hills creating deep valleys parallel to each other. As the glaciers disappeared so the valleys were filled with rivers all running from north to the seas in the south.

These inhospitable lands were very sparsely populated until the 18th and 19th century. Then it was discovered they had all the natural resources to become the powerhouse of the industrial revolution: first iron ore and then coal – as well as the means to transport the goods cheaply by water and then railways. There was a huge growth of all kinds of industry in the area, especially coal mining, and the population exploded with people coming from all over the UK.

In every valley the characteristic terraced company houses sprang up alongside the coal mining infrastructure; furnaces, chimneys, viaducts and slag heaps. Urbanization requirements were also squeezed into each valley; shops, schools, chapels as well as the necessary roads and canals. Interaction with the people in other valleys was difficult due to the steep hills in between. The hard work and the poor wages created a tight knit community; a tough, rugby playing, choral singing and radically minded society. This image of the South Wales Valleys is the one usually evoked for most visitors.

These former mining communities were devastated during the 1980s with the bitter strikes and closing of the mines. Since then the slag heaps have been systematically flattened whilst the iconic mining landmarks have been dismantled or left to decay with many of the communal buildings becoming derelict. Some, though, have become tourist attractions or part of museum exhibits. Yet somehow the spirit of the Valleys lives on.

In the intervening years various regeneration schemes have been suggested with the aim of connecting the history and culture which pervades the area with the new ventures

Fishing is one of the many activities offered at Parc Bryn Bach Country Park.

and to provide easy access to as many opportunities as possible for the people. It has also been important that the surrounding countryside remains unchanged to allow it to be enjoyed and appreciated. Two such schemes are Parc Bryn Bach Project which developed 340 acres into a local nature reserve and activity centre with a stunning lake as the centre piece. The other is Dare Valley Country Park. Here, too, the land was developed into a recreational space, but at the same time environmental sustainability, conservation and education were equally as important. The popularity of these places suggest they have achieved their aims.

This area is well worth a visit to understand a little of the impact of the Industrial Revolution, for the stunning scenery, and the warm welcome.

Parc Bryn Bach Campsite

This campsite exemplifies why scrutinizing possible locations is essential, despite all the information that may be available. I had high expectations; a lovely lakeside location; visitors' centre and café onsite and lots of routes up to the moors. The campsite location was, as stated, next to a wonderful lake with amazing views of the hills. It was, therefore, such a shame so little customer service was accorded to the campsite patrons. It was difficult to find someone upon arrival to check in. Once the booking was confirmed the introductory process was very brief; the necessary keys were handed over with a short account of their function, and a comment to return if there were any problems. There were various issues, and trying to find someone to resolve them was not easy. A map of the campsite would have been useful. It appeared the showers were used during the day by other customers and there was no designated chemical toilet.

The onsite visitors' centre and café was a hive of activity, seemingly all day, not only offering food but also offering a huge variety of activities. It would have been helpful to have information as to how to access the activities available, as would a map of the complex showing the various cycling and walking routes and location of the activities. It was such a shame so little information as to the services available

Wonderful walks from dog-friendly campsites on a budget

were offered at the check in. There was so much potential to make this a lovely spot to spend some time.

PEARLS OF WISDOM 🐾

Ooooh water! A huge lake! Swim time. But no. Not allowed. Not sure why. Maybe it is all the ducks or the boats or the strange large round coloured balls bobbing about. Exploring around the lake was interesting; lots of new, mostly doggy and duck, smells but I would have liked to roam further afield than the lead allowed. If I did, it was something to do with my owner being fined. But I'm a good girl and always come when called. During the day it was very busy around the lake; bikes, scooters, runners with lots of people and dogs. I enjoyed going up to the moors because then I was free to explore, except for one place where there were so many of these pesky sheep so it was lead time again. Just a shame there was so many hard paths and uncomfortable stony places. An interesting place quite different from other places.

RATING ££££
PRICING STRUCTURE; (SEE CHAPTER 3) – FLAT RATE
PROS:
- Good location
- Café on site
- Simple easy pricing
- Places to walk nearby
- Variety of activities on offer

CONS:
- Lack of map of newly designated walking routes
- Several sheep proof stiles
- Lots of sheep on heath
- Lack of nearby green space for ball throwing
- Essential to keep dogs on lead around lake
- Poor customer care
- No designated chemical toilet

The campsite is beside a wonderful lake with amazing views of the surrounding hills.

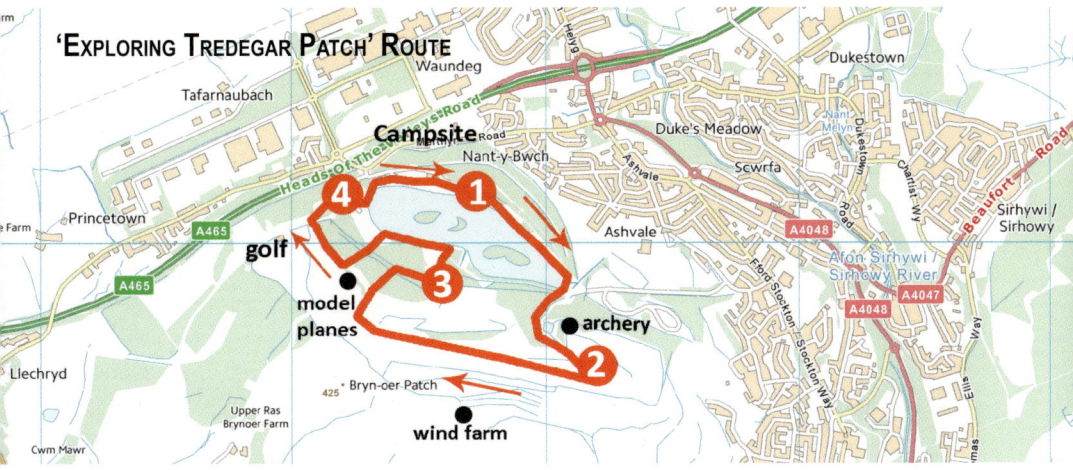

SHORT WALK – EXPLORING TREDEGAR PATCH

Distance: 3mi (4.8km)
Duration: 1.5hr (Easy)
Terrain: Footpaths, stony tracks, paths, gates, climbs

Section 1: 0.75mi (1.2km)
- Exit campsite via Portakabins in left corner onto lakeside path
- Turn left, following path round right bend, ignoring paths leading off, over bridge
- Turn left through gate, turning immediately right through second gate onto wide stony track, passing kissing gate in fence on right
- Follow path winding uphill, passing archery compound on left
- Continue along path, round to left, then right bend up slope onto wide stony track

Section 2: 0.75mi (1.2km)
- Turn right towards wind turbines, following track to junction by metal barrier
- Turn right downhill along tarmac track, turning right again through kissing gate into field
- Bear slightly right through kissing gate in right corner onto wide track, and through second kissing gate onto path

Section 3: 0.75mi (1.2km)
- Follow path down to lakeside path turning left
- Turn left again after recycling area onto earth path, going uphill through kissing gate by model flying club, and onto tarmac access road
- Turn right downhill through gate

Section 4: 0.75mi (1.2km)
- Turn sharp right onto path at boulder, following to metal barrier
- Turn left along lakeside path, passing visitors centre on left, to campsite.

Wonderful walks from dog-friendly campsites on a budget

Passing one of the wind turbines on the hills

Long Walk – Hunting for the Heath
Distance: 6.25mi (10km)
Duration: 3hr (Easy)
Terrain: Footpaths, stony tracks, paths, gates, climbs

Section 1: 1mi (1.6km)
- Exit campsite via the visitors' centre, turning right along lakeside path, passing car park on right
- Turn right through metal barrier, passing another car park on right
- Follow path round left then right bend to huge boulder
- Continue straight ahead, passing another car park on right, golf house on left, BMX park on right through two kissing gates
-

Section 2: 0.75mi (1.2km)
- Turn left along tarmac track, round left bend uphill
- Turn right before top, along earth path between trees, through metal gates out to tarmac access road
- Turn right, zig-zagging downhill through metal barrier to houses

Section 3: 0.75mi (1.2km)
- Turn sharp left through kissing gate, passing rear of houses on right

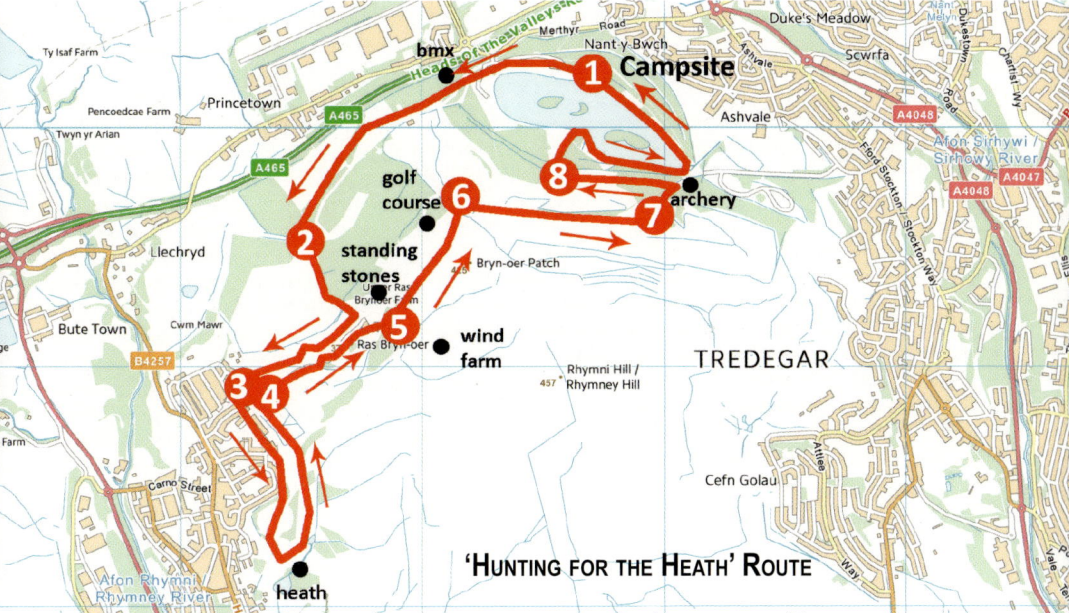

'HUNTING FOR THE HEATH' ROUTE

- Take right fork though gate onto heath (climbing up the hill gives views across the gully to the hills beyond, all dotted with numerous sheep. There were no clearly defined footpaths just animal tracks criss-crossing the hillside)
- Bear right close to trees on right, down slope to gully
- Turn left along gully on right, skirting pond onto stony track
- Turn left uphill, following path back through gate into lane (this reconnoitre around the gully to the pond confirmed the decision to enjoy the experience and backtrack)
- Follow lane to left, passing houses on left out to road

Section 4: 0.75mi (1.2km)
- Turn immediately right, up road though barrier, uphill to houses at top
- Turn left through metal cage-gates, following path to wide tarmac track

Section 5: 0.75mi (1.2km)
- Turn right, passing wind turbine farm on right, and circle of standing stones, through two kissing gates into golf area
- Continue along path through three gates

Section 6: 0.75mi (1.2km)
- Go straight ahead, passing path off to left, onto very wide grey stony track through barrier
- Turn left along wide stony track, going down first, round left, then right, then left again, passing archery compound on right

We found a circle of standing stones with a flat piece in the middle, possibly for offerings.

Section 7: 0.75mi (1.2km)
- Follow path downhill, through kissing gate in fence on left, onto narrow path
- Follow path uphill, keeping close to fence on left, through gate
- Continue along path, with fence now on right, through gate in right corner

Section 8: 0.75mi (1.2km)
- Follow path down to lakeside path
- Turn right with lake on left
- Follow path to campsite

IN THE VICINITY OF PARC BRYN BACH
BIRDWATCHING/WILDLIFE
There are plenty of birds, especially ducks, to see around the lake. With binoculars you can also see plenty from the campsite, especially if on a lakeside pitch or from one of the many benches situated around the lake. Exploring some of the paths leading uphill offers the opportunity to study the local flora and fauna.

CYCLING
An easy ride around the lake especially for young inexperienced cyclists. For more skilled cyclists there are forest tracks and dedicated routes to nearby towns, such as Merthyr Tydfil. A special BMX track is also onsite, together with the services of an instructor for novices.

FISHING

Dotted all around the lake are specially designated stations for anglers.

GOLF

Besides a regular golf course onsite, there is also a driving range and mini golf. Details can be obtained at the golf club.

ARCHERY

The archery programme can be accessed at the visitors' centre.

WATERSPORTS/WILD SWIMMING

Information regarding the activities available, and when, can be obtained from the visitors' centre.

BRECON MOUNTAIN RAILWAY

This heritage railway leaves from Pant Station just north of Merthyr Tydfil and journeys up the mountain past Pontsticill Reservoir to Torpantau Station, then returns. Public transport is available to get to Pant Station (two buses), and it is possible to walk back to the campsite (approx 9mi/14.5km) from Torpantau Station along the Cambrian Way

BEDWELLTY HOUSE & PARK

Just two miles away in the town of Tredegar are Bedwellty House and Park. They were built in the early 19th century for the owners of Tredegar Iron Company. In 1900 they were gifted to the people of Tredegar, and since then they have gradually been developed to provide a place for relaxation and fun. It is also an historical memorial, as Aneurin Bevan, the architect of the NHS, is associated with the building. In 2000 it was updated and is an ideal place to enjoy a day out and learn about the local history.

Walks in North East England
(Lincolnshire, North Yorkshire, Northumberland)

Lincolnshire – The Humber Estuary

OS MAPS: EXPLORER 281 ANCHOLME VALLEY; EXPLORER 284 GRIMSBY, CLEETHORPES & IMMINGHAM

The village of New Holland in Lincolnshire is one of the many towns and villages on the south bank of the River Humber. A local person informed me it was so called because people from Holland were asked over to drain the fens, so that the village could be built. Once the work was completed, several of the Dutch workers decided to remain, hence its name New Holland. This of course may just be a local legend.

The River Humber itself is a misnomer. It is in actual fact a 40+ mile (64.3km) long tidal estuary that has carved its way eastwards from the North Sea to the confluence of the River Ouse and River Trent. Like all estuaries, it gradually gets wider as it tumbles down to the sea. At its widest point it is a staggering seven miles across, and a surprising one mile (1.6km) wide in many other places.

This deep water tidal estuary has had a considerable impact in the area, and still does today. It is so wide and deep it can accommodate large ships, even the enormous modern container ships. It is a vital gateway, spawning a series of settlements along the bank, as well as a variety of industries including power stations and oil refinery complexes. There are three major ports: Immingham and Grimsby near the mouth of the estuary, and Hull further inland, as well as several smaller ones, including New Holland. This has the added advantage of having a pier jutting out into the estuary, so can take the larger vessels. These days New Holland's primary cargo is timber.

Being so wide and long the estuary is a natural border between Lincolnshire in the south and Yorkshire to the north. For many years the quickest way to cross the estuary was by ferry, usually in paddle steamers. These ran from Barton-upon-Humber across to Hull. Then in 1848 a second ferry service to Hull was established from the newly built pier at New Holland, initially as a terminus for stage coach passengers. With the advent of the railways, the pier assumed even greater importance as a rail terminus allowing rail passengers to transfer to a ferry for a quicker journey to Hull.

Even though it was common knowledge that a bridge across the Humber would have enormous benefits, discussion and planning took many years. It was not until 1981 that a bridge across the estuary was finally officially opened by Queen Elizabeth II, nine years after construction started. By then, of course, all ferry services ceased.

At the time, the bridge was a feat of modern engineering, and was the longest single-span suspension bridge in the world, which cyclists and pedestrians can also use.

A very large ship on the Humber Estuary.

Because of its innovative engineering and inspiring design it has been designated a Grade 1 listed structure. At the last count in 2006, an average of 120,000 vehicles used the bridge per week. Without doubt its impact has been significant, especially now there are no tolls to pay.

Besides providing commercial opportunities, the Humber Estuary is also a haven for wildlife. Its large coastal plain created by the huge tidal range is the second largest in the UK, and also supports an abundance of wildlife. So much so, in fact, that UK and European law has awarded it various conservation designations.

This is surprising considering how brown and dirty the water looks flowing under the Humber Bridge. (I certainly would not want to swim or fish in it). The mucky colour is not due to pollution or chemicals, as heavy industry along the banks of the Humber has declined considerably over the years. It is the result of boulder clay being swept into the river further upstream. This silt and sediment is then deposited along the banks, so creating the important coastal plain. A perfect illustration of how deceptive appearances can be.

Marshland Alpacas Campsite

This is an unusual campsite because, as the name suggests, it is situated almost in the middle of an alpaca smallholding on the edge of a small Lincolnshire village. The alpacas graze in the adjacent field, and at feeding time wander into the enclosure between the campsite and bar. The close proximity of the alpacas offers the opportunity to learn about these intriguing animals, from feeding them to stroking some of them if you're lucky, maybe baby ones too (I saw one being born). They are very tame and placid (no spitting, even over food). It is a small campsite with 16 pitches of which only 15 are used, to allow grass to recover by rotation. The site is well organized, with dishwashing, recycling, etc, conveniently located by the toilet block. Recently, a small bar was opened in one of the barns, which is a bonus. Dogs are welcome, but because the alpacas are nervous of them, it is essential they are kept on leads.

Wonderful walks from dog-friendly campsites on a budget

Pearls of Wisdom 🐕

What an odd smell: what odd animals. I was a bit nervous, so glad I was on the lead. Even so, I would have liked to have been able to take a closer inspection; not allowed. Shame. Seems these odd creatures were more afraid of me than I was of them. Luckily my son and I could still have our walks, but we had to go along a street and very carefully over an odd bit of road with metal strips in it. My owner said something about a rail crossing. It was worth it, as there was a wonderful huge green open space; lots to explore, lots of smells and, best of all, space to chase my frisbee; hooray. The walks were great even though there were some roads; they were very quiet so we could still explore. We even went on a train ride. The water was so tempting but too mucky for a swim.

Rating ££

Pricing Structure (see Chapter 3) – Flat rate (additional charge for awnings etc)

Pros:

- Interesting location on alpaca farm
- Alpaca feeding every morning
- Simple fee structure (£2+ for weekends)
- Excellent price during school holidays
- Bar on site
- Good amenities (hedges border each pitch)

Cons:

- Dogs under close control
- £1.00 charge for showers
- Dog exercise area 15 min walk away

Feeding the alpacas at the campsite

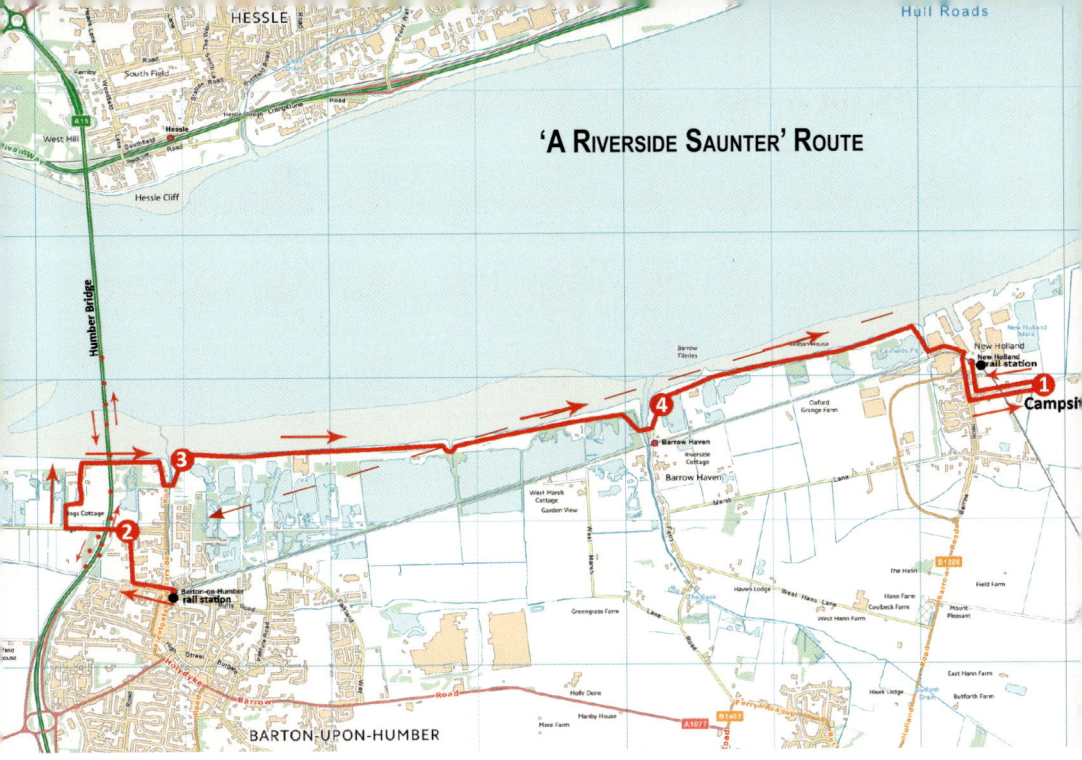

'A RIVERSIDE SAUNTER' ROUTE

SHORT WALK – A RIVERSIDE SAUNTER
Distance: 5.75mi (9.2km)
Duration: 4hr (Easy)
Terrain: Train station, rail tracks, steps, footpaths, riverside path, tracks, kissing gates, roads, bridges, Humber Bridge (busy but wide pedestrian path)

Section 1: 0.75mi (1.2km)
- Exit campsite to road, turning left, cross rail tracks, past playing fields on left, (good place for a short dog exercise) to T-junction
- Turn right along road to railway station on right
- Catch train to Barton-upon-Humber
- Exit station to bus terminal, by notice board with town map, small supermarket across road
- Turn right along Waterside Road (B1218), crossing at bollards
- Turn right, then left along Dam Road
- Turn right along Humber Road, with bridge ahead to T-junction
- Turn left along Far Ings Road (pavement on opposite side), under bridge

Section 2: 1.25mi (2km) – bridge partway
- Turn left immediately after bridge, onto tarmac path up to bridge (noisy and windy)
- Continue along path for view of surrounding countryside and river
- Retrace steps to road (1mi/1.6km, turn left)
- Continue along Far Ings Road, passing house on right
- Turn right along driveway to Garden Centre, café, etc, signposted
- Follow driveway to restaurant main entrance

The Humber Bridge is visible for many miles.

- Turn right into car park towards field
- Bear left to corner, through gate, onto stony path with unusual wall on left made of tiles, through gate, up slope to riverside path (Viking Way)
- Turn right along Viking Way
- Turn right along road just after Viking Way Coffee Bar
- Turn left, cross road, up steps and ramp over footbridge
- Turn left before steps, along pavement with black railings on left, round left bend, right bend, passing huge green building on right (a kind of river watch station)

Section 3: 2mi (3.2km)
- Continue along path as it snakes along with river on left, passing tile works on right
- Take left, passing lakes and sailing club on right
- Follow path round right bend, beside inlet, with timber yard on opposite bank, to rail crossing
- Through gate, turn left along rail line to road (take care)
- Turn left along road, passing yard on left, house on right, through kissing gate beside large green gates, through timber yard, towards river
- Follow path round right bend, with timber yard now on right, onto wide stony track with river on left, through gate

Section 4: 1.75mi (2.8km)

- Continue along path beside river with lakes on right towards five large silos and pier out to open gravelly space
- Bear right crossing footbridge round right bend with sheds on left round left bend
- Continue along path with rail tracks on right over level crossing to rail station on left
- Go straight on along Barrow Road passing Memories café on left
- Turn left along Oxmarsh Lane over rail crossing to campsite entrance

LONG WALK – AND SO TO GOXHILL

Distance: 7.5mi (12km)
Duration: 5hr (Easy)
Terrain: Footpaths, fields, tracks, rail tracks, footbridges, gates, stiles roads (mostly quiet)
NB – No refreshment stop available on this route

Section 1: 1mi (1.6km)

- Exit campsite to road, turning left, crossing rail tracks
- Turn left through gate beside tree, into playing fields
- Cross fields bearing slightly left, passing derelict hut ahead on right, through gate onto lane

There were many rail crossings, some manned but most just with gates and notices.

- Turn right along lane, passing garage on left, to road
- Turn left along road, left again at pub, along Peploe Lane, crossing rail tracks ahead (take care)

Section 2: 1mi (1.6km)
- Continue ahead along wide grass track, along edge of field, keeping close to hedge on left, then between crops, crossing footbridge
- Turn right in 30yd (27m), bear left, round bend onto very narrow path between crops
- Continue ahead across field, keeping close to ditch on right, out to wide stony track, West Marsh Lane
- Turn right along track, round left bend

Section 3: 0.5mi (0.8km)
- Turn right across footbridge into field, signposted, onto grass path
- Straight on at corner, into field, along narrow path, turning left in 50yd (46m) through gap in hedge cross footbridge
- Continue ahead, along edge of field, hedge still on left, through gate, then kissing gate
- Bear right, through gate into field, across three fields, cross footbridge into field
- Turn left along edge of field, through gate to road

- Bear right, across road to grass track
- Follow track to road
- Bear left along Ruards Lane

Section 4: 1 mi (1.6km)
- Turn right, along stony lane, onto grass track, to junction
- Turn left, passing houses on left
- Turn right, along path beside allotments, across playing fields, over footbridge, onto stony path
- Follow path, round bends, onto tarmac path, out to road
- Bear right, across road, to Stothards Lane
- Turn right at T-junction, along Westfield Road, through gates, onto narrow path between fences, out to Ferry Road

Section 5: 0.75mi (1.2km)
- Turn right, along road, passing Manor Lane on right
- Turn left, opposite mushroom sculpture in garden, over stile, into field, onto footpath between fences, over stile into second field
- Go straight on, passing signpost at hedge corner, into another field, to cross rail tracks ahead, into field
- Bear slightly right, across field, over footbridge
- Turn right, then left, along edge of field, keeping close to hedge on right, out to road, East Hann Lane

Section 6: 1.25mi (2km)
- Follow lane to B1206
- Turn left, then right, onto West Hann Lane, passing farm on right, New Hann farm on left
- Turn right opposite West Hann Farm, between hedges, beside gate, onto narrow path

Section 7: 1mi (1.6km)
- Continue straight ahead, along edge of field, keeping close to hedge on right, through gap in hedge in corner, into second field
- Go straight on, along edge of field (Humber Bridge visible on left), over footbridge, out to road
- Turn right along Marsh Road, crossing bypass onto minor road
- Turn left, onto path between hedges

Section 8: 1mi (1.6km)
- Follow path, turning right onto narrow path, just before road
- Continue along path into open green space, turning left through overgrown bicycle exit beside gate, onto road
- Turn left, following tarmac path through trees, out to road, opposite Memories Café
- Turn right, then left, onto Oxmarsh Lane, passing playing fields on right, to campsite

Wonderful walks from dog-friendly campsites on a budget

IN THE VICINITY
CYCLING
There are several cycle routes, which are available online: some crossing the Humber Bridge and around Water Edge Country Park.

BIRDWATCHING
With Nature Reserves along the banks of the estuary, there is plenty of opportunity for birdwatching.

GOXHILL
Just three miles to the SW is the village of Goxhill. It has some impressive buildings, some of which are listed. The parish church of St Giles Church is Grade 1 listed, with parts of it dating from as early as 13th century. Surprisingly, there are no pubs in the village so nowhere for refreshments. Goxhill is most noted for its old air base, located to the east of the village. It has a long history having been established during WW1 and then used extensively during WW2, especially by the Americans. Local legend has it that one of the pilots stationed here was Clark Gable! Though it was decommissioned in 1962, it is still remarkably unaltered

BARTON-UPON-HUMBER
This town has long been an important place on the banks of the Humber estuary. In 1066, at the time of the Domesday Book, Barton-upon-Humber was already a large prosperous place with a church, a market and even a ferry service across the estuary to Hull. Over the years it has grown considerably. Now there are two churches and several chapels, schools, a variety of shops, both chains and independent ones; roof tiles are still manufactured in the town (though not as many as in years past), and the rail line terminates at Barton now with a special bus service over the modern Humber Bridge to Hull. There are many interesting Victorian and Georgian buildings scattered around the town, and it has managed to retain its charm

WATERS EDGE COUNTRY PARK
This was established in the 1990s on land previously used as quarries for clay. It now has an enormous green visitors' centre which overlooks the Humber Bridge. This houses an information centre, café and various displays and information about the area. Though dogs can explore the 110 acres (44.5ha) of the country park, they are not allowed inside the visitors centre.

VIKING WAY
This long distance trail starts near the Waters Edge Country Park. Its 147mi (236.6km) route crosses Lincolnshire to Rutland

ROPEWALK
The old Rope works building just north of the railway station is a Grade 2 listed building.

This unusual building, stretching an enormous ¼-mile (0.4km) along the road, was built in 1767. The factory eventually stopped production in 1989, and has been an important regional centre for the arts since 2000. It houses an eclectic mix of enterprises including a theatre, cinema, artists' studios and exhibition galleries, as well as a café and a museum which chronicles the history of the building and the people who worked in it.

HUMBER BRIDGE COUNTRY PARK
On the north side of the Humber Estuary, on the outskirts of Hull, is the Humber Bridge Country Park. The 52 acre (21ha) site has a long history, having been a chalk quarry from as early as the 13th century until the 1960s. The Country Park opened in 1986 but it was not until 2003 that it was designated a nature reserve, in recognition of the variety of habitats which support a profusion of wildlife, and the different nature trails which meander through the landscape. An added bonus is that dogs are welcome.

THORNTON ABBEY
Situated just five miles (8km) south of New Holland, and one train station away, are the Grade 1 listed ruins of Thornton Abbey with its magnificent gatehouse. The abbey was founded in 1140, and over the years became wealthy enough to build the stunning gatehouse. Surprisingly, the abbey and gatehouse survived the suppression of the monasteries in 1539, and was reassigned a secular college for priests. In 1547, however, this too closed, and slowly over the years the abbey building deteriorated, though the gatehouse remained remarkably intact. In 1938 the complex was gifted and is now managed by English Heritage. Dogs are, unfortunately, not allowed in the grounds.

HULL
The Humber Bridge links North Lincolnshire with the Yorkshire city of Hull, or, to give it its proper name, Kingston-upon-Hull. It lies at the junction of the River Hull and the north bank of the Humber Estuary. It is one of the UK's most important ports with a long history and is an interesting, vibrant place. William Wilberforce, who in the 1800s was instrumental in ending slavery, was born in Hull, and it was the UK city of culture in 2017. Lots to see and do.

CLEETHORPES
Easily reached by train, Cleethorpes is the result of the unification of three small villages, Litterby, Oole and Thrunscoe. Originally it was a fishing village, but became a popular seaside resort during the 19th century, with a host of attractions including a long sandy beach, ideal for various water sports.

North Yorkshire – More than just Moors
OS MAPS: EXPLORER OL27 NORTH YORK MOORS (EASTERN AREA)
Just over 20mi (32km) to the north-east of York lie the North Yorkshire Moors. These moors were designated a National Park in 1952. Here in the UK, unlike most other countries, the lands of National Parks are mostly privately owned. Areas designated as

Wonderful walks from dog-friendly campsites on a budget

National Parks in the UK are funded by the government to:

- Conserve and enhance the natural beauty, wildlife and cultural heritage
- Promote opportunities for the understanding and enjoyment of the special qualities of national parks by the public

The North York Moors National Park is a precious landscape for the public as well as the residents to enjoy, so any proposed changes and developments are carefully vetted by the authorities. The title of 'Moors' is somewhat misleading, as the 554 square miles (1435km^2) of the North York Moors National Park includes four main types of landscape, with clearly defined characteristics caused by different underlying geology:

- The stereotypical heather-clad hills, signified by seasonal purple and brown colours
- Woodland, which covers a surprising 23% of the area; over 100sq mi (259km^2) mostly in the south of the National Park. Some of the oldest trees in northern England are located here
- The coastal belt, which stretches 26mi (41.8km) along the eastern border, with some stunning views, amazing beaches and charming villages
- Green pasture land, an unexpected contrast

The wildlife is as varied as the landscape, taking advantage of the habitats best suited to its needs.

The distinctive valleys, or Dales as they are called locally, and the hills and ridges were formed by melting glacial waters gushing southwards, crumbling any limestone encountered. So it is that most of the rivers today flow across the moors north to south in steep valleys.

Despite its rugged landscape, history has left its indelible mark upon the North Yorkshire Moors from the earliest times. There is evidence of habitation from 600BC, with the remains of Iron Age hill forts. Then by 71AD the Romans reached Yorkshire, as they continued their push northwards. With their usual efficiency, in over three centuries of occupation, they established forts and roads, eventually leaving in 410AD.

Being in such a northerly position, the North Yorkshire Moors are very close to the Scandinavian countries, with only the North Sea separating them. The hiatus left by the departing Romans was soon filled with the Angles, Saxons and Jute tribes from Europe. They bought with them their religion, worshipping a variety of gods, but then from 627AD Christianity became the accepted religion, with the conversion of King Edwin of Nothumbria, and the building of numerous churches, cathedrals and monasteries. Many of these were ransacked by the Vikings, but eventually they too settled in the area and adopted the accepted religion, Christianity. Evidence of these invasions can be seen in the artefacts left behind, and the names of many of the places in the area.

With the arrival of the Normans huge castles were built as a symbol of their power, as well as the building of more and grander monasteries and abbeys. These religious houses were given land and money for various reasons. They used this wisely, acquiring more

The North Yorkshire Moors are stunning.

land and so becoming very rich and influential, wielding a great deal of power. This all changed between 1536 and 1541 when Henry VIII closed them down and confiscated or sold all their land and money, leaving many of the buildings in ruins

The coming of the railways in the 1800s changed things again. The iron ore, which had been mined for centuries, could now be easily transported, leading to a booming industry. It even became viable to mine other low grade minerals including the semi-precious 'jet', which is only found in this area. Most of the mines have since closed. Some of the railways have become heritage lines, and mostly transport tourists across the area.

Agriculture is still important, as it has been for centuries, as is fishing off the east coast There is some mining, but nothing significant. Nowadays the economy depends on tourism. There is plenty to see: the castles, churches and all the many ruins of once-impressive monasteries and abbeys, museums, pretty fishing villages and towns, and of course beaches. This is in addition to the outdoor pursuits on offer. With over 1400 miles (2253km) of paths and tracks crossing the National Park there is plenty of opportunity to explore the landscape, including Dalby Forest which features in a TV programme on Channel 5, *Secret Life of the Forest*.

White Swan Campsite (North Yorkshire)

Behind the White Swan pub are two wooden cabins with space for cars, then a long field divided by hedges into two sections. Most of the 20+ hardstanding pitches are lined up on

Wonderful walks from dog-friendly campsites on a budget

The campsite stretches behind the pub, with vans on each side of the access road.

the left and are occupied by seasonal caravans. The other side of the path is mostly grass, available for tents as well as tourers, and a couple of hardstanding pitches. There are a few electric hook-ups in the first field. Some are used by the seasonal caravans, so at any one time there are only about four hook-ups available for tourers and tenters. The facilities block is clean, modern and well organized, and is attached to the back of the pub, so is quite a distance from some of the pitches. The campsite is located in a quiet village with just the one pub. This opens limited hours and, at present, does not serve food regularly though it does have special events including pizza and beer evenings or curry evenings etc. Unusually the pub is part of a terrace of houses. The side entrance is narrow so entry to the campsite requires care.

PEARLS OF WISDOM

A strange place. Despite there being lots of those machines similar to my owner's it was oddly silent. Didn't matter; there was enough space for me to chase my frisbee and the walks were brilliant. We did not even have to go out to the road; through a small gate into a lane which led to a bigger lane. There was quite a lot of hard tarmac, but it was very quiet, so my son and I did not have to go on the lead. The walk through the woods was sooo steep; we didn't mind. The puffing engine we got on was not my favourite activity. Even at the end of the ride there was little space for us to run never mind explore; too many people; everything squashed up. I think my owner called the place Whitby. Anyway the trip back was great; lots of time and space to run and explore once we got off the puffing machine.

RATING ££

PRICING STRUCTURE; (SEE CHAPTER 3) – ITEMIZED (ELECTRIC CHARGED ON USAGE)

PROS:
- Simple fee structure (bargain for solo travellers)
- Excellent price during school holidays
- Bar on site
- Very quiet site

CONS:
- Charges per person (expensive for multiple occupancy)
- Lots of seasonal caravans
- Very steep walk to train station
- Some of the footpaths on map are actually tarmac access roads

SHORT WALK – SURPRISE SURPRISE – NO HILLS

Distance: 5mi (8km)
Duration: 3hr (Easy)
Terrain: Footpaths, tracks (stony, grass and tarmac), fields, lanes, quiet roads,

Section 1: 1.5mi (2.4km)
- Exit campsite towards entrance, turning sharp left through small gate onto narrow footpath opposite huts
- Follow path with campsite on left, out to wide track
- Turn right along track, passing footpaths signposted both sides, farm on right with track now tarmac

Easy walking in fields for a change.

Section 2:1.5mi (2.4km)
- Turn right at T-junction, along Ruddings Road to main road
- Turn left along Yatts Road verge (busy, take care)
- Turn next right, along road with sign Haugh Rigg Farm, following its zig-zags

Section 3: 1mi (1.6km)
- Turn right at junction with grassy track, staying on tarmac track, passing campsite on right
- Go straight on at fork and left bend

Section 4:1mi (1.6km)
- Turn right, onto narrow footpath, into field
- Continue straight on, along edge of field, keeping close to hedge on right
- Turn left at corner, then right in 30yd (27.5m), along path through middle of very large field with different crops in various sections (some short gentle climbs)
- Turn right at T-junction, then left fork out to wide track
- Turn left, climb steadily, out to road with pub opposite on left

LONG WALK – MOORS? (I THINK WOODS)
Distance: 8.25mi (13.2km)
Duration: 5hr (Moderate)
Terrain: Footpaths, tracks, woods, fields, lanes, quiet roads, kissing gates, some steep climbs (refreshments not available en route, take sandwiches for picnic at Roman Camp)

MOORS? (I THINK WOODS) ROUTE

TABULAR HILLS WALK

This trail marks the southern boundary of the North York Moors National Park. The name comes from the distinctive table top shape, as they rise up gently from the south and ends abruptly in a series of steep north facing headlands known as 'nabs'.

Section 1: 0.75mi (1.2km)
- Exit campsite via entrance, out to road, turning right
- Bear right at bend, keeping dog bin on right, onto grassy path going downhill into woods (amazing trees), passing farm sheds, stile on right through gate

Section 2: 1.25mi (2km)
- Turn right, cross stream, up path opposite (steep short)
- Follow narrow path strewn with boulders, through ferns, shrubs and trees
- Go straight ahead at junction, passing grass track on left, out to byway, by house Middle Farm, signposted
- Go straight on through gate, onto wide grass track, passing house on right, onto narrow footpath, out to wide stony track
- Turn left along track, round metal barrier, out to road

Section 3: 1.mi (1.6km)
- Turn left along road, passing sign for Stape on right
- Turn right along wide stony track, signposted
- Turn left at right bend, onto wide grass track

There are many woodland areas dotted about the moors.

Section 4: 1mi (1.6km)
- Follow track out to driveway
- Cross through gate opposite into field (blue waymarker on gate)
- Bear right across field, through gate, ahead onto narrow footpath between ferns, into woods, crossing footbridge

Section 5: 1mi (1.6km)
- Bear right uphill, out to road
- Turn left, uphill along road to junction
- Turn left, along road to driveway of Cawthorn Roman camp

Section 6: 1mi (1.6km)
- Turn left along driveway, round right bend into car park, bearing left to noticeboard
- Turn left along gravel path
- Take left fork and follow path round to viewpoints, returning to car park

Section 7: 1mi (1.6km)
- Exit via car park entrance, turning left along road
- Continue straight ahead into cul-de sac at left bend
- Go straight on at right bend onto wide grass track
- Take left fork uphill in 30yd (27.5m)

Section 8: 1.25mi (2km)
- Turn sharp left at junction

- Turn right in 30yd (27.5m), onto narrow footpath, into field
- Continue straight on along edge of field, keeping close to hedge on right
- Turn left at corner, then right in 30yd (27.5m), along path through middle of very large field with different crops in various sections (some short gentle climbs)
- Turn right at T-junction, then left fork, out to wide track
- Turn left, climb steadily out to road, with pub opposite on left

IN THE VICINITY

CYCLING

There are plenty of opportunities for all kinds of cycling, as most of the roads are quiet and the forests have tracks criss-crossing them. Beware, there are some steep hills.

WILDLIFE/BIRD WATCHING

The North Yorkshire Moors is an ideal location to watch birds and wildlife, though they aren't always easy to spot as there are plenty of places to hide.

NEWTON-ON-RAWCLIFFE

This is a typical North Yorkshire Moors village, with attractive stone cottages dotted along both sides of a long main street. Also to be found whilst wandering along the street is St John's Church, a play area and football field. Newton is special in that firstly there is a small campsite behind the pub; ideally located to explore the Moors. Secondly, in the middle of the small village green opposite the 18th century White Swan pub, is a wonderful duck pond. An ideal place to sit and admire the view.

CAWTHORN ROMAN CAMP

The site of the remains of a Roman camp, which the long walk passes, is one of the best in Yorkshire. The only access to the camp is the entrance on the road to Cropton, which leads to the car park in the woods. There are several paths around the site (wonderful for dogs) with information notice boards, leading to viewpoints of some of the significant areas of the camp such as barracks etc. Unfortunately the scenic viewpoint from the edge of the escarpment overlooking Elleron Lake was obscured by trees when I visited. It is also disappointing that from here there is no footpath to the Tabular Hills Walk and viewpoint, which is just a few hundred yards north-east.

PICKERING

This charming market town is a fascinating place to explore. As well as its independent shops and wonderful cafés, there is the Beck Isle Museum, the medieval wall paintings in St Peter's and Paul's churches, and many interesting historic buildings, as it is thought Pickering is the oldest settlement in the area. It has a long and intriguing history; especially its name. Legend has it that King Peredurus, the town's founder in 270BC, lost a ring. It miraculously reappeared in the fish, a pike, which the king had for his supper; hence Pickering. The Normans originally built the castle, then over the centuries various inhabitants have enlarged and strengthened it, and it is now maintained by

Wonderful walks from dog-friendly campsites on a budget

English Heritage. In the centre of town is the 1930's themed railway station; this is the terminal of the North Yorkshire Moors Heritage Railway. (It is possible to take the train to Pickering and walk back across the moors to the campsite, approximately five miles.)

NORTH YORKSHIRE MOORS RAILWAY

The Heritage Railway runs from Pickering northwards along Newton Dale, beside Pickering Beck, to Whitby, and was first opened in 1836. This was to allow goods and passengers easier access to Whitby harbour. Then in 1965 it was closed. A group of enthusiastic volunteers began the long process of reinstating train services, which was finally achieved in 1973 with trains running the whole way to Whitby from 2007.

From Pickering this 24 mile stretch has four stations en route:

- Levisham Station is 1900's style, with various attractive station buildings and railway cottages that are available to hire. A steep road leads from the station to Levisham village, though it is in fact closer to Newton-on-Rawcliffe and the campsite, but only via a really steep footpath. To go by road is much longer via the town of Pickering.
- Newton Dale Halt is a remote stop that is not accessible by road. It was requested by walkers for easier access to the many walks in Cropton Forest.
- Goatland Station is known locally as the 'celebrity' station, as it has featured in many TV programmes and films including the first Harry Potter film, as the fictional village of Aidensfield in the 1990s programme *Heartbeat*, and more recently *Mission Impossible* with Tom Cruise, no less, and an Indiana Jones film.
- Grosmont Station. For train enthusiasts, this 1950s themed station is probably the best one, as it is the operating hub, with locomotive workshops where the trains and engines are maintained and restored.

The line terminates at Whitby mainline station with its own special platform. Unusually, there are a huge number of circular walks possible from most of the stations. Information can be obtained from Pickering and Grosmont Stations or Tourist Information.

WHITBY

This coastal town is most striking, as the River Esk meanders between the headlands out to the sea and the bustling harbour. Overlooking the cobbled streets, houses built into the hillside, and a sandy beach are two headlands: one with the magnificent abbey ruins and on the other the statue of explorer Captain James Cook – a steep climb to each. The town and abbey ruins are also of interest to visitors, because according to the author Bram Stoker this is where Dracula entered the country! The town hosts an annual vampire gathering in the autumn. Whitby is easy to reach from the campsite by the Heritage Railway, and is a wonderful place to explore with lots to see. Beware, it is a popular destination and is very busy during the holidays. Visiting with dogs can be problematic as the streets are so narrow, and dogs are not allowed on the beach during summer months.

THE HOLE OF HORCUM

Just five miles from the campsite across the moors is this landscape anomaly formed by a bubbling spring. Various walks around it can be found online.

CROPTON BREWERY

In the village of Cropton, five miles west of the campsite, is a local brewery that has been producing beer of one kind or another for centuries. Its beers are sold in the village pub, The New Inn.

Northumberland – A Betwixt and Between Place

OS MAPS: EXPLORER OL16 THE CHEVIOT HILLS (JEDBURGH & WOOLER)
EXPLORER 340 HOLY ISLAND & BAMBURGH (WOOLER, BELFORD & SEAHOUSES)

Snaking up the north-east coast, and with its western border squeezing past Scotland, is England's most northern county: Northumberland. Despite being such a large county, it is somewhat tucked away in a corner, being surrounded by the North Sea to the west, Cumbria to the east, County Durham to the south, and, of course, Scotland to the north.

Its geographically isolated position is compounded by the physical landscape. Stretching along its western border with Cumbria are the North Pennine hills and moors, together with the deep river valleys that carve their way through to the sea. Then, along the Scottish border, are the Cheviot Hills: rounded uplands of heights from 1000 to 2500ft (300-700m). To put this in context, in the UK any hill over 2000ft (610m) is considered a mountain; Scafell Pike is 3209ft (978m). The Cheviot Hills may not be classified as mountains, but they are nevertheless very high and a significant barrier.

Mainly rural and sparsely populated; agriculture is important, especially sheep.

Wonderful walks from dog-friendly campsites on a budget

As a consequence, geography dictates the routes of roads and rail. The more densely populated urban, commercial and industrial areas are situated mainly in the south of the county. Following the Romans' example, most of the transport links run east and west, south of Hadrian's Wall. In the rest of the county they run north to south because of the terrain. The rail-line and main A1 meander northwards along the coast and the A697 runs in a north-westerly direction along river valleys and lowlands.

Northumberland is sparsely populated and mostly rural, but because it is so large there is a huge variety of landscape. To the far south of the county there are many residential and commercial buildings dotted about. Along the coastal plain it is fairly flat, so more suitable for agriculture, and here are located the much smaller settlements that are generally associated with the county. Inland are the rugged hills and moors that are really only suitable for sheep and a very few small towns and villages.

One such place is the small town of Wooler. Being situated on the edge of the Northumberland National Park, close to the Cheviot Hills, it is spread over three terraces. The lowest one is in the valley of Wooler Water, and, in addition to the main A road passing through, there are several commercial businesses as well as the school, a cricket club and a large caravan park. The next level is up a steep climb to the High Street with lots of small independent shops and businesses, including a very interesting bookshop specializing in all printed matter about the area. There is another steep climb, passing houses of all descriptions to the top terrace, where the campsite is situated along with some large houses. Surrounding the town are the hills and moors of the National Park, which are steep in places but reward walkers with magnificent views. The steep hills of Wooler and its environs must help keep the inhabitants very fit.

To many people, Northumberland is considered the 'cradle of Christianity' in England. Monks from Iona, a small island near Mull in Scotland, were invited by the King of Northumbria to convert his people. They established a monastery on Lindisfarne, a small tidal island just north of Bamburgh in 634AD. This was also the home of one of the first Christian Bishops, St Cuthbert, though because of Viking invasions he is buried in Durham Cathedral. The island was an important Christian centre during this time, producing the Lindisfarne Gospels around 700BC and, as a consequence, is frequently referred to as Holy Island.

Northumberland has a long and very bloody history, with various invaders from over the North Sea as well as from Scotland plundering the area. As a result there are more castles and fortifications in Northumberland than any other English county. They are scattered along the coastline, overlooking towns and villages, and poised on rugged islands. Its position, so far from the capital London and the south, and its proximity to Scotland, has had a profound influence which continues today, eg, the local folk instrument is the bagpipes. This is hardly surprising as Edinburgh, the capital of Scotland, is a mere 45 minutes from its northern border. Without doubt a betwixt and between place.

HIGHBURN HOUSE CARAVAN PARK

This campsite is situated on a small farm on the outskirts of Wooler. Just like this small Northumberland town, it is spread over several sloping fields. The area has been very cleverly landscaped into informal terraces with flat hardstanding pitches on different levels. It is a spacious, attractive campsite with plenty of green space, some of which is available for tents, and a special section for static caravans. There is a stream which runs though it that can be crossed in two places; a large bridge for motorhomes and caravans and small charming footbridge. There is one modern facilities block near the entrance which also houses a laundry and dishwashing area. Access to this is easier as gravity helps (going down) but more of an effort returning to your pitch (going up). The campsite is efficiently organized and maintained.

PEARLS OF WISDOM 🐎

What's this scurrying away!!! Rabbits!! I want to chase! But I can't, I'm on a lead (my owner knew, so put me on the lead before I knew. She's always smart). Not only did I have to put up with these maddening rabbits roaming about, but there were also ducks waddling about everywhere, even checking out my bowl to see if I had left any food. The cheek of it. I would have shown them who was boss if only I had been allowed. It wasn't all bad though. There was a fabulous field nearby for my son and me to explore and chase balls and frisbees. It was odd as there seemed to be lots of comings and goings. My owner mentioned something about a footpath. No idea what she meant. A fun place even so.

Through the gate from the campsite into the large dog walking field. The resident ducks can be seen on the left.

RATING ££
PRICING STRUCTURE; (SEE CHAPTER 3) – VARIABLE (HIGH AND LOW)
PROS:
- Simple fee structure
- Excellent price during school holidays
- Quiet site, spacious and well organized
- Large dog walking area
- Near an interesting town

Wonderful walks from dog-friendly campsites on a budget

Cons:

- Charges displayed on website
- Pitches flat, but site steep
- Lots of hills everywhere, so lots of climbs
- Resident ducks okay for humans, not so for dogs

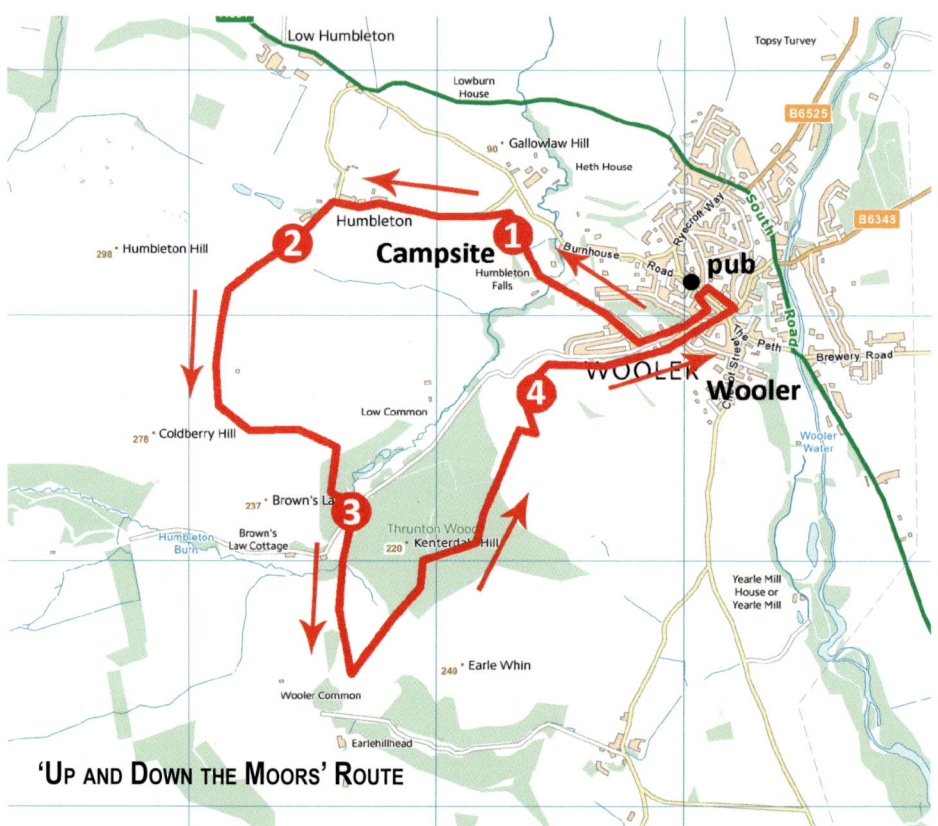

'Up and Down the Moors' Route

Short Walk – Up and Down the Moors

Distance: 4.25mi (13.2km)
Duration: 3.5hr (Tricky)
Terrain: Footpaths, tracks, woods, moors, lanes, quiet roads, kissing gates, many steep climbs and descents of varying length

Section 1: 0.75mi (1.2km)

- Exit campsite via kissing gate into dog walking field
- Bear right towards right corner at top slope, onto narrow path, through kissing gate, onto path
- Follow path out to minor road

Moors all around the surrounding hills.

- Turn left, passing cottages on right to T-junction
- Turn left along cul-de-sac, onto stony track, through gate, passing signed path on right (good place to detour into field for amazing views)

Section 2: 1mi (1.6km)
- Continue along track, climbing steadily, through gate onto grass track
- Follow wide grass track, round left bend, through gate (less hilly), through another gate into woods
- Continue straight ahead, going down to tarmac path
- Turn right, crossing footbridge into car park, out to access road

Section 3: 1.25mi (2km)
- Turn right, then take left fork signposted St Cuthbert's Way, onto narrow path, passing Wooler Common on right, through gate
- Bear left along path beside wall, climbing steeply (again) onto wide grass path
- Continue ahead, along path between hills, ignoring narrow ones leading off
- Turn left at junction, downhill through gate

- Turn right, following path climbing thorough woods, round right bend at junction at top of hill
- Continue along path downhill, through gate, going straight ahead, still down hill
- Bear right at next two junctions, straight on at third, onto wide grass track down
- Turn right at next junction, passing derelict stone building up ahead on right, down steep narrow path to valley
- Continue straight ahead towards house on right

Section 4(a): 1.25mi (2km) – If going into town for refreshments
- Turn right through gap in fence, then left through gate beside white house, onto stony path
- Follow path out to road by signpost
- Continue straight ahead, down Common Road into Ramsey Lane, passing Oliver Road on left, to Market Place with the Co-op opposite on right
- Turn left to No1 Hotel for refreshments (ideal after hilly walk)
- Exit hotel turning right, and right again along Ramsey Lane
- Take second turning right along Broomey
- Go straight ahead at bend, crossing field through gate in left corner
- Bear right, down steep slope, through gate into static caravan park, out to access road
- Turn right follow road over bridge into campsite

Section 4(b): 0.75mi (1.2km) – Avoiding town
- Continue straight ahead down Common Road
- Turn first left along Broomey Road
- Go straight ahead at bend, crossing field through gate in left corner
- Bear right, down steep slope through gate into static caravan park, out to access road
- Turn right, follow road over bridge into campsite

Long Walk – Up to a Trig Point
Distance: 7.5mi (13.2km)
Duration: 5.5hr (Tricky)
Terrain: Footpaths, tracks, moors, lanes, quiet roads, streets, kissing gates, gates, some very steep climbs and descents

Section 1: 0.75mi (1.2km)
- Exit campsite keeping amenities block on right, going down steps, across bridge, up through gate, out to access road
- Turn right into static park, taking left fork up slope between caravans
- Turn left at right bend onto grass between two caravans, through kissing gate, into field
- Bear right up steep path, passing houses on left
- Bear left at top, through kissing gate into another field
- Go straight across field, passing more houses on left, out to road
- Continue ahead along road to junction

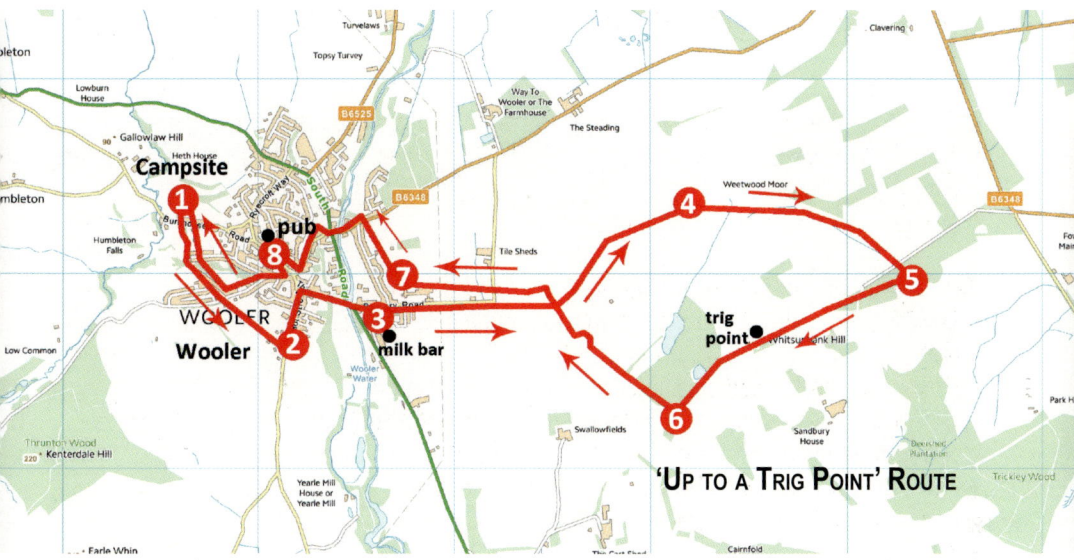

'UP TO A TRIG POINT' ROUTE

- Cross road to driveway, keeping right, onto footpath beside wall on left, going down to road
- Turn left, along road to church on right, chapel on left, tower ahead
- Go straight on along lane to road

Section 2: 0.5mi (0.8km)
- Turn right along The Peth to A697
- Turn right, cross bridge, then immediate left onto road passing Milk Bar on right, restaurant on left

Section 3: 1.25mi (2km)
- Continue along road, passing school on left, cricket club on right
- Straight on at junction, climbing steadily
- Turn left at bend onto narrow footpath, through gate onto moor (amazing views)
- Turn right at junction at top of hill, then immediately left along path, going away from Wooler signpost

Section 4: 1mi (1.6km)
- At junction turn left, then right towards blue waymarker 50yd (45.7m) ahead
- Take left fork at junction by blue waymarker, through gate
- Continue along path ahead, passing gate on left, then through gate onto access road

Section 5: 1mi (1.6km)
- Continue straight ahead at bend onto wide track through kissing gate
- Follow path with heath and trig point on right, round left bend through gate
- Turn sharp right through gap in wall into field

We found a trig point to rest at for a moment.

- Go straight on along edge of field, with wall on right, passing pond and wood on right, through another gap in right corner, out to grass track

Section 6: 1.25 mi (2km)
- Turn right along track, onto tarmac road with radio mast on right
- Continue down road (steep), round left bend to Wooler, passing cricket field and school

Section 7: 1mi (1.6km)
- Turn right along road just after Riverside pub on right, passing garden centre and Budgens on right, onto green
- Bear right round play area, on to car park, passing bowling club on left, out to road
- Turn left, cross bridge to A697, crossing to road opposite
- Continue up Church Street, passing church and Co-op on left
- Turn right at top into Market Place, to No1 Hotel (good place for refreshments)

Section 8: 0.75mi (1.2km)
- Exit hotel, turning right and right again along Ramsey Lane
- Take second turning right along Broomey Road
- Go straight ahead at bend, crossing field, through gate in left corner
- Bear right down steep slope, through gate into static caravan park, out to access road
- Turn right, follow road over bridge into campsite

In the vicinity

Cycling/Mountainbiking

All types of cyclists are catered for; both road users and those with mountain bikes who seek out challenging rides. There are plenty of cycle routes from Wooler to be found on the internet, providing the opportunity to pass through some amazing scenery.

Birdwatching

The ideal place to see moorland birds such as black grouse and golden plover. Maps, reviews and comments from other birdwatchers are available from https://www.alltrails.com/en-gb/england/northumberland/wooler/birding.

Wooler Common

On the outskirts of Wooler, on upper third terrace level, there is an access road to Wooler Common car park, which is passed on the short walk. From the car park a path leads round two small lakes and a picnic area. There is also is a noticeboard in the car park and a small memorial plaque. Besides open common there are also areas of mature trees, with a network of footpaths criss-crossing the area, as well as St Cuthbert's Way.

Doddington Dairy Milk Bar

This milk bar might look like it just specializes in ice cream that uses the milk the Maxwell family produces from its farm in Glendale Valley, but it offers so much more. Not only does it now sell its own cheese, but it has extended its menu to include breakfasts and light lunches, as well as drinks and a range of delicious cakes. It is conveniently situated on the A697, by the bridge that crosses Wooler Water on the lowest terrace, for passing trade as well as walkers and cyclists. This charmingly small but perfectly formed 1950s themed café, with inside and outside seating, closes at 4pm but opens at 8am.

Glendale Show

If you are lucky enough to be in Wooler over the August Bank Holiday weekend, pop along to the Glendale Show held on the Showground North Middleton, 2mi (3.2km) south of Wooler on the A 697. A shuttle bus runs from Wooler bus station. This is one of the most important shows in Northumberland, celebrating all things agriculture from farming to life in the countryside, with sheep classes, cattle classes, and a dog show. Lots to see and do.

Ad Gefrin (closed Tuesday)

Situated at the junction of the A697 and the bridge which crosses Wooler Water on the lowest level of the town is Ad Gefrin, a new museum devoted to the Golden Age of the Kingdom of Northumbria during the less well known Anglo-Saxon period. As a result of a nearby archaeological dig, it houses many unique and interesting artefacts including a replica of the Great Hall at Yeavering. It is also home to a whisky distillery, the first to open in the county for 200 years. There is a café where tea and coffee is available. Tickets are available for the museum and a tour of the distillery. Though dogs are allowed in the grounds and outdoor areas, they are not allowed inside.

Walks in North West England
(Cheshire, Cumbria, Lancashire)

Cheshire – Meandering through Cheshire with the River Weaver
OS Maps: Explorer 257 Crewe & Nantwich

Frodsham town is situated on the west bank of the River Weaver. Like most long rivers, 50 mile+ (80.5km+), the nature of this Cheshire river changes as, like its name, it weaves across the countryside. The River Weaver is one of huge contrasts; at times it gurgles through quiet wooded areas, while at others it slinks past huge industrial sites. It rises near Ridley, burbling southwards to Wrenbury, where it is totally overshadowed by the Llangollen Canal, becoming in contrast a mere stream passing unnoticed under the canal and past a pub. It winds its way southwards, bypassing Wrenbury village, towards Audlem.

During the journey southeast to Audlem, the river waters gradually increase in volume. Before reaching the village it swings northwards, this time tumbling under the Shropshire Union Canal a few miles north of the Audlem. On it snakes across the Cheshire plain, its impact gradually becoming more noticeable, so by the time it reaches Nantwich and Winsford it is an important landmark.

It continues its journey northward, roaming around the Cheshire countryside in huge loops, unhurriedly expanding and deepening. Not only does this necessitate the building of ever bigger bridges, even a viaduct, it also influences the growth and development of Northwich town. Eventually the river spills out into the River Mersey, close to the Manchester Ship Canal

The River Weaver is tidal, but only navigable for about 10 miles (16km) along the section from the Manchester Ship Canal past Frodsham to Winsford. Even this small part was not a very efficient method of transport. It snaked about the countryside, and was not deep enough to be a viable option for the salt mines past which it flowed. From the early 18th century there was extensive work all across the county, not only to improve the flow of the River Weaver by the building of locks and channels, but also the building of several canals. Some of the canals ran parallel to the River Weaver, and others crossed the river.

One place this happens is at Anderton, on the northern edge of Northwich where the River Weaver flows 50ft (15m) below the Trent and Mersey Canal. At this point, the route to the River Mersey and the Manchester Ship Canal is faster navigating along the River Weaver, so in 1875 the Anderton Boat Lift was built to allow boats to move up and down between the river and the canal. This operated until 1983 when it was closed on safety grounds. As is often the way, a group of enthusiasts managed to refurbish it, and in 2002 it reopened.

The River Weaver is one of the longest rivers in Cheshire.

Over the last 300 years the river has seen many changes as a navigation route. Nowadays it offers the opportunity for many people to enjoy all kinds of leisure activities: fishing, rowing, sailing and cruising. It is quiet and peaceful, and yet is as attractive as it has always been with many signs of its long history still visible. In addition there is a profusion of wildlife, especially in those parts of the river now unsuitable for boats, such as Frodsham Cut.

The charming market town of Frodsham itself is rather overshadowed by its neighbour Runcorn, with its location on the banks of the River Mersey, halfway between Manchester and Liverpool, and its proximity to good transport links. However there is much to see in Frodsham. It has a long history, being mentioned in the Domesday Book, with many interesting buildings, and every Thursday a market is held on the main street, a tradition that has continued since 1661. Frodsham is a vibrant community with a host of small businesses, a variety of pubs, cafés and restaurants, and with an abundance of activities on offer. The views over the Mersey to Liverpool from the sandstone Frodsham Hills are incredible.

Wonderful walks from dog-friendly campsites on a budget

The campsite is large and very spacious.

LADY HEYES CAMPSITE

This is a large spacious campsite spread over 14 acres, and offering a variety of camping options besides the 85 hardstanding touring pitches, all of which have electric hook up and drainage. There is a field for tents, a designated hot tub area, together some with hardstanding pitches and glamping pods. There is only one comprehensive modern facilities block. Besides toilets and showers which have underfloor heating, there is a laundry room and vegetable preparation/dishwashing room. The site is cleverly arranged in circles and semi-circles of varying sizes. Consequently nowhere is too far from the facilities block; there are open green spaces dotted about, and each pitch has a degree of autonomy. Situated between the campsite and the road are a series of barns that house the Lady Heyes Craft Centre; various small independent shops and workshops including an indoor play area restaurant and bar. There is even a small shop in campsite reception. To ensure a smooth flow of traffic there is a crucial one way system, so take care when entering the campsite for the first time.

PEARLS OF WISDOM 🐕

This place with a designated dog walking area was splendiferous. The field wasn't very big, but we were free to run and explore, and it was big enough to chase my frisbee. Sometimes we even met other doggy companions. Occasionally my owner managed to find other areas we could potter around and sniff out exciting smells. On the walks we came across fields and some amazing woods; thankfully no silly sheep or fearsome cows. It was just a shame some of the paths were a hard surface; tarmac, my owner said. Not so many intriguing smells here, but I love inspecting new places.

RATING **££**

PRICING STRUCTURE (SEE CHAPTER 3) – FLAT RATE

PROS:
- Good location
- Pub and shop on site
- Simple easy pricing
- Plenty of places nearby to walk dogs

CONS:
- Complicated online booking process
- Cows in some of the fields
- Access route unclear

SHORT WALK – INTO THE WOODS

Distance: 4.5mi (7.2km)
Time: 3.5hr (Easy)
Terrain: Footpaths, tracks, woods, fields, some climbs, kissing gates, stiles, roads (busy ones have pavements), bench (for picnic)

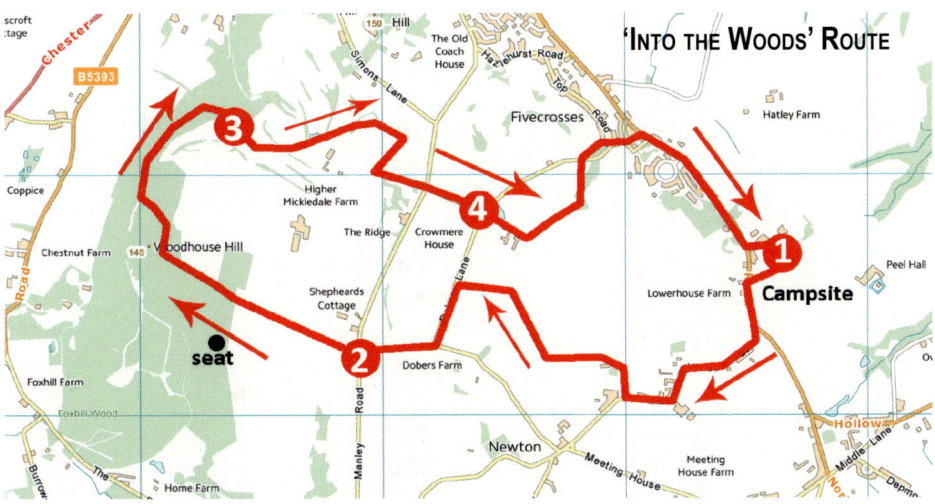

Section 1: 1.5mi (2.4km)
- Exit campsite via entrance, passing café and bar, out to B5152
- Turn left (pavement), then right uphill along Hillfoot Lane
- Follow road round two bends
- Turn right, to track beside house on right, signposted
- Continue ahead along path, passing driveway and gate into field, to T-junction
- Turn left along path between fences, passing building on right, go through kissing gate
- Turn sharp right through second kissing gate into field
- Go straight on along edge of field, with hedge on right, and through kissing gate in right corner

- Turn right along edge of field, with hedge still on right, through kissing gate in right corner into another field
- Continue straight ahead, passing phone mast on left, through gap out to wide track
- Bear left along track, out to road, turning left
- Turn right along stony track at left bend, onto narrow path, out to road

Section 2: 1mi (1.6km)

- Cross road to stony access road opposite, go through kissing gate, onto narrow path into woods, to noticeboard with map
- Detour (if wanted) – 1.5 mile (2.4km) Turn sharp left at notice board onto footpath, continue along edge of wood with fields visible on left, to viewpoint and bench (good place for a picnic). Retrace steps to notice board, turning left downhill
- Continue straight ahead at junction, passing bench on right, skirting field on right onto Sandstone Trail, signposted
- Continue ahead ignoring left fork, round right bend
- Bear left onto path leading away from field, with low stone wall on right
- Go straight on at junction, passing 'Welcome' board on left, down steps bearing right
- Turn left at bottom of hill, past a bench and another viewpoint on left, along Sandstone Trail, signposted
- Follow path downhill taking right fork

There are some fabulous woods nearby.

Section 3: 1mi (1.6km)
- Bearing right, cross the field, on opposite side follow path round right bend, with hedges on left
- Continue along grass path, round a left bend, passing under tree
- Turn left onto wide grass track across field, passing close to trees on right, hedges on left
- Continue along wide grass track, up round left bend, through a belt of trees
- Go straight on at junction, still following wide grass track, up slope and across wide junction
- Take right fork, going down slope and crossing another track onto narrow grass path between another belt of trees
- Follow path across field, passing buildings on right, towards a third line of trees and joining another path
- Bear right along path onto stony track
- Turn left at junction, go through gate ahead onto access road
- Cross road onto wide grassy track opposite
- Continue ahead, taking left fork, heading towards hedgerow, go through gate opposite in hedge
- Turn right along narrow fenced path, following short diversion into field then back onto path
- Turn left, over stile in fence into field
- Continue straight ahead, along edge of field with fence on right, and through the gate to road

Section 4: 1mi (1.6km)
- Cross to Sutton Lane, following to junction
- Cross to stony track opposite, passing pond on left, through gate ahead at bend, then onto grass track
- Follow narrow path through copse, go through kissing gate onto wide track
- Turn right down to road
- Turn right down Dobers Lane to junction
- Turn right, then left, then right again to B5152
- Follow road (pavement) to campsite

LONG WALK – ALONG THE RIVER WEAVER
Distance: 6mi (9.6km)
Time: 5hr (Easy)
Terrain: Footpaths, tracks, woods, fields, some climbs, kissing gates, stiles (one sheep proof), roads (mostly quiet), slurry patch around one stile. (Walk slightly shorter than planned, due to cows in fields)

Section 1: 1mi (1.6km)
- Exit campsite via main entrance

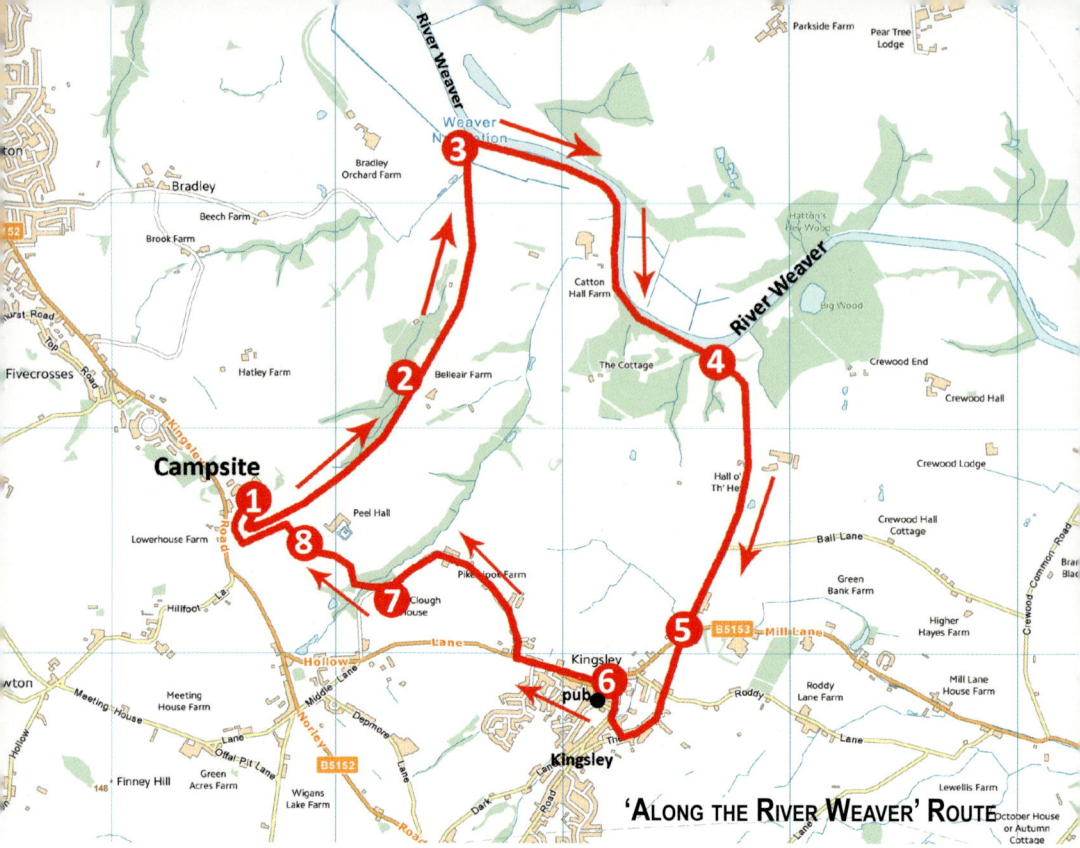

- Turn sharp left along tarmac access road opposite bar, before B5152
- Go straight ahead at junction, passing stile on left through gate into farmyard
- Bear left into field immediately after gate

Section 2: 1mi (1.6km)

- Cross field, passing hedges and houses on right, through kissing gate in middle of hedge opposite, into another field
- Bear left across field, passing telegraph pole in middle of field, go through kissing gate on right of large gate, signposted NCW (North Cheshire Way)
- Bear left, keeping telegraph pole in middle of field on right
- Keep bearing slightly left, go through kissing gate on right brow of dip, into third field
- Still bearing slightly left, cross field down through kissing gate, into road
- Cross road to field opposite
- Go straight on along edge of field, with hedge on left, through kissing gate in left corner into field
- Continue straight ahead, along wide track across field, and round right bend
- Go straight on at next bend, up slope onto riverside path.

Section 3: 1mi (1.6km)

- Turn right, with river on left
- Follow path beside river, going across two fields, through kissing gates, passing buildings on right

There are some great swimming places for dogs along the River Weaver.

- Bear left through kissing gate, onto narrow path close to river
- Follow path over several footbridges (one footbridge good place for dogs to swim), through kissing gate and out to field

Section 4: 1mi (1.6km)
- Turn right away from river, onto wide track between large hedges, going uphill, and through gate
- Continue along track, through kissing gate and farmyard, out to tarmac access road
- Bear right along road, out to minor road turning right, continuing to B5153

Section 5: 0.5mi (0.8km)
- Turn right, then in 50yd left, over stile into field
- Follow narrow path between fence on left and hedge, over stile (sheep proof), out to road
- Go straight on along The Hurst, turning first right along Well Lane, following to main road and pub on left (only open in afternoon, but a good place for a picnic)

Section 6: 0.75mi (1.2km)
- Exit pub gardens, cross road along The Cross following to B5153
- Turn left along road (busy but pavements) passing school and Co-op on left, church on right
- To avoid slurry, turn right along Pike Lane, round left bend, passing Pike Nook Farm on

left, turning sharp right to stile on left, signposted (footpath is further on), up steps and over stile into field. Bear left along edge of field to stile in left corner at slurry patch, cross next field, go over stile out to road. Turn right, keeping left, to stile, signposted on left

Section 7: 0.5mi (0.8km)

- Cross stile onto narrow footpath.
- Bear left, down path through copse, over footbridge into field
- Follow path uphill, over stile, turning right along wide grass track, over stile into field
- Go straight ahead along edge of field, with hedge on right, over another stile on right at end of brick wall, onto wide stony track

Section 8: 0.25mi (0.4km)

- Turn left along track to tarmac access road
- Turn left along road to campsite entrance, bar and café

IN THE VICINITY

CYCLING

Many of the cycle routes around Frodsham are part of the National Cycle Network. In fact maps of cycle rides from Frodsham have been specifically assembled by the Weaver and Sandstone Cycle Forum, sponsored by Frodsham Town Council, showcasing places of interest around the town.

FISHING

The River Weaver is an ideal place for all standards of fishing with a diverse range of fish, and it is a popular activity with several clubs to be found along its length. Non-members need to obtain the relevant day permit. These can be obtained from Northwich Angles or from My Gilly on mygilly.com/venue/river-weaver-cheshire. Note the river is closed from 15th March to 15th June.

BIRDWATCHING/WILDLIFE

All along the river, a variety of birds and wildlife can be seen; binoculars are advised. A particularly good place to spot birds is Frodsham Marshes, a huge area of sludge beds, north of the town and on the other side of the motorway.

SANDSTONE TRAIL

Starting at the obelisk by the Bear's Paw on Main Street in the centre of Frodsham the Sandstone trail is a 34mi (55km) walking route. It follows the sandstone ridges southwards across Cheshire, ending at the Georgian town of Whitchurch just across the border in Shropshire.

This is a relatively new walking trail, as only part of it was opened in 1974. Since then it has been extended several times, but its current length was not viable until the 1990s. It explores the county's amazing scenery, passing though open woodland, ancient forest and farmland, as well as places of historical interest.

Dutton Viaduct/Anderton Boat Lift

Many of the structures built to improve water transport have significant historic value because lots of them were built during the 18th and early 19th century. As a result some are listed. Dutton Viaduct and Anderton Boat Lift are of special interest

Dutton Viaduct carries the rail-line over the River Weaver and can only be reached on foot via the riverside path. It is approximately 4mi (6.4km) from the campsite but easily accessible via several footpaths.

It is made of local red sandstone and has 20 wide segmented arches. The engineers were Joseph Locke and the man who built the first train, George Stephenson. The viaduct was built in 1837 and has been in regular use since then, the only modification being in the 1960s to accommodate electric trains. Then in the 1990s It was classified a listed structure

The Boat Lift is 11mi (17.7km) southeast of the campsite, on the outskirts of Northwich, though it is possible (at time of writing) to reach the town of Northwich by a bus which passes the campsite. This amazing structure is one of the 'Seven Wonders of the Waterways'; a remarkable feat of engineering. It lifts boats and barges from the River Weaver to the Trent and Mersey Canal. It is possible to see it in action today thanks to the restoration work of dedicated volunteers. Information about the lift and its history, as well as refreshments, are available from the adjacent visitors' centre

Cumbria – A Dale in the Yorkshire Dales

OS Maps: Explorer OL2 Yorkshire Dales
Explorer OL19 Howgill Fells and Upper Eden Valley

So what is a dale? It is a term used in the north of England, especially in Yorkshire, for a valley that has usually been formed many ages ago by glaciers. It is thought to be an Old Norse method of identifying places. Frequently the dale, or valley, is named after the river which flows through it, for example Ribbledale after the River Ribble and Wharfedale after the River Wharfe.

This is the case for most of the 40 or so named dales of the Yorkshire Dales, but occasionally the dale is identified by the largest settlement in the valley. One such place is Dentdale. Though the river Dee flows through the dale, it takes its name after the charming village of Dent, which is the largest settlement in the dale. Confusingly, although Dentdale is geographically a typical 'dale' in the northwest part of the Yorkshire Dales, since 1974 it has been an administrative part of the county of Cumbria.

Dentdale originates at Dent Head on the northwest perimeter of Blea Moor, which is uniquely marked by the Dent Viaduct of the Settle to Carlisle Railway. The dale slices through the Pennines wandering 10½mi (17km) across some spectacular landscapes, continuing in the east-west direction to Sedbergh. Here the Dee flows into the River Rawthey and eventually drains out to the Irish Sea. In the flatter areas of the valley is an idyllic patchwork of fields, divided up by legendary local dry stone walls with a few farmhouses and barns scattered about. From there, the sides slope steeply to some of the highest hills of the National Park.

The village of Dent is situated on the lower slopes of Cragg Hill, with the River Dee

The cobbled streets and the colourful cottages of Dent are very picturesque.

curving round it like a protective arm, so some parts in the village are over ¼mi (0.5km) from the river. Because Dent is the largest settlement in the dale it is the main shopping and social area of Dentdale, but with a population of just 750 it is a quite a small village. Nevertheless it is a dynamic community with many amenities and activities. Besides the magnificent 12th century church of St Andrew's, there is a school, a village shop, two pubs and two cafés. In addition there are reading rooms, an art and craft studio, and meditation centre, as well as large playing fields and a Heritage Centre full of artefacts and information about Dent, also with a café for refreshments. This is surprising because the first impression of the village with its narrow cobbled streets and brightly painted cottages suggests a reserved conventional community. This does not appear to be the case, with several events on the calendar including the Music and Beer Festival in June and the Dentdale Show in August.

The relative isolation of Dent has resulted in many historical upheavals bypassing the village. Though the Romans did know of the dale there is no evidence that they established a settlement. It was the Norse invaders who discovered the dale in the 10th century and decided to stay awhile. Farming is the main occupation of Dentdale and has been for many, many years. For a time in the late 18th century, the local limestone was polished up into an attractive marble that was used all over the world. Unfortunately this ceased by the very early 20th century when tariffs on Italian marble were relaxed. The village did not really gain any benefits from the coming of the railway in 1877, as Dent Station was established over 4mi (6.4km) further along the dale. In fact it contributed to the demise of the marble industry, as it allowed easier quicker transport of imported Italian marble.

Then there were the 'knitters' of Dentdale. There is much information in the Heritage Centre about these people, both men and women, who found a way to diversify their income stream in the 18th century. There is also a 'Wool Shack' which sells all manner of woollen items.

Probably the most significant event which took place in Dent was the birth of Adam

Sedgwick at the Old Parsonage in Vicarage Lane in 1785. He used to wander around the surrounding countryside collecting rocks and fossils. Though he was educated at the Grammar School in Dent, he gained a place at Trinity College Cambridge, and in 1810 was elected a fellow of the college. His early interest in rocks continued throughout his life and so it was he helped establish the new science of geology. He never forgot the village of Dent, and on the main street near the church is a memorial fountain to him.

Despite still looking much as it would have 100 years ago, there is plenty to see and do in Dent. There are lots of walks, with something to suit all abilities. Information and details about these can be found in the Heritage Centre.

HIGH LANING CAMPSITE

Situated on the outskirts of the charming village of Dent is this small campsite. It is part of High Laning farm; a typical Yorkshire Dales Farm. (I saw a quad bike transporting two sheep in a trailer, complete with sheep dog). The campsite comprises two fields; one on either side of the road. The lower field is for tourers and tenters. On one side of the field near the road (no noise as so little traffic), are the hardstanding pitches, both gravel and some grass, all with electric hook-up. The rest of the grass is set for tents. The amenities block is modern and well organized including facilities to purchase tea/coffee from a vending machine. There are several toilets for both men and women but only one unisex/family shower and dishwashing area

The upper field across the road behind the Heritage Centre also run by the farm is mostly seasonal caravans and leads to the farm itself. Here is a bigger amenities block with more showers. All showers are coin operated.

PEARLS OF WISDOM 🐎

Lots of green open spaces, but according to my owner also lots of notices about using leads. Where can we dogs have a really good run? Beside the river was fun; there was even a space for us to have a swim, but those pesky sheep again; this time with small ones. Sometimes they would follow us and stamp their feet. Bit disconcerting. I wish they would go away so I could have some freedom from a lead and be able to chase my frisbee now and again. Wandering through the village was okay, despite some odd stony roads. Walks were good but too many irksome sheep for my liking.

RATING £££

PRICING STRUCTURE (SEE CHAPTER 3) – FLAT RATE

PROS:

- Good location
- Café and shop on site
- Simple easy pricing
- Lots of footpaths nearby
- Roads narrow but very quiet

CONS:

- £2.00 charge for each dog (so not such good value)

Wonderful walks from dog-friendly campsites on a budget

The campsite is on the outskirts of Dent, surrounded by fields (with sheep!) and hills.

- Lots of sheep in the fields
- Numerous notices prohibiting dogs (locals seem to ignore)
- Lack of nearby green space for ball throwing

SHORT WALK – BIMBLING ALONG THE DALES WAY
Distance: 4.25mi (6.8km)
Time: 2hr (Easy)
Terrain: Footpaths, fields, tracks, riverside paths, footbridges, spring gates, quiet roads (beware: sheep)

Section 1: 1.25mi (2km)
- Exit campsite via main entrance, turning left along road, left again along lane, signposted, through narrow gate, then larger green one, passing house on left, through another gate onto path beside wall on right, through gate into field
- Turn sharp right, cross field through gate opposite into another field
- Continue straight ahead along edge of field, passing treatment plant on left, onto track leading into field
- Go straight ahead along edge of field, through kissing gate, onto wide track, passing building on right
- Follow track out to road
- Turn left along road, then bear right at playing fields, through gate onto path leading to river
- Follow riverside path with river on left, then go through gate into field

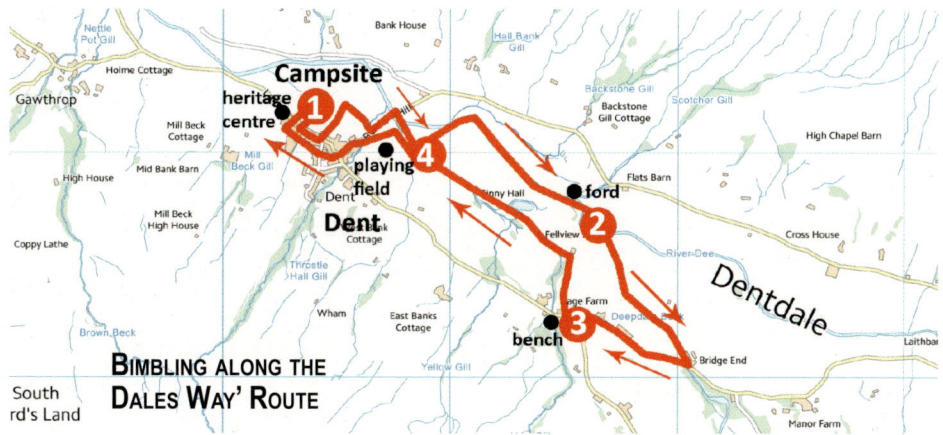

BIMBLING ALONG THE DALES WAY' ROUTE

- Cross field keeping close to river on left, turning left over footbridge
- Continue ahead across field, bearing slightly right, skirting fence corner, go through wooden gate onto path beside stone wall on left
- Follow riverside path through five gates or stiles, passing stepping stones of ford on left, then crossing footbridge ahead and through another gate

Section 2: 1mi (1.6km)
- Continue along Dales Way beside Deepdale Beck, crossing footbridge, going through two gates into field
- Go straight on along edge of next two fields, keeping close to Beck on left, go through gate onto wide stony track, out to Bridge End
- Turn right along road, uphill to junction and small green bench

Section 3: 0.75mi (1.2km)
- Turn right along track, passing house on left, signposted Double Croft Lane
- Turn left at bottom of hill, through a small wooden gate in wall, before Fell View Barn
- Continue along edge of field, close to wall on right, go through gate in wall into another field
- Turn sharp left along edge of field, go through gate
- Cross track, going through the gate opposite (note wooden sign on left)
- Follow path along edge of field, around left bend, passing pond on right and crossing field though gate ahead, over footbridge
- Turn sharply onto path beside Beck, between the trees
- Bear right just before gate under tree, onto gravel path

Section 4: 1.25mi (2km)
- Continue straight ahead, passing a ford on the left, and through gate into field
- Cross field, keeping close to Beck on left, go through gate onto fenced path
- Follow path, passing footbridge on left, through gate
- Turn left over footbridge, right along edge of field, through the gate onto riverside path

The Dales Way passes by Dent, and has many stiles with 'paddle' gates for dogs.

- Continue along path, passing playing fields on left out to road
- Go straight on along road, passing church on right, onto cobbled street, passing The Sun Inn on the left
- Follow road passing Meadowside Café on left (good for refreshments), to campsite entrance

Long Walk – Following the River to Dent
Distance: 7.25mi (11.6km)
Time: 4hr (Moderate)
Terrain: Footpaths, fields, copse, tracks, riverside paths, footbridges, stiles, spring gates, kissing gates, some short climbs, quiet roads (beware: sheep), streets, bus ride
***NB:** Buses run on Wednesdays and Saturdays only, check timetable before setting out!*

Section 1: 1mi (1.6km)
I always give the dogs a short walk before getting on buses or public transport.
- Exit campsite via main entrance, turning right along road, passing rear entrance to campsite on right
- Continue along road, passing field (of sheep!) on right, to corner
- Turn right along footpath, down towards river
- Bear right through kissing gate onto narrow footpath (Dales Way)
- Go straight across next four fields (possibly sheep), keeping close to river on left, over stiles as necessary, and out to road
- Turn right along road, passing playing fields on left
- Turn right along stony track

'FOLLOWING THE RIVER TO DENT' ROUTE

- Follow track, passing barns on right, bearing right round building (gym) and small car park
- Bear left onto lane, passing works on right, into field
- Go straight across field, and through gate on left onto narrow path
- Follow path between houses out to road
- Turn left along road to school on right, with car park, public toilets and bus stop on left

Section 2: 0.75mi (1.2km)

- The bus stops in Sedbergh outside Cumbria Council Offices on Main Street
- Turn right along Main St (there are several cafés there, I stopped at Gun Dog Café for obvious reasons)
- Continue along Main Street passing shops, toilets, market in car park (if market day), and Tourist Information/bookshop on left to junction with A684 (50yd left along the A684 is Westwoods Books)
- Turn right, cross road onto Vicarage Lane, passing playing fields on right
- Go straight on at bend, through the gate into a field, signposted Millthrop
- Continue ahead uphill, through gate, across access road, through another gate into field
- Continue along edge of field, bearing right, downhill, through narrow gate in wall
- Follow path along edge of field, close to wall on right, and out to road

Sedbergh is the nearest town, at the head of Dentdale.

Section 3: 1mi (1.6km)
- Turn left along road, downhill, cross bridge, round right bend
- Turn left, uphill, along minor road to T-junction
- Turn right towards telephone box, passing houses
- Turn left along stony track at Fell Garth Cottage
- Follow track uphill, passing house on right, then downhill over stream and round to right
- Take left fork uphill, signposted, through gate into field

Section 4: 1mi (1.6km)
- Continue along edge of field, close to wall on left, through gate onto wide path, ignoring other paths leading off
- Follow path through three gates, into field
- Cross field through farmyard, onto to stony track, signposted Millthorp, to T-junction
- Turn right down hill to road
- Bear left across road, onto track between walls
- Follow track over two footbridges, turning right
- Go straight ahead, bearing left through farmyard, out to road

Section 5: 1mi (1.6km)
- Continue along road to farm buildings on right
- Turn left over footbridge, then right onto narrow path, with river on right

Section 6: 1mi (1.6km)
- Follow path through gate into field
- Continue straight ahead, along path on top of dyke, close to river on right, passing through gates of four fields
- Up steps, through the gate, then through copse out to road

Section 7: 1mi (1.6km)
- Turn right along road over bridge
- Turn left though gate part way along bridge wall (very narrow), down steps into field
- Go straight across field, with river now on left, over footbridge through gate opposite, into another field
- Bear right across field to bend in river on left, go through gate over two footbridges into field
- Continue along edge of next two fields, with river on left, then through gate and out to road

Section 8: 0.5mi (0.8km)
- Turn left, and follow road back to campsite

IN THE VICINITY (DENTDALE)

CYCLING
There are several interesting cycle routes that can be found online.

FISHING
It is possible to fish in the River Dee, but a day or weekly ticket is required. This can be obtained from Sedbergh Anglers.

GOLF
Visitors are welcome at Sedbergh Golf Course, subject to availability. Check the website for details.

DENT HERITAGE CENTRE
This small museum is housed in the old filling station. The various rooms of the museum are packed with information and artefacts about the social customs and working lives of local Dales people from the 16th century onwards. Margaret Taylor was the curator when I visited, but volunteers from the village also support the venture with videos and scale models of significant features of the area. It is an interesting place to spend a couple of hours and to obtain maps and pamphlets about Dent, then to recuperate and study them with refreshments at the café.

Wonderful walks from dog-friendly campsites on a budget

SETTLE TO CARLISLE RAILWAY

This 73 mile (117 km) long main railway line in northern England opened in August 1875, initially just for freight traffic. It was an amazing feat of engineering, because the route crosses some of the most remote and difficult terrain in England; 14 tunnels and 22 viaducts, including some really spectacular ones, were needed, and high engineering standards were the priority during construction. As a consequence many stations along the route were several miles from the actual settlement. Dent is a typical example of this. This did not prevent passenger services being introduce from April 1876.

British Rail proposed closing the line during the 1980s. One of the reasons for this was the high cost of maintaining the line; particularly all the tunnels and viaducts. However, a diverse group of people and organizations opposed this, and in 1989 the decision was retracted. This decision has proved correct as since then passenger numbers have increased to 1.2 million in 2012. Eight stations that had been closed were reopened, and the line has provided vital support to some local businesses. Even though the line is operated by a commercial company, it is one of the most popular rail lines, with all kinds of trains using it.

DENT STATION

This is a typical example of the village being situated a long way from the station, being four miles (6.4km) away from Dent. It is in fact the highest station in England at 1150ft above sea level and with amazing views of the countryside, especially from the viaducts at Dent Head and Arten. On both platforms there are waiting rooms, but the station is unmanned. In fact one of the buildings has been converted into a holiday let, so is private property.

COWGILL

This is another small village in Dentdale, much closer to Dent railway station than Dent itself. The village pub The Sportsman Inn dates from the 17th century. The church, St John the Evangelist was built in 1837.

SEDBERGH

Located at the start of Dentdale, is the stone built market town of Sedbergh. As well as being a good starting point for various outdoor pursuits, walking, cycling etc it is also an interesting town to explore. There are a variety of small independent shops on the main street as well as numerous book shops. In 2003 it became England's book town. Of particular note is Westwood Books on the edge of the main street, which has over 70,000 books and the Sedbergh Information and Book Shop which is run by volunteers. An ideal place to look and browse.

FARFIELD MILL ARTS, CRAFTS AND HERITAGE CENTRE

Just a mile along the A684 is this Craft and Heritage Centre. It is busy most days with workshops, displays, demonstrations etc. The heritage loom is still used to weave textiles for the local people. Again there is a café, where you can take some time to appreciate the work of the centre.

SEDGEWICK GEOLOGICAL TRAIL

In 1985 this trail was created to celebrate the bicentenary of the birth of the geologist Adam Sedgwick in Dent. It starts at a car park on the A684 about 2mi (3.5km) east of Sedbergh. Each of the 12 rock exposures is numbered on a wooden post. Be aware that part of the trail crosses private land.

Lancashire – Betwixt and Between
OS MAPS: EXPLORER 287 WEST PENNINE MOORS

Surrounded by the sprawling conurbations of the former Lancastrian mill towns of Bolton, Chorley, Blackburn, Darwen, Accrington, Burnley, and Bury, and dissected by road and rail, is the lesser known West Pennine Moors. This 90sq mi (233km²) area is in sharp contrast to the nearby towns, offering a 'wild space' with unspoiled countryside, dense woodland, lakes, reservoirs, moors, diverse habitats for wildlife, and attractive villages.

One such place is Rivington Village, situated about halfway between Chorley in the northwest and Bolton to the southeast. What's more, it is squeezed between the flatter Lancashire plain to the west and the high moorlands of the West Pennine Moors to the east. It was originally a small rural village in a quiet backwater, with the main occupations being farming, home-based spinning and weaving, and just a handful of miners working the small mines and quarries in the area. All this changed during the 19th century with the construction of the reservoirs, built to address the health problems experienced by the people of Liverpool. Eventually, after much discussion, The Rivington Pike scheme,

One of the many reservoirs at Rivington

designed by Thomas Hawlsey, and still supplying clean water to Liverpool today, was agreed. Construction finally started in 1850. Initially this led to a fall in the population, but the influx of workers resulted in a change in the character of the village, with more pubs opening. Once the reservoirs were completed there was a growth in tourism, partly to see the engineering wonder of the time, but also as an escape for the factory workers. This was fuelled by the growth of cheap rail transport.

The scheme proposed the building of five reservoirs. The water of the two smaller ones, Rake Brook and Lower Roddlesworth, was carried south by a man-made channel, a 'Goit', to the three main, large ones, Anglezarke, Upper Rivington and Lower Rivington. These were formed by flooding three valleys, which dramatically changed the landscape of the area. Upper Rivington and Lower Rivington reservoirs are really one large body of water separated by a long wide embankment, along which runs Horrobin Lane, permitting access to both sides of the reservoirs.

The scheme was expanded several times with the construction of smaller reservoirs in the area, including Yarrow Reservoir, which was started in 1867. At this time it was the largest reservoir complex ever built, and became the template for similar projects all over the world.

In 1902, in order to secure water supplies, the then local council, Liverpool Corporation, suggested the further expansion of the project, which would have necessitated the demolition of the entire village of Rivington. This caused a huge outcry from local people. Nevertheless, properties in the village were acquired by Liverpool Corporation. The support of William Lever, who had purchased the lands of Rivington Hall resulted in a rethink. As a consequence, the project for the village on the eastern shore of the reservoir around the Hall was scaled down.

Part of the lands that William Lever (who later became Lord Leverhulme) bought at Rivington were to be his rural retreat. The rest he gifted to the town of Bolton, which he would develop at his own expense, and from then on known as Lever Park. He had grand plans for the area, despite it being the side of a steep hill leading up to the moors. He was able to realize this, having become a very successful business man as part owner of Lever Brothers. Beside plans for a grand house and formal gardens for himself, he also wanted to build lakes, ravines, bridges, refreshment huts, garden terraces, a zoo, and many other 'follies', all connected by paths and steps; lots of steps. It was a really ambitious project, and a work in progress from the moment the park opened in 1904 until his death in 1925, after which all work ceased and it was decided to sell everything.

The land was bought by Liverpool Corporation, who did not know what to do with it and so just left everything. Over the years the park fell into disrepair and became dangerous, so it was agreed the best option was to demolish everything. This process began, but fortunately only slowly. In 1974 the situation was reassessed, due to the enormous reorganization of local government (Liverpool Corporation was abolished) and greater awareness of preserving places of significance and extensive local interest. So began a programme of restoration. Again, because the original plans were so all-encompassing, the restoration is also a long process and still a work in progress. It is a particularly interesting place to visit, as there is something different to see each time.

Nowadays, like when the reservoirs were first built, thousands of people come to Rivington to either explore the West Pennine Moors, to admire the incredible engineering feat of the reservoirs via the profusion of footpaths, or to visit the amazing Lever Park, its gardens, lakes and unusual outbuildings.

RIVINGTON BREWERY CAMPSITE

This is a Camping and Caravanning Club CS (certificated site), a small site with just 10 pitches, all hardstanding, situated in a semi-circle around a lovely green area, and overlooked by the trees os Rivington Country Park and Lever Park. One water tap can be found near the entrance, and the facilities block is conveniently located on one side at the top of the semi-circle. It is perfectly functional and kept spotlessly clean. On the other side of the semi-circle, well out of the way, is the chemical disposal. On the sloping bottom part of the field are bell tents. With the brewery taproom and farm using the same driveway as the campsite there is an interesting flow of traffic; horses during the day as there is a livery stable on site, and in the evenings visitors to the taproom. The taproom is a converted barn with a large outside seating area and several street food vans.

PEARLS OF WISDOM

How lucky we were. There were actual woods on site. Fabulous to explore, but oh not much of them; a few sniffs and we were done. However, a bonus was the large green space down the hill; great for chasing my frisbee. There were lots of other woods to explore and some water for swimming – hooray! But we had to go along a narrow tarmac bit beside a busy road to reach them. But then, so many different ways to go; down to the water or up to the tower, and lots of other dogs to meet and greet. What fun, fun, fun.

The campsite overlooks the amazing Rivington country Park and Lever Park.

Wonderful walks from dog-friendly campsites on a budget

RATING ££
PRICING STRUCTURE (SEE CHAPTER 3) – FLAT RATE
PROS:

- Good location
- Brewery on site
- Simple easy pricing (Sat/Sun & Mon-Thur)
- Dog walk on site (small)
- Plenty of easy accessible off site walks
- Places for a dog swim

CONS:

- Some steep hills
- Short busy road with narrow pavement
- Several tarmac routes (quiet)

SHORT WALK – CASTLE HUNTING

Distance: 4.25mi (6.8km)
Time: 2.5hr (Easy)
Terrain: Footpaths, tracks, woods, some steep climbs, castle ruins, kissing gates roads (quiet)

Section 1: 1mi (1.6km)

- Exit campsite via main entrance, turning right and crossing bridge
- Continue along road, passing Rivington Tea Rooms on left

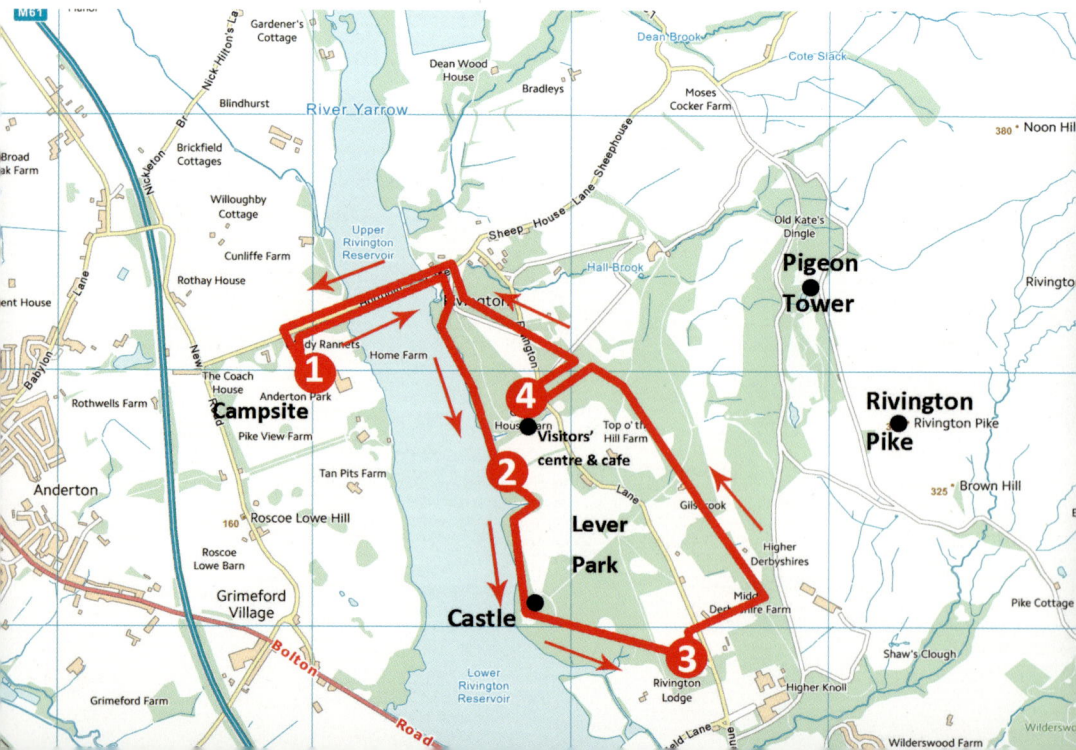

Part of 'Liverpool Castle' at Lever Park, neither of which were ever finished.

- Turn right along road, passing school on left, into car park
- Turn right down path between wooden fence and bin, towards large notice board
- Follow path, keeping close to fence on right
- Take right fork, passing footbridge on left, then left fork along path parallel to water on right, and stone wall on left, passing GoApe structures on left

Section 2: 1mi (1.6km)
- Continue along path, with wooden fence now on right, over a footbridge, and up slope
- Take left fork away from fence, onto path parallel to water (that can be glimpsed on right through gap in wooden fence), ahead onto narrow path winding along water's edge, over wooden fence onto wide cobble path
- Turn right, then right again in 50yd (45.7m), through gap in fence and back into woods
- Bear left onto path parallel to cobbled track
- Take left fork onto wide path, with fence on right and close to water on right (excellent dog swim), passing bench on left
- Bear slightly left onto wide well-used path
- Take left fork up to stony track
- Turn right, then right again at junction, onto wide track towards stone building (castle turret)
- Turn left along path round turret to castle entrance (free to explore, dogs allowed)
- Exit castle via entrance
- Continue straight ahead at junction onto wide track ignoring all paths leading off towards road

Section 3: 1mi (1.6km)
- Turn left along path immediately before road, then left at junction, out to road
- Cross road to path opposite between school on right and fence on left, climbing (long steady climb)
- Round left bend, still climbing, out to wide stony track
- Turn left along track, straight on at four-way junction, through gate
- Turn left at next four-way junction, downhill, passing bench on left

Section 4: 1.25mi (2km)
- Bear immediate left, through cycle gate, onto narrow path, down to road
- Cross road to Great House Barn for refreshments
- Exit/retrace route across road onto path, uphill through cycle gate, bearing right to wide track
- Turn left along path to road
- Cross road onto wide track opposite, through car park, passing school on right, and out to road
- Turn left along road, continue over reservoir bridge
- Turn left into campsite entrance

LONG WALK – WATERING LIVERPOOL
Distance: 7mi (11.2km)
Time: 3.5hr (Moderate)
Terrain: Footpaths, tracks, narrow stony path woods, kissing gates, stiles (one stone wall), some climbs, roads (quiet)

Section 1: 1mi (1.6km)
- Exit campsite via main entrance, turning right and crossing bridge
- Continue along road, turning left along cul-de-sac, passing Rivington Tea Rooms on right
- Follow access road, with water on left, and passing fishing gate on left
- Take left fork through gate, along stony track, towards reservoir embankment on right

Section 2: 1mi (1.6km)
- Take right fork, keeping close to reservoir and view of aqueduct on right, continue to road
- Turn left down road to junction
- Turn sharp right, keeping water on left
- Continue straight ahead at right bend, through two gates, still keeping close to water on left

Section 3: 1mi (1.6km)
- Follow tarmac path with water still on left, between stone gateposts, ignoring all paths off to right, continue uphill and go through gate
- Continue along path, out to field, round right bend, onto downhill stony track and through gate

Section 4: 0.75mi (1.2km)

- Straight ahead at junction, uphill through gate onto 'moor'
- Go straight on, cross footbridge, passing seat on right, through kissing gate onto path through woods, over wooden walkways, down steps, across footbridge and up through kissing gate, out to road
- Turn left along road over bridge, passing house on left, over second bridge, go through kissing gate

Section 5: 1 mi (1.6km)

- Turn left along path, then left again at end of wooden fence
- Turn right, continue along narrow path with stone wall on right (take care of large stones), water on left
- Follow path round left bend, then right bend, with fence now on right, passing notice board on left, and out to reservoir embankment with houses on right

Section 6: 1 mi (1.6km)

- Continue along top of embankment, round to left, then down over gate (care with big dogs), into road
- Turn left along road, to main road with pub opposite (Yew Tree Inn – a good place for refreshments)

Section 7: 0.25mi (0.4km)

- Exit pub onto road, turning right along Knowsley Lane
- Turn right along access road immediately before bridge

Section 8: 1 mi (1.6km)

- Continue along track out to main road, with water still on left
- Turn right to campsite, entrance on left

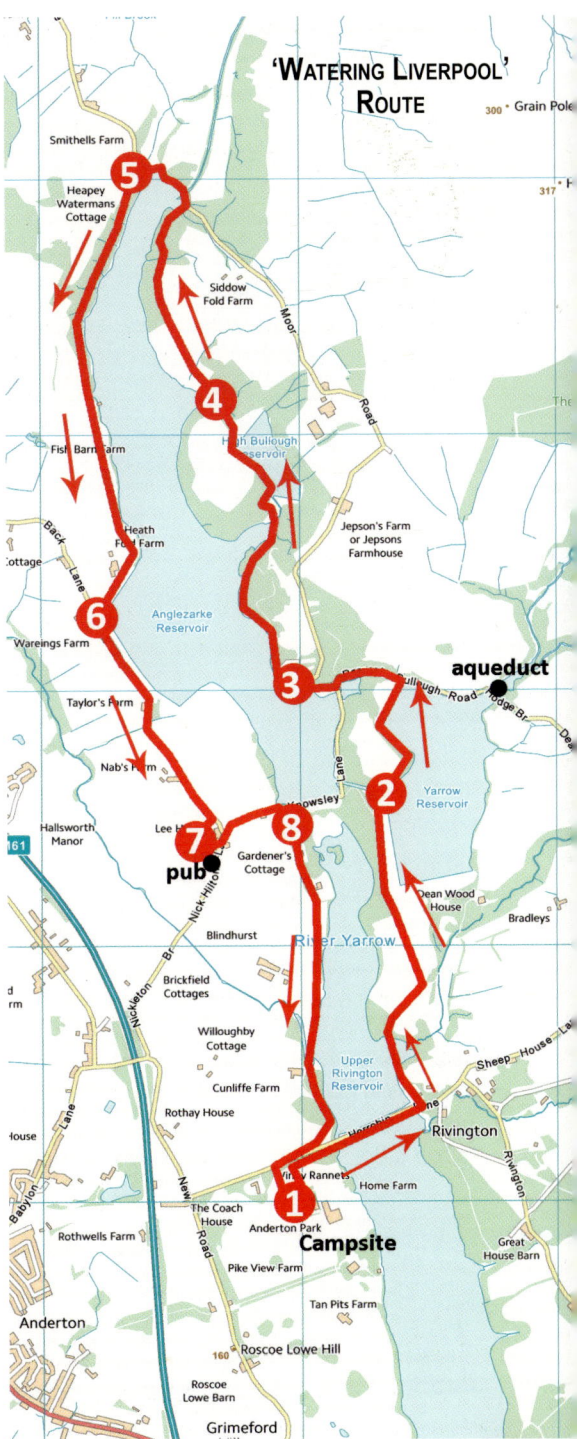

'WATERING LIVERPOOL' ROUTE

The viaduct from Yarrow reservoir.

IN THE VICINITY

CYCLING

There are lots of possible cycle routes around Rivington and the reservoirs, for all abilities and with many suggestions online. Beware, the route up to the West Pennine Moors is very steep!

FISHING

The reservoirs around Rivington are extremely popular with anglers and several fishing clubs use this fabulous facility. The rules are very strict to prevent contaminating the waters, and because there are conservation areas along the shores. Information and Day Tickets can be obtained from the Great House Barn information centre at Rivington, Crown Tackle & Bait, Coppull Anglers or via Adlington Angling Centre, Facebook page.

BIRDWATCHING/WILDLIFE

Both the West Pennine Moors and the Rivington reservoirs support a wide variety of birds and wildlife, with both environments in some way unique.

GREAT HOUSE BARN TEA ROOMS/GREAT HOUSE FARMHOUSE INFORMATION CENTRE

The barn is an excellent example of a medieval tithe barn. It was used to store food and shelter cattle. In the 1900s William Lever sympathetically refurbished it to provide refreshments for visitors. After WW1 the barn reopened as a café and provides light meals and snacks for visitors.

The adjacent farmhouse was also renovated by William Lever, and now houses an information centre where information about the area and maps of Lever Park can be obtained, which is essential as there are so many paths and steps that lead to interesting places. Both places are listed.

RIVINGTON HALL/RIVINGTON HALL BARN

The current Rivington Hall is a Georgian fronted building on the same site as the one demolished in 1774. The council bought the Hall and Barn when William Lever died. They were used as billets during WW2, but then were left and became quite dilapidated. The Salmon family leased them for some time, and the Hall is now a private residence, but Hall Barn is now a café and a wedding venue. Both places are listed.

PIGEON TOWER

This was built by William Lever as a present for his wife. It is situated at the top northwest edge of the terraced gardens, with the top floor as a small sitting room where Lady Lever could sew or play music, and look out at the boating lake. The other floors were home to doves and pigeons. The three floors were accessed by a solid narrow circular stone staircase. Volunteers open it to the public on holidays.

WINTER HILL

This is the highest point of the West Pennine Moors, as indicated by the trig point near the TV masts and towers over Rivington. Rather than a single summit pointing to the sky it is a raised moorland plateau of several smaller hills, and is popular with walkers.

RIVINGTON PIKE

One of the smaller hills on the West Pennine Moors is Rivington Pike. It is especially prominent because a tower was built on it in 1733; originally used as a hunting lodge, the three windows and door are now blocked. When owned by Liverpool City Council it was neglected to such an extent that in 1967 the only option was to demolish it. This provoked fierce opposition and a legal challenge. Eventually ownership was transferred to Chorley Council and restoration work began. Even though it is not possible to climb the tower, the views are spectacular.

LIVERPOOL CASTLE/LEVER CASTLE/THE CASTLE

This castle ruin is known by different names. It is a replica of Liverpool Castle, which no longer exists. It is one of the 'follies' that William Lever built, so is sometimes called Lever Castle, and locally it is known simply as The Castle. Construction began in 1912, but was slow. William Lever had ambitious plans for it to include a terrace overlooking the reservoir and tea gardens. However, work stopped when he died in 1925, and was never resumed. It is free to visit, but be careful as the ground is uneven and some stones are loose. Nevertheless it is an impressive structure.

Walks in Central England
(Herefordshire, Nottinghamshire, Oxfordshire)

Herefordshire – A Hidden Gem

OS Maps: Explorer OL13 Brecon Beacons National Park

Despite its close proximity to the large conurbations of the Midlands, Herefordshire is a very rural county with Wales on its western border, and has a historic connection to Wales as part of the Welsh Marches. These days this term is merely descriptive of the borderland region between England and Wales; however, historically it has been a contentious issue, and was once a wild and turbulent frontier. Squeezed between the mountains of western Wales and the rivers of England, control of the Welsh Marches ensured a buffer from marauding invaders, often the Welsh Celtic tribes. So, in the 8th century, Offa, King of Mercia, built a dyke to keep the Welsh out! It was the Normans, however, who, hoping to subdue the Welsh and secure the area, built castles and fortifications all over the counties on either side of the Welsh border, thus reinforcing the unique region of the Welsh Marches. As a result it has the highest concentration of all types of castles in the UK.

In fact what happened is that this geographically somewhat isolated rural area developed a unique identity, a hybrid of Welsh and English. This persists today, with a blending of identity still evident in the more remote rural areas of the Welsh Marches and the county.

The River Wye, the fifth longest river in the UK, is considered to be a Welsh river. Yes, it does rise in Cambrian Hills of central Wales, but during its 135 miles (217km) it winds its way into western Herefordshire, encompassing amazing views and charming villages. It is a significant feature of the county as it meanders around the countryside before slipping out of the southeast corner back into Wales. This is the largest river in Herefordshire, but, as it drifts through the landscape, several other rivers drain into it, many of them quite large such as the River Lugg and River Frome. On the western side of the county the River Dore, which passes the campsite, carves its way southwards to the River Monnow, meeting the magnificent River Wye just as it flows into Wales.

Despite so many waterways, river transport in Herefordshire was not important or efficient. Even the new canal technology of the 19th century was unable to harness the rivers. There were plans for canals, and two were even started, but they were not successful. Similarly, with the industrial revolution: there was some mining, and a few mills and industrial works along the rivers, but by and large the county remained an industrial backwater, with agriculture remaining important and farming as the main occupation.

The amazing views and charming villages of Herefordshire, in a diverse landscape created by the many rivers in the county.

The county is known primarily for its produce. Cider production, especially, is important. It is thought the cider orchards of Herefordshire provide over half of all cider consumed in the UK. Strongbow cider is made by Bulmers, which has its headquarters in Hereford. Also important is fruit production. Recently soft fruits, such as strawberries have become viable due to the introduction and use of polytunnels, which allow the growing season to be extended. Then there is cattle – or rather beef. Hereford beef cattle are very common and these gentle and hardy animals can be found all over the world.

This unassuming region has much to discover: farms, wooded river valleys, small villages, half-timbered buildings, castles, as well as historic market towns and, of course, the cathedral town of Hereford. Tourism is increasing here, no doubt due to the peaceful atmosphere and stunning scenery.

POSTON MILL CAMPSITE

This very large campsite is part of a chain, Morris Leisure, which runs five other similarly large campsites in this western area of England and Wales. Poston Mill campsite has 59 pitches, all hardstanding. With several static caravans in a large section on the other side of the access road, the facilities are considerable. In addition to a modern heated shower block there is a dishwashing and vegetable preparation area, laundry, a shop

Wonderful walks from dog-friendly campsites on a budget

housed in reception, an on-site pub (with restricted opening times), pitch and putt golf, fishing, dog washing facilities, dog grooming and a huge 10 acre (4ha) dog exercise area. As the campsite stretches out along the River Dore, there is also a delightful stroll along the river bank and adjoining golf course. It is a well organized and efficiently run campsite.

Pearls of wisdom 🐕

So many places to investigate just a sniff away, but, oh confusion. Sometimes we were on leads in wide open spaces that we were keen and eager to explore, but in other places we could run free. I loved those. So much to sniff out, even though we went there several times. All very exciting. There was even somewhere close by to chase my frisbee. Perfect! The walks were good too, though in the fields beside the river there were often these big animals, cows I think. They do rather spoil things for us, but we get by. Though there was a river so close, having a swim was not possible. Shame. The field was a-maz-ing!

Rating £££
Pricing structure (see Chapter 3) – Complicated
Pros:
- Brilliant dog walk on site
- Well organized
- Special offers available

Cons:
- Price not available until booking process complete
- On site pub and café only open during summer
- Cows in nearby field

The large dog exercise area next to the campsite.

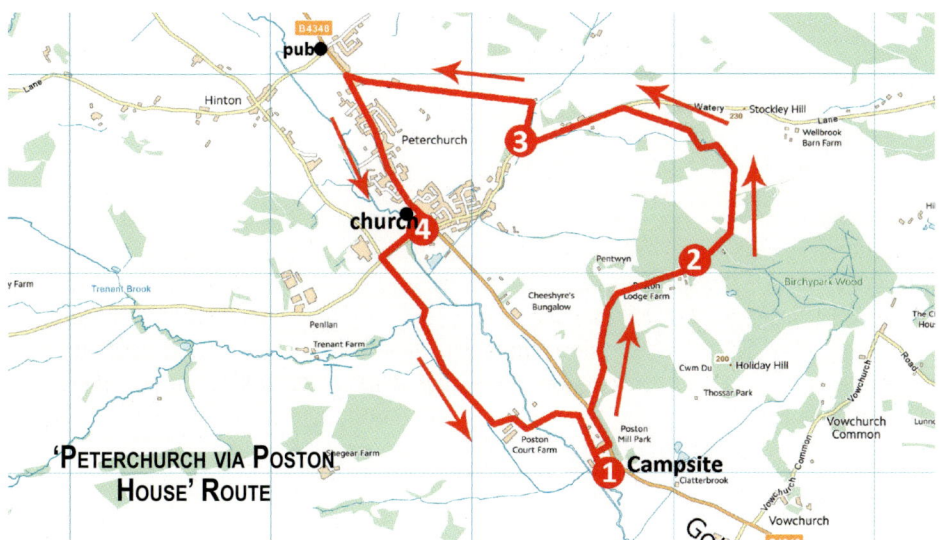

'Peterchurch via Poston House' Route

Short Walk – Peterchurch via Poston House

Distance: 4.5mi (7.2km)
Time: 2.5hr (moderate)
Terrain: Footpaths, tracks, fields, woods, footbridges, some steep climbs, gates, stiles (several sheep-proof), roads (mostly quiet). Also watch for cows in fields

Section 1: 1mi (1.6km)

- Exit campsite entrance through barriers, onto road B4348
- Turn left along grass, passing 'The Mill' and bus stop on left, to driveway
- Cross road over stile opposite, signposted, onto narrow footpath between trees, over stile and into field
- Turn left along edge of field, keeping close to fence, following it round to right, passing stile, up slope to corner
- Continue straight ahead and uphill to tarmac driveway
- Turn left along driveway (amazing views)
- Take right fork, still climbing, through gate onto gravelly path, passing big house on right
- Continue straight ahead, go through gate between buildings, passing tennis court on right, and through third gate
- Take left fork onto grass path, signposted Stockley Hill
- Follow path over stile into field

Section 2: 1mile (1.6km)

- Bear left across field, towards gate, go over metal stile at side
- Go straight ahead, and over   stile in hedge on left
- Bear left for 50 paces, over stile in fence, onto overgrown path
- Bear right, going down to join wide track

The River Dore that flows along Golden Valley.

- Turn right along track
- Turn left in 50yd (46m), signposted with yellow waymarker, downhill, passing two more yellow waymarkers on right
- Continue along footpath, close to fence, on right over stile
- Cross track, bearing slightly right, over stile into field
- Bearing slightly right, cross large field, heading towards right corner, over stile or through gate to road
- Turn left along road onto wide stony track on right
- Follow track to left bend

Section 3: 1.25mi (2km)
- Continue along track towards garage
- Turn left, passing house on right, onto narrow footpath then wide grassy track
- Go straight ahead along footpath, passing hedges on either side and purple gate on right
- Cross junction onto wide track, with buildings on left and stile on both sides, out to B4348

- Turn left along road (to the right along B4348 is a pub, but it doesn't serve food), into Peterchurch, passing church on left (has a café) and school on right, to junction with Closure Place

Section 4: 1.25mi (2km)
- 20 paces after the junction, turn right over stile in hedge
- Turn left, cross field bearing slightly right, cross stile in hedge out to road
- Turn right along road, cross bridge over stile immediately on left, onto footpath through copse, then over stile into field
- Cross field, keeping trees on left, over the stile in corner to wide track and river bank
- Bear slightly left to cross footbridge ahead, through gate on left, and into field
- Bear left along edge of field, keeping close to river on left, through the gate into another field
- Continue along the edge of the next three fields, following the river, passing farm on left, and go through gate
- Over footbridge, and through gate into another field
- Bear left, going through small gate onto narrow path, with fence on right and river on left
- Follow path over footbridge to campsite entrance

LONG WALK – THE HEREFORDSHIRE TRAIL
Distance: 7mi (11.2km)
Time: 4hr (moderate)
Terrain: Footpaths, tracks, fields, woods, footbridges, some steep climbs, gates, stiles (several sheep-proof), roads (quiet). Also watch for cows in fields

Section 1: 0.75mi (1.2km)
- Exit campsite via footbridge onto narrow path
- Follow path through gate into field
- Turn left along edge of next two fields, and out to road
- Turn left along road to bend
- Continue ahead, passing house on left, and through gate into field

Section 2: 1mi (1.6km)
- Turn right across field, through gate, over footbridge, into field
- Bear left across field, uphill, over stile, and into wood
- Continue through wood, uphill (steep in places), go through gate
- Bear left between trees, out to field
- Continue ahead along edge of field, with hedge on left, through copse, across small field and through gate into another wood

Section 3: 1mi (1.6km)
- Follow path, go over stile in fence on left, into field
- Cross field, bearing slightly right, away from wood, downhill, across stream with stepping

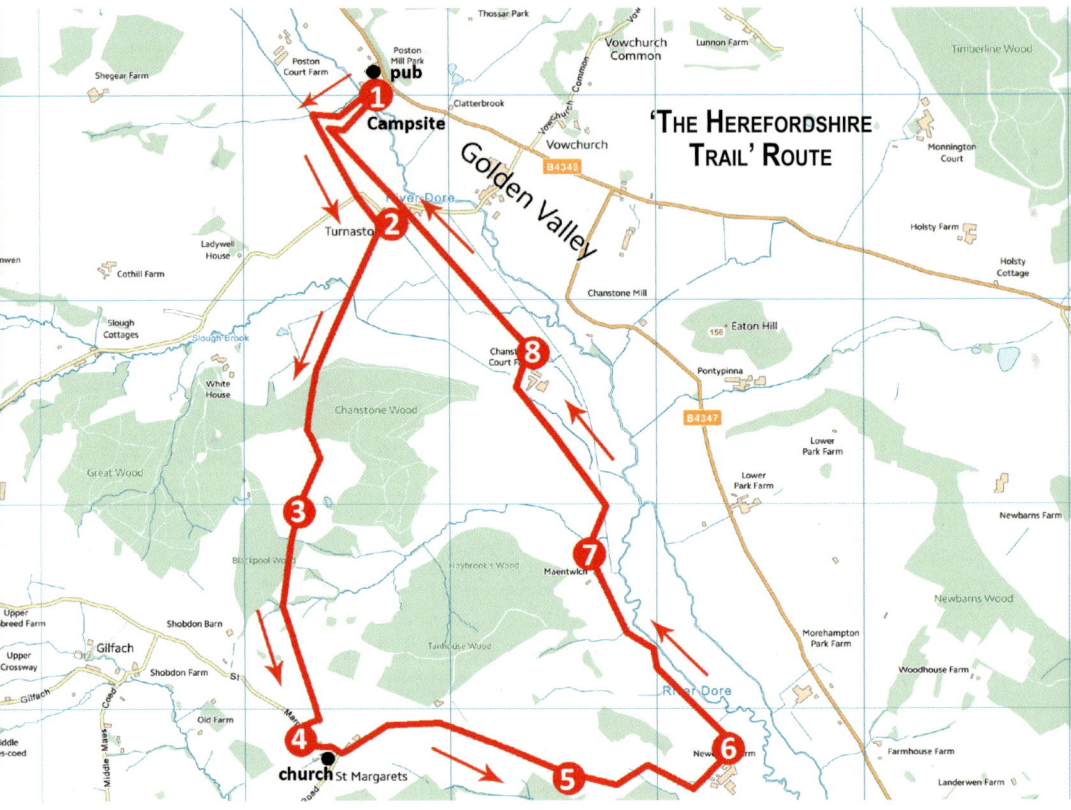

stones, uphill and over stile ahead (gate beside), into field, through gate at top of hill
- Bear left through gate ahead
- Cross field, bearing left, to top left corner, go over stile (gate beside), onto track
- Follow track out to field, bearing right, across to building in right corner
- Turn sharp right, then continue along track, passing building on right, through the gate out to road

Section 4: 1mi (1.6km)
- Turn left along road, past church (open to visitors, and a good place to sit in porch for break/food), to bend by Fountain Cottage
- Turn left along road, signposted, through gate, passing stiles in fence on right, going round left bend
- Turn right through gap in fence, before grey barns and after stile on right
- Bear right across field, passing clump of trees on right, over stile by three trees
- Continue straight on across field, towards fence on left, over stile (very difficult for dogs to jump/hole in fence on left – alternative route is: straight on through gate keeping close to fence on left; through gate in left corner)
- Turn right along edge of field to right corner, then left

Section 5: 0.5mi (0.8km)

- Continue downhill, with woods on right, through gate, towards farm and through another gate
- Turn immediate left, following hedge down to farm
- Continue straight ahead through farmyard turning left between barns through gate ahead out to access road
- Follow road away from farm turning left through gate into field, signposted

Section 6: 0.75mi (1.2km)

- Continue along edge of field, with hedge on left, bearing right as field narrows, passing two gates on left, then go through gate into field
- Cross field, keeping close to hedge on right, go through gate out to track
- Turn left, passing barn on left, through gate on right into field

Section 7: 1mi (1.6km)

- Cross field over footbridge ahead (difficult for dogs/small gap in fence) into field
- Turn right around two sides of field, through gap into second field
- Turn right around two sides of this field
- Straight ahead at right corner, and cross track into another field
- Turn right along two sides of field, with hedge still on right
- Turn right at corner, through gate to track

Section 8: 1mi (1.6km)

- Turn right, continue along track, and through farmyard
- Turn left along tarmac road, passing house on right, through gate onto wide track

As a rural county farming is important, so there is livestock in many of the surrounding fields.

- Follow track through gate into field
- Straight on across field, with hedge on left, through gate, then over footbridge
- Continue ahead, through gate, along edges of two fields, then through gate
- Along edge of field, turn right over footbridge, passing farm and gate on right, out to road
- Go straight on along road to left bend
- Continue ahead, through gate into field
- Go straight on along edges of next two fields, with hedge on right
- Turn right, go through small gate onto narrow footpath
- Continue along path to campsite

IN THE VICINITY

FISHING

With so many rivers in the county, fishing is very popular. The campsite is situated beside the River Dore, so there are opportunities for fishing. Enquire at reception for further information.

CYCLING

There are plenty of cycle routes from Peterchurch and the campsite, for a variety of abilities. These can be found online. The county has many interesting places, some of which are suggested in the cycle routes.

BIRDWATCHING

With seats dotted about the large campsite there are plenty of places to sit and lookout over the Golden Valley for birds.

PETERCHURCH

The B4348 runs along the Golden Valley beside the River Dore, so the village is strung out along it in a roughly north-south direction. At the northern end is the pub, The Nags Head, a typical local country pub which, surprisingly, doesn't offer food. At the other end of the village is the school and St Peter's church.

ST PETER'S CHURCH

Legend has it that the village took its name from the church, which was dedicated by St Peter on his way to Rome. It seems a strange route to take, but then it is not known where he started. It is also thought that the church was founded by King Offa (there are lots of hypotheses). What is known is that the church is Norman in origin, but was restored during Victorian times. It has recently been updated with part of it converted into a more accessible community space, including providing refreshments during the day. The magnificent spire is visible from many parts of the surrounding area. Most unusually it is made from fibreglass, though it is difficult to tell.

ST PETER'S WELL

East of the church, along Bazley Lane, is St Peter's Well. This is a spring, which again according to legend, was blessed by St Peter so that baptisms could be held there. It is easy to miss, as all that is visible are a few mossy steps and bubbling water.

ARTHUR'S STONE

About 6mi (9.6km) north of the campsite is a Neolithic burial chamber called Arthur's Stone. It is said to be the site of one of King Arthur's battles when he defeated a giant.

SNODHILL CASTLE

The remains of this castle, north of the campsite along the Golden Valley, have recently been acquired by Historic England after many years of neglect. It is now being restored and made safe for visitors. It is also being carefully studied and catalogued in order to discover more about it.

BUSES

There is a bus stop outside the campsite. Buses go to Hereford and Hay-on-Wye. Check times and destination at reception and online.

Nottinghamshire – Robin Hood's Home

OS MAPS: EXPLORER 270 SHERWOOD FOREST

Mention the name Nottingham or Nottinghamshire to just about anyone in the world and they will immediately respond 'Robin Hood'. Most people would be able to recount the bare bones of the legend: a man who hid in Sherwood Forest, with his band of merry men, to rob the rich and give money to the poor. This has been embellished throughout history with details added to the story to make it more interesting and exciting, especially by the entertainment industry. Many films and TV series featuring Robin Hood have been made.

Mystery still surrounds Robin Hood, despite thorough scrutiny of evidence. There is even doubt that he actually existed. The name Robin Hood and various derivatives are used in a range of bygone myths and legends, and so he became an established folklore figure which was then incorporated into literary and historical sources.

Certainly during the 12th century life was hard; Robin or Robert Hood was a common name, and there were many outlaws so called. The forest in Nottinghamshire was enormous, stretching from Nottingham in the south to Doncaster in the north. Within the forest were meadows, villages, fields, and commons, as well as trees. An ideal hiding place for outlaws. There are some who believe Robin of Sherwood was a real person, based on evidence from a grave in Kirklees Hall in Yorkshire. The gravestone has the inscription, 'Here underneath this little stone / Lies Robert Earl of Huntington / Never archer were as he so good / And people called him Robin Hood / Such outlaws as him and his men / Will England never see again'. Whatever the true story, it has captured the imagination of generations of people.

Nottinghamshire is a landlocked oval-shaped county, surrounded by Leicestershire, Derbyshire, South Yorkshire and Lincolnshire. Because the foothills of the Pennine range butt up against the western edge of the county, the terrain is squashed into a mostly north-

It's easy to imagine how Robin Hood could have hidden out in this forest.

south direction, as are the road and rail transport links. This has resulted in three quite distinctive separate regions in the county.

The southwest of the county changed enormously during the Industrial Revolution, as this is where the much need deposits of coal and iron ore were discovered. Mining and various other associated industries sprang up. It was a period of growth and innovation, with the founding of cotton and lace industries, and construction of canals and railways. Many innovations resulted from this region including tarmac and traffic lights, and Nottingham is also well known for Raleigh bicycles. It is still a densely populated area with a range of industries.

In contrast, the central region is relatively sparsely populated. During the medieval period the huge forest of Sherwood covered the area. Over the centuries it was divided up into new forest plantations or various estates with huge mansions and landscaped surroundings. One of these estates is Clumber Park now managed by The National Trust.

The third section is around the Trent River in the east of the county. This is an important agricultural area. Beside arable farms growing sugar beets and cereal, there are also several dairy farms, many of which are involved in the production of cheese, Stilton in particular.

Nottinghamshire is also notable for its successes in many different sports. It was here that the ice dance champions Torville and Dean, as well as rowing supremo Sir Steve Redgrave trained. Nottinghamshire Cricket Club is first class; its ground is Trent Bridge. There are two football teams, Nottingham Forest who play in the Premier League and Notts County in League Division 2. Nottinghamshire is an enjoyable place and a remarkable county with a long, interesting backstory, in addition to the Robin Hood legend.

CLUMBER PARK CARAVAN AND MOTORHOME CLUB CAMPSITE

This is a large and very spacious Club campsite situated deep in the woods of Clumber Park, which is owned and managed by The National Trust. The facilities are of the usual high club standard, but having recently been refurbished they are modern and quite luxurious. There are two of these swish blocks on the site. As it is so large, there are three gates around the perimeter of the site that lead directly into the woods .The 188 pitches are divided into three catagories: grass + EHU; hardstanding + EHU, and Premium (everything supplied at pitch, water, EHU etc.) The price of each pitch varies accordingly, with grass the cheapest and Premium the dearest. A couple of things to be aware of: first, the phone signal is non-existent on the campsite and in much of the woods, with the exception of a few 'hotspots', one being near reception. The club hopes to remedy this in the near future. Second, it is an isolated site. The nearest shop is several miles away in Worksop, and the nearest refreshment establishment is about 2mi (3.2km) away in the Clumber Park Activity 'hub' near the remains of the house. With over 4000 acres (161.9ha) of woodland and parkland, there is plenty to explore.

PEARLS OF WISDOM 🐾

Amazing! Two tail wags and we were through a gate into woods – mind you, my owner often took a while fiddling with the catch to open it. Where to go? So much choice: wide paths, narrow ones, stony ones, grass ones, and even the occasional tarmac. Were they roads? My son and I were not put on leads as there did not seem to be any vehicles. Surprisingly we did meet cows, big ones with huge horns, and sheep. My owner found a wonderful route through the woods that avoided them, so I didn't have to worry about being inspected. We even managed to have a swim and find a space among the trees to have the occasional frisbee chase. It was a fantastic place even when it rained.

RATING ££££

PRICING STRUCTURE (SEE CHAPTER 3) – ITEMIZED AND SEASONAL

PROS:
- Well organized
- Usual high Club standards
- Direct access to the large wood
- Good price for solo members in low season
- No charge for dogs

CONS:
- Sharp price increase for couples and families.
- Price not available until booking process complete
- No pub or shop locally

One of the three gates leading directly into the forest from the campsite.

Wonderful walks from dog-friendly campsites on a budget

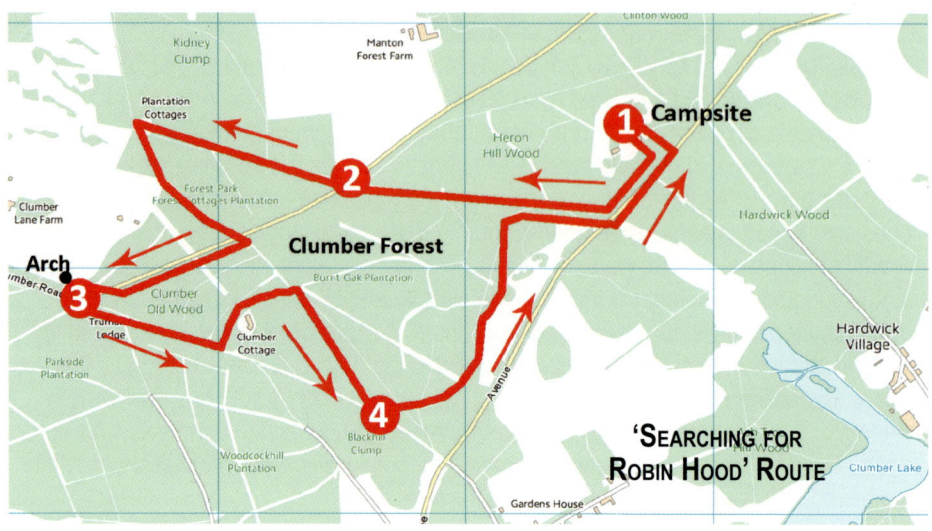

Short Walk – Searching for Robin Hood
Distance: 4.5mi (7.2km)
Time: 2.5hr (Easy)
Terrain: Footpaths, tracks, woods, some short gentle climbs, kissing gates, roads (mostly quiet; one busy)

Section 1: 1mi (1.6km)
- Exit campsite via gate near pitch 34
- Go straight on along path, out to Limetree Avenue, turning right
- Turn right again in 300yd (274km), go through gate (opposite gate on other side of Avenue) onto wide path
- Follow path as it meanders through shrubs and trees, then through double gates numbered 16
- Continue ahead, taking right fork at junction, straight on to road

Section 2: 1.25mi (2km)
- Cross road onto path opposite
- Follow path in woods, through gate round wooden barrier passing house on right
- Turn left opposite house, onto wide track, continue to junction
- Bear left along very wide path to road
- Cross road to track opposite, going round metal barrier
- Turn immediately right along very narrow footpath, parallel to road on right, to junction
- Turn right, follow path round several bends, and out to road on right

Section 3: 1mi (1.6km)
- Turn left along road to main road, left again to Clumber Park Gate
- Go through arch along road (take care, busy)

- Turn left along track beside post No 19, to four-way junction (wide track)
- Turn right at next junction staying on Robin Hood Way
- Continue ahead, ignoring path to left, No 18
- Take second path on left (check out amazing tree shapes)

Section 4: 1.25mi (2km)
- Follow path (around fallen tree, if still there), across open space onto path opposite, to junction No 17
- Go straight on along path, towards junction post No 16
- Turn right, through two pairs of gates, along path, out to Limetree Avenue
- Turn left, then first left, onto narrow path.
- Follow path to campsite gate

Taking a break after looking for the elusive Robin Hood in the forest.

LONG WALK – EXPLORING CLUMBER PARK
Distance: 6.5mi (10.4km)
Time: 4hr (Easy)
Terrain: Footpaths, tracks, woods, kissing gates, roads (mostly quiet)

Section 1: 1mi (1.6km)
- Exit campsite via gate near pitch 34
- Go straight on along path, out to Limetree Avenue, turning left
- Turn right in 500yd (457m) onto footpath, into woods, over a large fallen log, then a smaller one

- Continue along path to junction, turning left out to road
- Cross road to path opposite, then immediate right, along wide path, to junction

Section 2: 0.75mi (1.2km)
- Turn right, then left before gate, to next junction
- Bear right onto wide track, then left up slope
- Take right fork onto narrow path
- Continue straight ahead, over open space, beneath tree, onto tarmac lane
- Turn left, up slope, to main road
- Turn right along road into Hardwick village
- Follow road round right bend, through a car park, passing Park Inn to toilets and refreshment van with outdoor seating area beside lake

Section 3: 1mi (1.6km)
- Turn left with lake on right, go over weir bridge and around lake
- Take left fork, No 5, signposted 'all cycles'
- At right bend of cycle path go straight ahead, onto narrow footpath, into woods, and through gate

- 100yd (91m) past gate, turn sharp right, keeping to main path at junction in 30 paces, out to open space
- Bear left across open space to wide track opposite
- Turn left along wide grass track

Section 4: 0.75mi (1.2km)
- Take right fork at junction, and right again at next junction
- Follow wide grassy track, taking right fork at wide junction to join another track, bearing left through gate, ahead onto tarmac lane

Section 5: 0.75mi (1.2km)
- Turn right along lane, with view of church between hedges, to bridge (place for dogs to swim)
- Cross bridge, taking right fork

Section 6: 0.5mi (0.8km)
- Turn right on to wide path at signpost 'Laundry Yard'
- Follow path round to left, across open space, back onto wide path, with wooden fence on right, out to tarmac path
- Turn right along tarmac path, through gate beside notice board, towards church

Section 7: 0.75mi (1.2km)
- Bear left through gap in hedge to Activity Centre of Park, passing café on the right (a good place to stop for refreshments, with toilets on left)
- Continue straight on, passing buildings on left (these house various activities that are well worth investigating)

The 'Hub' and café in the outbuildings of the house.

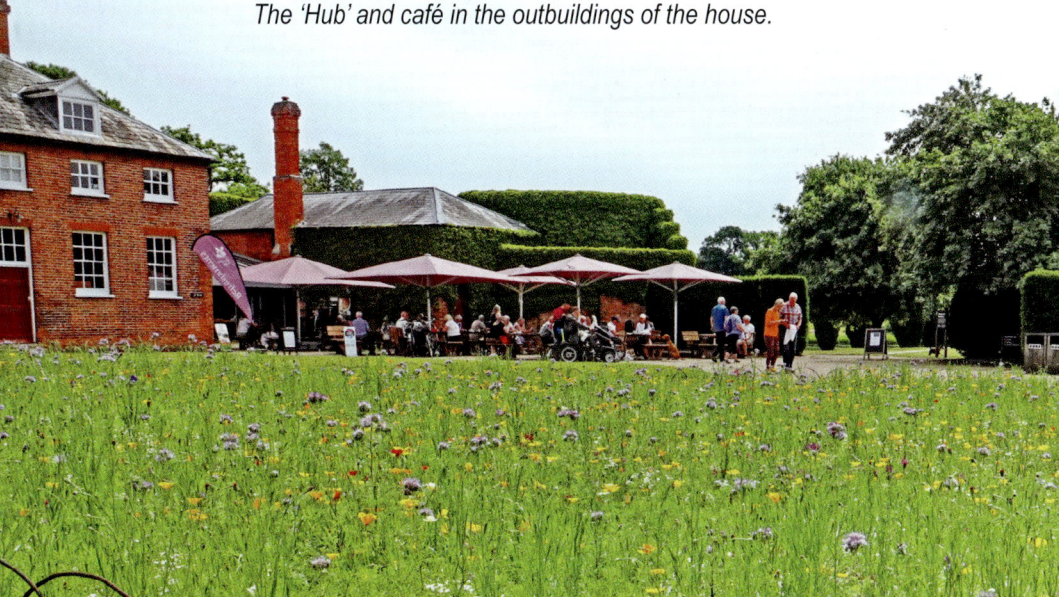

Wonderful walks from dog-friendly campsites on a budget

- Bear left through large gates by shop (also worth a visit)
- Turn right and immediate right again, along path between trees, out to car park
- Turn right, passing car park on left (paths off to the left lead to the Kitchen Garden and a special dog café called 'Central Bark' with activities for dogs in the outdoor area, signposted)
- Go straight on at bend into overflow car park field
- Bear left onto narrow grass path leading out to field
- Cross field passing large tree on left
- Bearing slightly right, go through gate in hedge (opposite second large tree on right)
- Go straight ahead along wide track between trees, joining another wide track

Section 8: 1mi (1.6km)

- Continue straight ahead at junction along very wide track, round barrier onto tarmac lane
- Cross lane, go through gate into field
- Follow path across field, and out to tarmac minor road
- Turn right along road over cattle grid
- Turn left round barrier onto path, crossing junction onto narrow path over two tree trunks, out to Limetree Avenue
- Cross road, turn left, take first path on right to campsite gate

IN THE VICINITY

CLUMBER PARK

This is one of the huge estates that were carved out of Sherwood Forest. It is over 3800 acres (1500ha) in size, which includes the house, lakes, formal gardens, open heath, rolling farmland and over 2250 acres (910ha) of woods. Like many large estates it has a long history. For over three centuries it was the home of the Dukes of Newcastle. In 1938 the house was demolished in part because of a fire, but also to avoid a tax bill, and the contents of the house were sold to pay off debts. Fortunately The National Trust was able to purchase the property in 1946 to restore it, and then open it to the public. Nowadays it is one of the most visited National Trust properties. It is a large park with lots to see, so it is a good idea to pop into the visitors' centre for maps and information.

CYCLING

This is an ideal way to explore the over 20mi (32km) of trails which criss-cross the different landscapes of the Park. There are routes suitable for all abilities and ages. Forgot your bike? No problem. The cycle hub located near the outbuildings of the old house has a large selection of bicycles and equipment. No need to book as it operates on a first come first serve basis. Further details available online.

BIRDWATCHING/WILDLIFE

There is an abundance of wildlife to spot in the parkland, whilst the walk around the lake offers the opportunity to see a variety of birds. There is even a bird hide in Ash Tree Hill Wood by the vehicle access to the overflow car park.

CHURCH OF ST MARY THE VIRGIN

Situated between the outbuildings and the lake, this 19th century church is an imposing building towering over the grounds. In many ways it seems out of place; too grand and opulent for only the family to use for worship. Even though there is no family now, services are held every Sunday. It is as marvellous inside as outside.

DISCOVERY CENTRE/MUSEUM/OUTBUILDINGS/VISITOR CENTRE

The house may have been demolished but the outbuildings weren't. The National Trust has converted these into different zones that inform and demonstrate the different aspects of the Park. There is a small museum with information about the history of the Park and the surrounding area. The 'Discovery' area is a series of activities illustrating the significance of the Park in the wider world. Other outbuildings are used to raise funds for the upkeep of the Park, with a shop, the sale of second-hand books and plants, as well as a visitors' centre. Adjacent to the outbuilding is a café which is housed in the only part of the house still standing, called The Duke's Study.

WALLED KITCHEN GARDEN

This 4 acre(1.6ha) horticultural interest is situated some distance north of the lakes, church and barns. The walled kitchen garden at Clumber Park is one of the most impressive surviving 18th century walled gardens. In its prime it was the finest garden for an elite family, providing employment for 30 people.

Quality produce is still cultivated in the gardens and the enormous greenhouses, but nowadays modern and organic methods are used. All food grown is used in the Park's cafés and restaurants, and is available for purchase in the barns. Also in the gardens is a museum of gardening tools.

CENTRAL BARK

Adjacent to the Kitchen Gardens is a dog café; Central Bark. It provides an enclosed play area for dogs; like an obstacle course, as well as special 'refreshments' for dogs. Oh yes, owners can get refreshments too.

HARDWICK VILLAGE

At the eastern end of the Clumber Lake is this small rural village, comprising a few cottages and a farm. It was originally built by the Dukes of Newcastle to house his estate farm workers. These days the properties are mostly occupied by commuters.

WORKSOP

This is a market town, known as the 'Gateway to the Dukeries' because it is surrounded by the large estates owned by various Dukes, including Clumber Park. The Worksop Heritage Trail provides information about the church and important buildings, as well as the Chesterfield Canal, which passes through the middle of the town. Markets are still held on three days, Wednesday, Friday and Saturday.

Wonderful walks from dog-friendly campsites on a budget

Oxfordshire – On the border
OS Maps: Explorer 206 Edge Hill & Fenny Compton

Oxfordshire is centrally located in the UK. It lies almost completely in the basin of the River Thames, with tributaries rippling down to swell the river as it courses southwards to London. Its capital Oxford is a renowned tourist city with its 'dreaming spires', and yet there is so much else to explore in the Oxfordshire countryside.

The Cotswolds spill over into the northwest section of the county, as evidenced by the quintessential small villages and towns of golden coloured stone cottages and buildings. In the south of the county the chalk hills of the North Wessex Downs stretch northwards, and to the southeast are the woods of the Chiltern Hills. All of these are AONBs (Areas of Outstanding Natural Beauty). In addition there are the charming towns and villages dotted along the River Thames.

Despite being so central, the county is mainly rural, with agriculture still essential to the economy. Wool has been and remains significant, but diversification has become a necessity, so there is mixed farming with many farms now organic.

Not far from the campsite in the northwest part of the county is Banbury, the second largest town after Oxford. If people have heard of Banbury, it is usually in connection with the nursery rhyme: 'Ride a cock horse to Banbury Cross, to see a fine lady upon a white horse'. It is not certain who the fine lady was. Some think Lady Godiva, others Queen Elizabeth I. Whoever it is, there is a statue of a 'fine lady' in the centre of the town.

There is just as much uncertainty about which cross is meant in the nursery rhyme. There were, in fact, three crosses dotted around the medieval town of Banbury. It is assumed the reference was to the most important one: the High Cross in the centre of the town. All three crosses were destroyed by the Puritans in the 1500s, and only one was replaced by the Victorians in 1859: the High Cross, which still stands tall today. Even this assumption is contested. Banbury is situated at the junction of two ancient routes; the Banbury Lane and Salt Way. Maybe the 'cross' refers to the historical crossroad.

Perhaps the town's position at this junction contributed to its prosperity. For centuries it has been a busy market town, benefiting from the establishment of canals and then railways. It is still an important centre of industry due to the proximity of the M40, having grown over the last few years.

On the border of Oxfordshire and Warwickshire is the Edge Hill escarpment. This was such a significant factor in the first major battle of the English Civil War between the Royalists and the Parliamentarians on Sunday 23rd October 1642 that the confrontation is recorded historically as the Battle of Edge Hill. The armies accidentally met here whilst the Parliamentarians were marching across the plain to Worcester, and the Royalist army were navigating the escarpment on their way to London.

The Royalist came down the steep slope to engage the Parliamentarians on the plain. The battle was long and bloody but ultimately inconclusive though both sides claimed victory. Had the Royalist continued immediately to London this may well have been the one and only battle. As it was the Parliamentarians reached London first and there were many more battles over several years before the conflict was finally resolved.

A view of the plain where the first battle took place between Charles I and Oliver Cromwell. The church in the middle has an exhibition of the event.

MOUNT FARM CAMPSITE

On the borders of Oxfordshire and Warwickshire, overlooking the charming precipitous village of Ratley, is Mount Farm. Being ecologically aware, the farmers have adopted 'regenerative' practices. Here soil health is the priority, so there is as little soil disturbance as possible and no pesticides or chemical fertilizers are used. As with many farms nowadays, diversification is essential. Some of the barns and outbuildings on the opposite side of the access road to the farmhouse are used as storage by local businesses. The campsite field is just beyond this. It is a large flat field, with 16 pitches that all have electric hook-up, but are not specifically marked, so it feels somewhat disorganized. Beyond this is another field for off-grid campers and tents, as well as being used for rallies. The amenities block is in the back of one of the outbuildings and some distance from the pitches, especially the rally field. It is, however, comprehensive and modern, with a laundry and dishwashing area.

PEARLS OF WISDOM 🐅

So we stayed on a farm. I though that meant there would be lots of those big smelly animals (cows, I think they're called) and umpteen sheep milling about, so I would have to be on the lead all over the place. But no! Lots of green space with only other dogs to meet. Even the field next door was just grass. We were allowed to check out this field, as well as investigating all the nooks and crannies. And at the entrance to the place was a playing field – frisbee time! Lots and lots to do. The walks were great too, with fields and even woods; a bit hilly though. That didn't worry me or Pippin.

RATING ££

PRICING STRUCTURE (SEE CHAPTER 3) – FLAT RATE

PROS:
- Brilliant dog walk on site
- Playing field nearby
- Modern toilet block
- Pub in village
- Informal, relaxed site

CONS:
- Toilet block across adjacent field
- Pub down a steep hill
- No shop

One of the fields beside the campsite where dogs can be exercised if no cattle or crops.

SHORT WALK – BATTLE WALK
Distance: 4mi (6.4km)
Time: 3.5hr (Easy)
Terrain: Footpaths, tracks, fields, steps, woods, gates, stiles, some very steep climbs, roads (quiet)

Section 1: 1mi (1.6km)
- Exit via campsite entrance onto Batchelors Lane

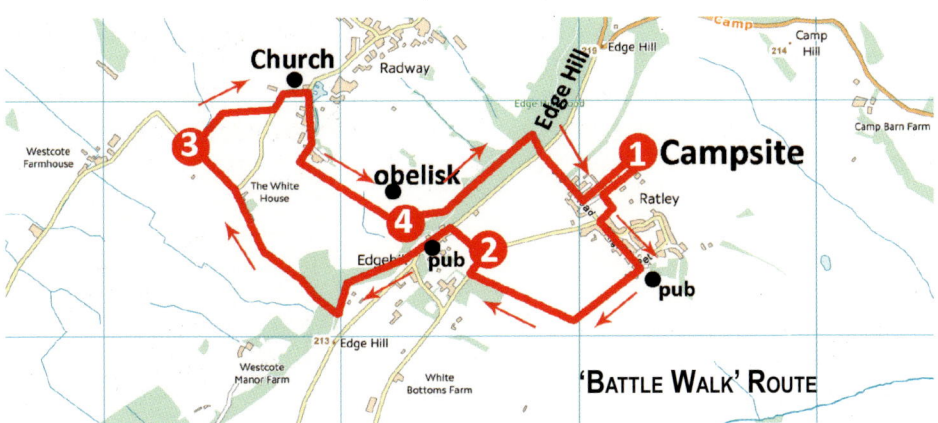

- Turn left onto playing field, crossing down slope to stony track
- Turn right along track to road
- Take second turning left, downhill, passing houses and post box on right
- Turn right along stony track towards gate, passing buildings on left, cross the stile keeping gate on left (bar to raise)
- Bear slightly right, uphill, across field, then down and through the gate
- Cross field bearing slightly right (steep uphill climb), towards right corner where field narrows, and over stile ahead onto wide stony track (Battlefields)
- Turn right along track, keeping close to hedge on right through gate out to road
- Turn right along road, left in 50yd (45.7m) onto narrow lane between drives, go round bends and out to road

Section 2: 1mi (1.6km)
- Bear left, cross road onto narrow lane beside telegraph pole, passing on right a magnificent tower that is now a pub, down steps across junction, where turning on left leads to pub car park
- Follow path downhill (steep), to wide junction, turning left along footpath, through woods to another junction
- Turn sharp right along wide track, still through woods, going downhill, and out to access road King John Lane
- Continue straight ahead, passing house on right, keeping left at junction along road
- Turn right through kissing gate into field

Section 3: 1mi (1.6km)
- Follow path across next four fields, through gates, and out to road (gate to road difficult to open – climb over, dogs can squeeze under)
- Turn left along road, round bend, left into churchyard, and church with Battle Exhibition
- Exit church, out to road, turning left, then right at junction, along Westend
- Follow road round left bend onto wide stony track, through gate then kissing gate into field

- Cross field, keeping close to fence on right, through kissing gate into second field, with hedge now on left
- Climb very steep hill towards tower and trees ahead (on left there is a possible detour to obelisk that commemorates the Battle of Waterloo), through kissing gate and into woods

Section 4: 1mi (1.6km)
- Direct route to campsite: Turn sharp left along path through woods, to wide junction with kissing gate, into field on left
- *or* detour to Pub Castle at Edgehill:
- Bearing left take middle path uphill (steep), with metal handrail on left
- Turn right at junction along stony track, towards tower, out to tarmac area, under walkway to entrance (good place to stop for views and refreshments)
- Exit castle, retrace steps under walkway to stony path.
- Continue straight ahead at junction along stony path, going downhill to junction
- Turn right along path, over fallen log, to wide junction with kissing gate on left
- To campsite:
- Take right fork at junction, up short steep hill to steps
- Climb long flight of steps and short path between, known as Jacob's Ladder, out to road
- Bear left across road to minor road
- Take second left, Batchelors Lane, passing playing field on right to campsite entrance

A replica of one of the soldiers who fought at the Battle of Edge Hill as displayed in the exhibition in the church.

LONG WALK – SWEET SMELLING
Distance: 7.25mi (11.7km)
Time: 5hr (Easy)
Terrain: Footpaths, tracks, woods, fields, gates, kissing gates, stiles (some sheep-proof), footbridges, some climbs, roads (mostly quiet, one difficult)

Section 1: 0.75mi (1.2km)
- Exit campsite via entrance, turning left across playing field down slope to track
- Turn left along wide stony track
- Go straight on at left bend, onto narrow path, passing gate on left
- Follow path through kissing gate across field to hedge opposite

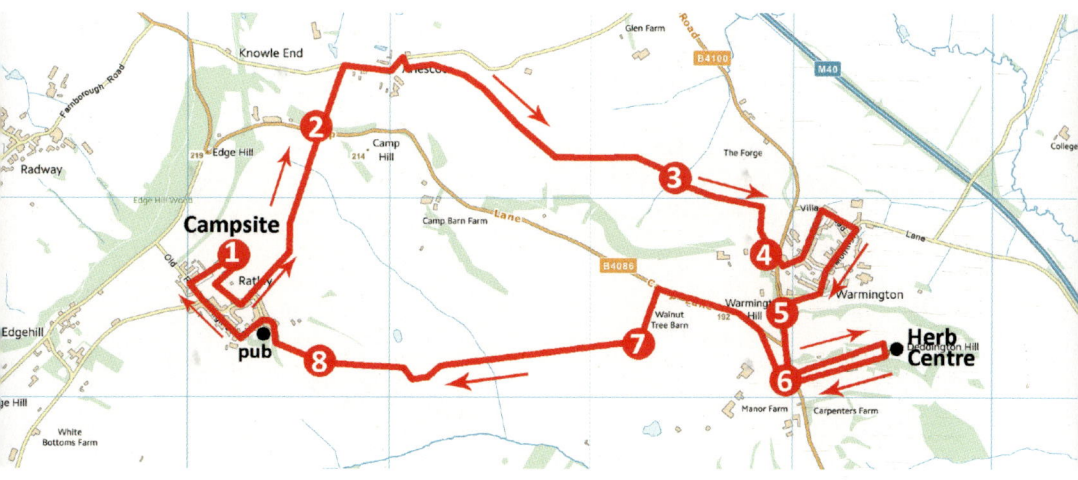

- Turn left along edge of field, along path between hedge on right, fence on left
- Follow path through kissing gate
- Cross field, bearing slightly right, crossing footbridge into another field
- Go straight across, out to B4086 (busy) via narrow steep footpath beside telegraph pole

Section 2: 1mi (1.6km)

- Cross road over stile opposite, onto narrow footpath, winding downhill through gate into field
- Go straight across field, through gate into another field
- Bear right over stile (might be a problem for fat dogs) to road
- Turn right along road, round left bend
- Turn right across green at next bend, through kissing gate
- Bear right across track, go through gate into small orchard, then through kissing gate opposite into larger field
- Continue ahead along edge, with hedge on left, through kissing gate, over footbridge (broken) into another field
- Go straight on along the edge of three fields, with hedges on left, through kissing gates as necessary
- In left corner of last field, go through kissing gate and over footbridge into field
- Continue ahead along edge of field, this time with hedge on right

Section 3: 1mi (1.6km)

- Go straight on at corner, across middle of field, cross footbridge in hedge opposite into another field
- Continue ahead, keeping close to hedge on left, go through gap in hedge in left corner into field
- Turn immediately right through another gap in hedge, cross the footbridge into field
- Go straight on along edge of field, with hedge now on right

The campsite is situated on the edge of the village of Ratley which has some very steep streets, including Chapel Street, seen here.

- Bear left across this field to just before large tree in hedge (two thirds of the way along), cross stile opposite into another field
- Continue ahead, along edge of field, with fence on right, over stile (take care, loose wire at bottom) opposite onto grass lane
- Follow lane over stile onto B1400

Section 4: 1mi (1.6km)
- Turn right along road (pavement), immediate left, down narrow road into Warmington, to T-junction, ignoring all roads leading off
- Turn right along Village Road, right again along Mollington Road, passing pond on left and pub on right
- Continue uphill, cross road at right bend, go through gap in hedge, onto footpath and up steps onto path

Section 5 (visiting Herb Centre): 1mi+ (1.6km+)
- Follow the path beside church wall, out to road B1400
- Turn left along road (pavement) to Herb Centre entrance on left (Herb Centre is an

interesting place to visit with an excellent café/restaurant)
* Retrace steps to Herb Centre entrance on B1400

Section 6: 0.75mi (1.2km)
* Turn right along road, then left along Camp Lane (no pavement but straight, and lane not too busy)
* Turn left along wide stony track, through gate, round right bend, and through another gate

Section 7: 1mi (1.6km)
* Turn immediately right, downhill, over stile at bottom of hill
* Continue straight across field towards tree in middle, go through gap in hedge
* Straight across next field, through gate onto wide junction
* Turn along track between trees, go round right bend
* Bear left at next bend, cross over stile (adjacent gate just tied) into field
* Bear slightly right, uphill, keeping telegraph pole on right, passing pond on right, through kissing gate at top of hill

Section 8: 0.75mi (1.2km)
* Bear right downhill keeping telegraph pole on left, waymarker on right, through gate on right
* Go straight ahead, uphill towards telegraph pole in middle of field, out to access road with building on right
* Continue down road, through gate passing pub on left, to Church Street, go straight on uphill, passing houses on left
* Turn right along Batchelors Lane to campsite entrance

IN THE VICINITY
CYCLING
This peaceful Cotswold area is ideal for cyclists, if somewhat hilly. There are many quiet typical villages to explore and Banbury is only 9mi (14.5km) away. Suggested routes can be found online.

RATLEY
The campsite is situated at the top of the hill on the outskirts of this charming Cotswold village. Its quirky layout is intriguing. The village hall is a beautiful converted barn, well used by the community. At the bottom of the hill is the historic Rose and Crown. Explore the village by following the Millennium Sculpture Trail based on the four elements; water (Groggs Spring), air (weather vane), earth (obelisk), fire (bonfire site), which is near the campsite. Details of these sculptures are available online.

RADWAY
At the foot of the escarpment very close to the Edge Hill battlefield is this village. It is a

long village stretched out along the road. At one end is St Peter's church. Though this is a relatively modern church having been built in 1866, it is on the site of previous church buildings. It houses a permanent exhibition about the Battle of Edge Hill and its effect on the local community. It is excellent and very informative.

THE WATERLOO OBELISK
Part way up the escarpment slope in the middle of a field is this curious obelisk. It was erected in 1854 to commemorate Fiennes Miller, who fought at the battle of Waterloo, but it is unclear why. However, its location is stunning, and the views are amazing.

CASTLE AT EDGE HILL
A building that grabs your attention whether driving, cycling or walking. Contrary to expectations it is not an ancient castle, having been built as a 'folly' in the 1740s to commemorate the centenary of the Battle of Edge Hill. The site was carefully selected, as it was King Charles I's headquarters prior to the battle. Inside is information about the battle, while the gardens overlook the battlefield. These days it is a hotel and restaurant. An ideal place for refreshments and to enjoy the spectacular view.

NATIONAL HERB CENTRE
A garden centre dedicated to all things to do with herbs. Not only are herbs sold, it is also a place of research, learning and education. On site is a café and bistro, which is very popular with the locals, a nature trail, shops, and, in the summer, there are guided tours. Dogs are welcome and admission is free.

UPTON HOUSE
The National Trust property Upton House is a fine example of a Cotswold mansion with exceptional gardens and an impressive art collection.

Walks in South East England
(Bedfordshire, Berkshire, Suffolk)

Bedfordshire – A Cluster of Grand Houses

OS MAP: EXPLORER 192 BUCKINGHAM & MILTON KEYNES

Bedfordshire is one of the smallest counties in England. It is situated just to the north of London, amongst the outer tendrils of the sprawling conurbation, and as a consequence the county is inundated with numerous roads and rail-lines that feed in and out of the city. These sustain the many 'bedroom' communities that have evolved to provide a workforce for London businesses. Half the population of Bedfordshire live in either the county town of Bedford or in Luton. This leaves a huge chunk of the county with many quiet places to explore.

For such a small county, it is surprising just how many grand houses there are: in excess of 30! One reason for this is also the reason why many people today live in Bedfordshire; it is possible to have a residence that suits your needs, and yet be close enough to London to commute for business or participate in activities there. During the 18th and 19th century it was possible for the nobility and wealthy merchants to have a stately seat together with an estate to provide income, and yet the journey to London for functions was not unreasonably long or arduous. Often, just like today, these houses were occupied mainly in the summer, but sometimes for longer periods when plague was rampant in the towns.

By and large the significant historical events of the country bypassed Bedfordshire, but a scrutiny of the 'grand houses' reveals a plethora of detail and insight into the social history, spanning decades and centuries.

When these houses were built varies enormously. Some date back to the time of the Norman invasion in the 11th century, and large dwellings continued to be built as late as the 19th century. Just like today, each resident of these houses modified the buildings, gardens and estates to suit their tastes, frequently using the renowned designers and architects of their time, if finances allowed. As a consequence the majority of these places are now listed.

Today in the 21st century very few of these 'grand' houses are private residences. Because of the huge cost of maintaining such a large historical property, and the taxes they incurred, especially during the 20th century, nearly all of their owners have sold off the land and turned the buildings into some kind of business. The method used these days to finance the upkeep of these huge impressive buildings varies; some are hotels, some are nursing homes, some are hired out for functions, particularly weddings, some are

Wonderful walks from **dog-friendly campsites** *on a budget*

Agriculture is important with many small farms and attractive villages

managed by charities such as the National Trust, some are now in ruins, but most fund the upkeep by encouraging paying visitors.

Each of the 30+ houses and halls have a different story, and most are well worth a visit. The ones that tend to pop up on tourist sites are:

Luton Hoo, the former seat of the Marquis of Bute. Its claim to fame is that the second wife of Henry VIII, Anne Boleyn, was born there, and in recent times Queen Elizabeth II often visited the owners. In October 2007, the house was converted into an upmarket hotel, while the surrounding lands are one of the busiest outdoor filming locations.

Wrest Park, the former seat of the de Grey family for over 600 years. It was sold in 1917, and had a very wretched history until 2006 when it was taken over by English Heritage, which started an ambitious restoration programme.

Harlington Manor, considered a 16th century building by English Heritage. It was owned by the Burwell family in the 1500s then passed to the Wingate family via marriage. Its most famous visitor was John Bunyan. Unfortunately it was not a pleasant visit, as he was interrogated and imprisoned there for a short time before transferring to Bedford gaol, where he wrote *The Pilgrim's Progress*. Currently, Harlington Manor is a luxury B&B. Occasionally group tours are organized.

Besides all these remarkable houses, Bedfordshire offers many exciting places to visit such as safari parks and zoos. Agriculture is also important, with many small farms dotted about. With flowing rivers, rolling countryside and attractive villages, there is plenty to explore.

Rose and Crown Ridgmont Campsite

There was little information available for this campsite, so I wasn't sure what to expect. First impressions were not promising. The entrance to the campsite is along a drive between the pub and a function room into a small untidy car park. There is no dedicated

The campsite is behind the pub, and is overlooked by fields and the church.

reception, so if the pub is closed it is necessary to phone for the padlock code to open the gate. This is a bit fiddly. Behind the pub is the camping field itself, which is flat, well maintained, well organized and spacious. The pitches are around the perimeter, leaving a large area in the centre free. On one side of the field is the toilet block with a shower, toilet and sinks; one side for men the other for women. From this, a path leads out through the hedge to the car park, pub and road. Everyone is so friendly and helpful, which makes any stay fabulous, despite the proximity of the M1. I didn't find the noise disturbing.

Pearls of wisdom

Tail-waggingly awesome. Lots of walks over fields, through wooded areas, along tracks; all so close; one even directly from the back of the field. Not many roads. So much to smell and explore. Plenty of space near us to chase my frisbee. Even the pub was great as so many people made a fuss of me – I loved it. Not so happy with all the sheep and deer roaming around in the park. It was a huge temptation – I just love to see them run. Just as well we were on leads. What were these large strange looking animals we met? My owner seemed to get quite excited seeing them – not me. I was glad they were behind a fence and we were on leads. This time I might have run away.

Rating ££
Pricing structure (see Chapter 3) – Flat rate (additional charge for awnings etc)
Pros:
- Pub on site
- Clean amenities
- Good walking
- Friendly, helpful staff

Cons:
- Entrance unclear and difficult
- No price available anywhere until booking
- Motorway close by

Short Walk – Over the Motorway

Distance: 5.5mi (8.8km)
Time: 3.5hr (Easy)
Terrain: Footpaths, tracks, woods, fields, kissing gates, roads (some very busy), bridges, short climbs

Section 1: 1.5 mi (2.4km)
- Exit campsite via front entrance, out to road
- Turn right, passing pub and café on right
- Turn right down steps, signposted, right again at bottom, along tarmac lane, going down
- Turn right opposite big house, Woodfall Cottage, onto narrow path, down steep short slope, round right bend, and out to field with M1 on left
- Turn left across field towards M1, signposted, through gap in hedge, onto uphill path
- Turn right at top, cross bridge over M1 (noisy)
- Go straight on, across bridge over A507, following path between fences, go through gap in hedge
- Turn right along edge of field, keeping close to hedge on right

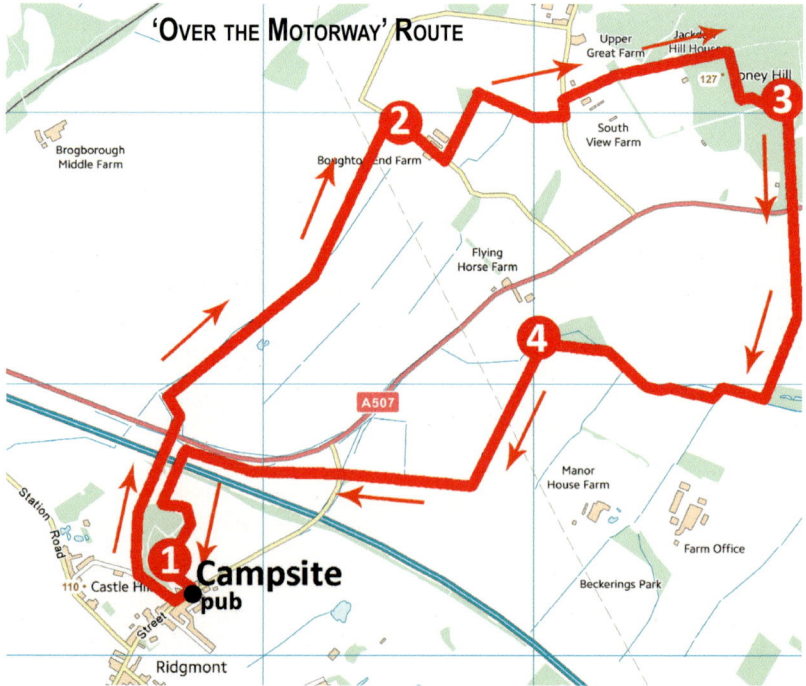

The busy M1 is nearby, with a footbridge across to access the countryside on the other side.

- Continue straight ahead at corner, and along edge of next four fields
- Straight on at bend, towards signpost, and out to road

Section 2: 1.25mi (2km)
- Turn right, then left after derelict building, along driveway
- Continue ahead, passing another derelict building, then a modern barn on left, onto track between fields, skirting woods
- Turn right immediately after woods onto path, across field into second field, keeping hedge on left, and out to road at corner
- Turn left, then right in 75yd (68.5m), signposted
- Continue along driveway, go through gate onto grass track, and out to tarmac driveway
- Bear right onto tarmac track, through gate of Jackdaw Hill House, into woods and out onto drive
- Go straight across drive, passing big house on left, go through gap in hedge ahead onto narrow path in woods, signposted
- Turn right at junction, following path through woods round past signal tower on left round right bend

Section 3: 1.25mi (2km)
- Turn right along track at junction, going slightly downhill, passing house on left, down to A507 (very, very busy)
- Cross road, bearing right to track opposite, through gap in fence signposted 'byway'
- Turn right at junction towards field, following path through trees, keeping close to fields on right

- Turn left at junction into field
- Bearing right, follow path around edge of field, with trees on right
- Turn right along track at junction, signposted
- Turn left at corner of field, then immediately right along edge of field, with hedge on right
- At corner, cross footbridge into second field
- Go straight on, keeping close to trees on right, round left bend at corner and out to road

Section 4: 1.5mi (2.4km)
- Turn right along access road to business park
- Cross road at junction, onto footpath between large round concrete blocks, signposted, through gate
- Continue along narrow path between roads, turning left at junction crossing bridge over M1
- Turn left through gap in fence, along path out to field
- Cross field, turning left at junction, along footpath at edge of field
- Follow path around right, then left bend at corner, passing church and campsite on right, out to road
- Turn right along road to pub

LONG WALK – A SAFARI VISIT
Distance: 7.5mi (9.6km)
Time: 4hr (Easy)
Terrain: Footpaths, tracks, woods, fields, open green spaces, animals, gates footbridge, streets, roads (mostly quiet)

Section 1: 1mi (1.6km)
- Exit campsite via entrance
- Turn right along road, passing church and school on left, continuing straight ahead at right bend, along wide grass verge, through gate into Woburn Estate
- Follow access road round right then left bend, down to Safari Park entrance, passing bison and camel enclosures on right

Section 2: 1mi (1.6km)
- Bear left across entrance, turning left onto wide track into woods
- Continue along track, going up slope, out to another access road
- Turn right, through large kissing gate by house
- Continue straight ahead, along the grass verge, keeping the road on the right for 300yd (274m)
- Bear slightly left towards yellow way-marker post, heading towards large patch of ferns
- Continue along path bearing left through ferns out to park entrance

Section 3: 1mi (1.6km)
- Turn right along access road, bearing left onto grass path parallel to road

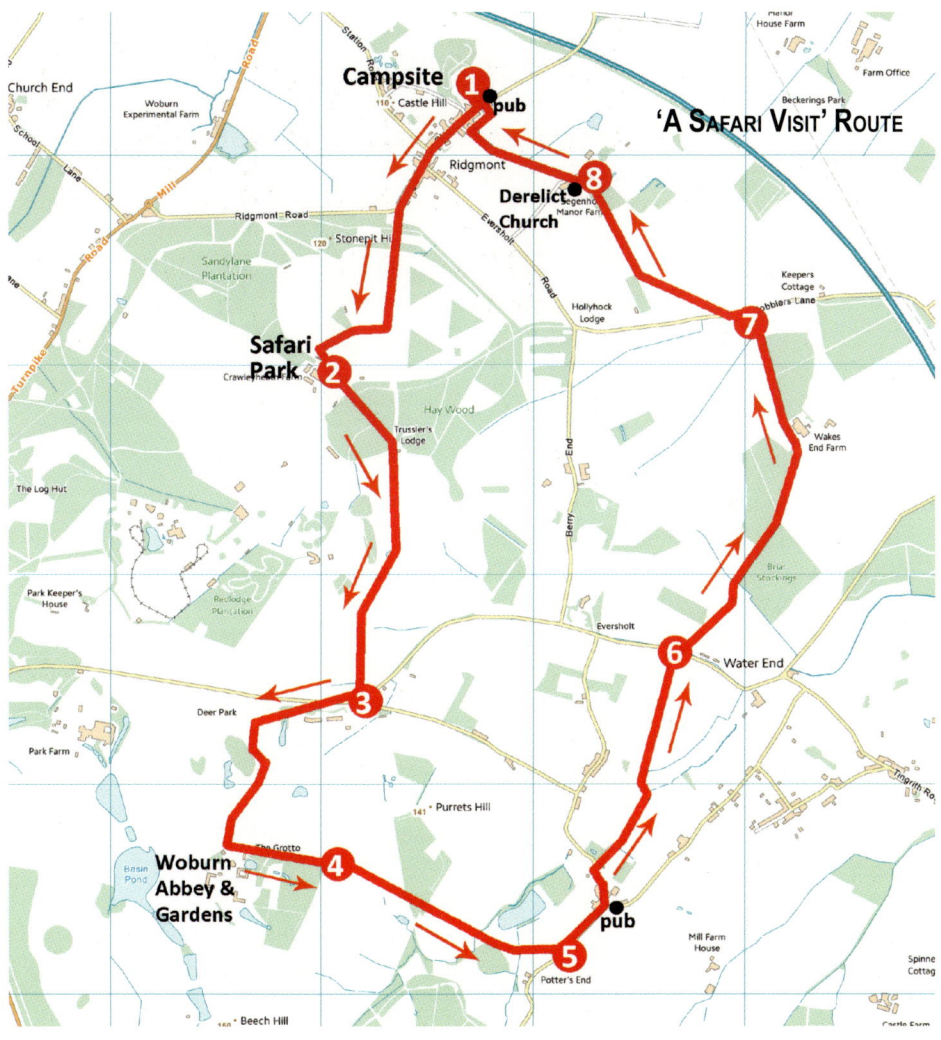

'A SAFARI VISIT' ROUTE

- Turn left at road, past barrier, along access road to Woburn Abbey and Gardens (closed when I visited)
- Turn left along access road, passing entrance gate and red phone-box on right
- Go straight on at junction, onto grass path

Section 4: 1mi (1.6km)
- Follow path across green, through large double gates, into woods
- Follow path through woods, out to field
- Bear right across field, through gap in hedge, and down step to field
- Continue round to left, up two steps into another field with signpost
- Go straight across two fields towards trees, through gap onto narrow path, through gate and out to road

Wonderful walks from dog-friendly campsites on a budget

With the footpath going through Woburn Safari Park, we passed quite close to some unusual animals, including these camels.

Section 5: 1mi (1.6km)
- Turn left along road, round bends, to pub on right (good place for refreshments)
- Exit pub, turning right along road, round right bend, passing church school and cricket field on left to corner
- Cross road, bearing right along Brook End, signposted, passing thatched cottage onto narrow footpath
- Turn left, cross footbridge, through gate, turning immediate right along edge of field, go through kissing gate into another field
- Continue along edge of field, with hedge on right, round corner, through another kissing gate onto footpath
- Turn left along path, ignoring signs and gates leading off both sides, go through gate ahead and out to road

Section 6: 1mi (1.6km)
- Cross road to track opposite, pass through three gates, onto narrow footpath between fences, and out to gravel driveway
- Go straight ahead onto grass path
- Follow path through woods, passing buildings on right, go through gate into field
- Continue ahead along edge of field, with hedge on right, go through gate out to road

Section 7: 1mi (1.6km)
- Turn left along road, then right into field
- Go straight on across field, through gate into another field
- Continue ahead along edge of field, with hedge on left
- Turn left at corner, along narrow footpath between fences, with woods on left, go through gap in fence into woods
- Follow path through gate, across field, through kissing gate into derelict church graveyard (parts of which are mowed)
- Bear left towards tower, out to road

Section 8: 0.5mi (0.8km)
- Cross road to path opposite along edge of field with hedge on right onto stony track with houses on right out to road
- Continue ahead to High Street turning right to pub on left

IN THE VICINITY
CYCLING
With many quiet country lanes, attractive landscapes and charming villages (many with pubs), exploring Bedfordshire by bike is ideal. Details of routes can be found online. For thrill-seeking cyclists there are the Woburn Bike Trails, winding around the 800 acres (323.7ha) of Apsley Woods between Woburn and Woburn Sands. This is just 3mi (4.8km) west of the campsite. To access these trails a permit is necessary. A day permit is approximately £5.00 and can be obtained online or from a park ranger.

AMPTHILL
Ampthill House was originally built in the 1680s for 1st Earl of Ailesbury, with the adjoining land forming Ampthill Park. The house and estate have had a long and very chequered history: some good and some bad. By the 1940s, the Bedford family who owned the house and park sold it to Bovril Limited. The company, in turn, sold just the Park to Ampthill Council in 1947, while the house was basically abandoned and became quite derelict. This changed in 1979 when the house was sold again, and refurbished as four large private homes. This listed building is only open to visitors on very special occasions. The Park, on the other hand, with parkland and woods of approximately 160 acres (64.7ha) is open for residents and visitors to use, including our four-legged companions.

RIDGMONT STATION HERITAGE CENTRE
Just over 1mi (1.6km) northwest of the campsite, on the other side of the M1, is the railway station and Heritage Centre which was built in 1846. It now houses information about the railway, a gift shop and tea rooms. Like most heritage railways it was part of the UK rail network, in this instance the Varsity Line, which ran between Oxford and Cambridge. It was closed in the 1960s. Subsequently, rail enthusiasts and local communities restored the Marston Vale part of the line, which now runs between Bedford and Bletchley. Since 2020 there have been plans to restore the entire Varsity Line.

FIRS CAFÉ
Situated on the High Street Ridgmont just a few yards from the campsite, this café is also a B&B so opens early to provide wonderful breakfasts for guests and visitors. They also do lunches, using local produce for all their meals where feasible. There is a lovely outside seating area where dogs are welcome.

WOBURN SAFARI PARK
Just ½ mile along the main road is the entrance to Woburn Safari Park. To see the animals necessitates driving though the various enclosures. Surprisingly, it is possible to take dogs

through parts of the safari park, so long as you stay on the recognized footpaths and keep your dog on a lead. Do take care though, as some unusual animals are passed en route – this is exciting for both people and dogs.

WOBURN ABBEY

One of the many 'grand' houses of Bedfordshire, Woburn Abbey is the seat of the Dukes of Bedford. The family has lived here for more than 300 years, with the 15th Duke of Bedford currently in residence. The 3000 acres (121.4ha) surrounding the house are open to the public, and there are many footpaths criss-crossing the estate. Though dogs are allowed in the grounds, it is not the most congenial of places for them, as deer, sheep, pigs and other animals roam freely, and often appear in the most unexpected of places.

Berkshire – Lambourn; Giddy Up

OS MAPS: EXPLORER 158 NEWBURY & HUNGERFORD; EXPLORER 170 ABINGDON, WANTAGE & VALE OF WHITE HORSE

Slicing through the county of Berkshire are some of the 231 square miles (598.2km^2) of North Wessex Downs AONB (Area of Outstanding Natural Beauty). The most well known part of these is the Lambourn Downs, probably because of its association with racehorses.

The chalk downs are not especially suitable for agriculture, though at one time it was used for breeding sheep. It is thought the name of Lambourn is derived from the practice of dipping lambs in the river. Over the centuries, the spelling of Lambourn has varied. Surprisingly, it was not until the early 20th century that a definitive spelling was finally agreed. Consequently, some of the other spellings can still be seen on old local signposts. The springy downland turf is perfect for horses, being less jarring than harder surfaces, and the wide open terrain provides plenty of space to exercise them; ideal for the training of racehorses. The area is known as 'The Valley of the Racehorse', with over 50 racing yards in the region, and in excess of 1500 horses in training. Lambourn is famous throughout the world for the training of racehorses.

It was in the 1700s that the involvement with horse racing began in the area. It was a keen interest of the Earls of Craven who owned nearby Ashdown House, and they organized various racing meets on the surrounding Downs. The first stables were in the village itself, at the Red Lion pub opposite the church. Soon other stables were established in the region, some even relocating from Newmarket because the going on the chalky downs was kinder to the horses. Although it was a popular training venue, it did not become important until the railway was built in 1898, and it became easier to transport horses. Nowadays, of course, the railway is closed, so horses are transported by road. One of the biggest horse transport companies in the area is run by Merrick Francis, the son of the author Dick Francis, who wrote numerous thrillers about horse racing

In 1750 the Jockey Club was founded by a group of people enthusiastic about horse racing. Initially founded in London, it moved to Newmarket in 1752, where it continued to grow. Today the Club is a large commercial organization, with a modern corporate system. It has many significant assets including 15 of Britain's racecourses. All profits are used to continue to support horseracing. In 2006 the regulatory responsibilities of the Jockey

Racehorses training on the gallops, usually very early in the mornings.

Club were taken over by the Horseracing Regulatory Authority (HRA), a new specialized administrative body. This was to enable the sport to adapt more effectively and efficiently to changing modern times.

Every day the various gallops on Lambourn Downs play host to a succession of racehorses, on average as many as 800 a month. They are all training to win races in the UK, including the big ones such as those at Cheltenham and Derby racecourses. The busiest time is very early in the mornings, as they process to and from the gallops. Throughout the day racehorses and their riders can be seen in the area, with as many as 120 additional horses a month using the facilities on a casual basis.

The village of Lambourn itself is situated in the river valley near the source of Lambourn River, in the NW corner of Berkshire. Because it is situated in the 'Valley of the Racehorse' all things 'horseracing' have a significant impact on this working village. The George Pub in the centre of the village, opposite the church, is the ideal place to rub shoulders with the racing fraternity, where there is always talk of horses. An important event is Lambourn Open Day, a huge fundraising event, held every Good Friday. In the morning the racing stables open their doors and welcome visitors into their yards to see the horses and learn about horseracing, and in the afternoon a country fair is held in the village. Here is the usual variety of stalls and trade stands and entertainment in the ring; often horse or dog related, and a dog show nearby. An interesting and exciting day.

But there is so much more to Lambourn. It has a long history dating back to Roman times and several interesting landmarks. The variety of events and activities that are hosted in the village indicates a modern, vibrant community.

FARNCOMBE FARM CAMPSITE

This is a small campsite on a working farm, close to the imposing house. The informality of the campsite allows choice of where to set up, which is useful as the field is quite sloping

Wonderful walks from **dog-friendly campsites** *on a budget*

The campsite field is opposite the imposing facade of a large house.

and levelling ramps are essential for motorhomes. The amenities are in a shed at the top corner of the site, comprising one toilet and shower kept spotlessly clean. The EHU is along one side of the field, so long cables are handy. Farmer John and his wife are friendly, welcoming and happy to assist. This is a lovely quiet place to relax with pleasant views, and red kites soaring in the sky above.

Though the family have been farming at Farncombe for generations, the campsite has only been a Camping and Caravanning Club Certificated Site since 1994. It is only in the past 17 years that the farm has been a conservation farm, with the fields turned into pastures, and cultivated without the use of chemical fertilizers or pesticides. The traditional Hereford cattle and Badger Face Welsh Mountain sheep are raised naturally without the use of hormones and antibiotics. John and Liz are so proud of their achievements that they are run farm 'safaris'. These are amazing and very informative. The food they produce can be bought from their farm shop.

Pearls of wisdom 🐕

A lovely little place. Though there is no specific area for me to stretch my legs there is plenty of space to chase my frisbee. Yippee! Lots of places to explore, mostly along wide tracks free of those pesky sheep and cows. We seemed to avoid those places where they were chomping. The tracks were littered with the wonderfully smelly droppings from those snorting animals that people sit on – horses? We only met them occasionally unless we were out really early. Loved, loved the woods we found and the pond to have a fun swim.

Rating ££
Pricing structure (see Chapter 3) – Flat rate (additional charge for awnings etc)
Pros:
- Friendly, helpful staff
- Free to choose pitch

- Tours (safaris) of farm available
- Clearly defined paths
- Good value during peak times

CONS:
- Sloping field (levelling blocks necessary for vans)
- Pricing only available when booking
- Long driveway
- Basic facilities

SHORT WALK – BIMBLING THROUGH THE LAMBOURN VALLEY

Distance: 6mi (9.6km)
Time: 3.5hr (Easy)
Terrain: Footpaths, tracks (mostly stony), woods, fields, pond, streets, roads (quiet), some steady climbs

Section 1: 1mi (2.8km)
- Exit campsite via main entrance
- Turn right along road (grass verge), past buildings on right, to wide stony track
- Turn right along track, signposted

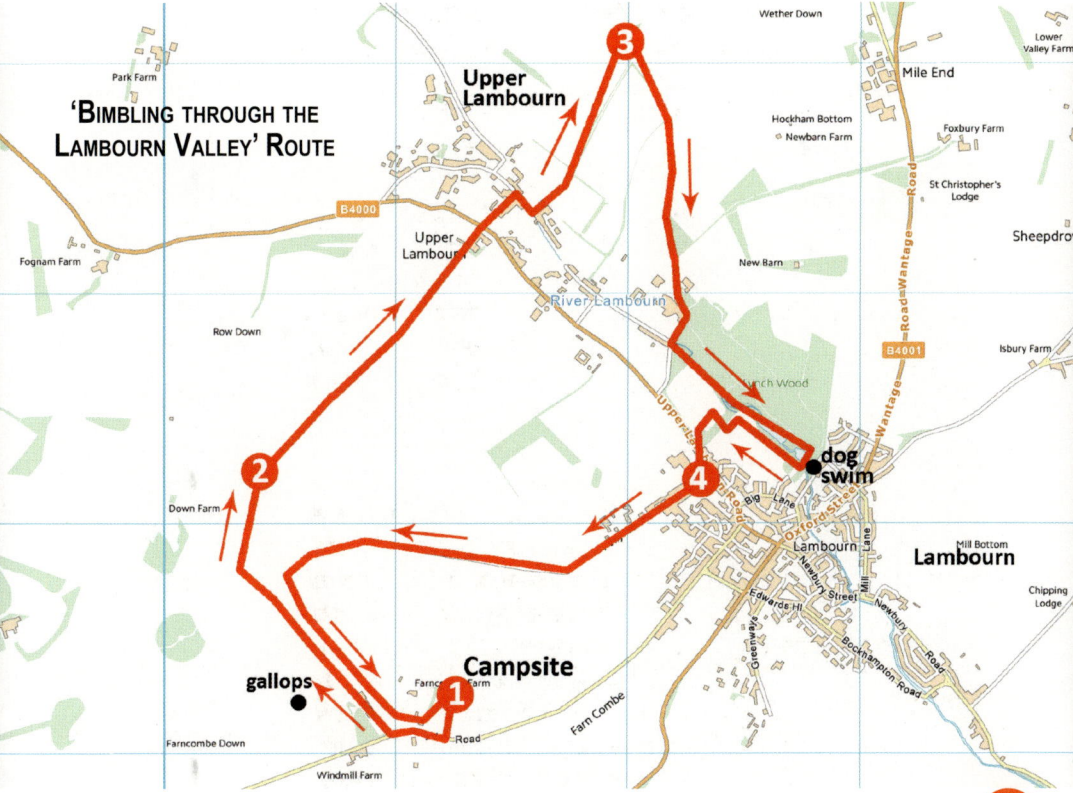

- Follow track, passing gallops in valley on left (you may see the horses training), to junction, going straight on
- Turn right at next junction, onto stony track

Section 2: 1.5mi (2.4km)
- Follow track, passing gallops on left, to road
- Cross to road opposite
- Continue along road to T-junction
- Turn right along lane, with fenced brook on left and buildings on right
- Turn left between houses after brook fence, continue along lane, climbing
- Turn right at junction along wide track, Lambourn Valley Way

Section 3: 1.75mile
- Continue along track, bearing right at fork, down towards buildings, and onto tarmac driveway.
- Follow driveway round to left, then right
- Turn left, go through gate into woods
- Go straight ahead along footpath through woods
- Bear right at fork, passing small pond on right
- Bear right again, towards pond by fallen tree where dogs can swim
- Retrace steps up slope to main path
- Turn left, passing footpath and fence, round small concrete area
- Turn left in 30 paces along narrow footpath

The footpaths passed the farmer's field with curious cows!

- Follow footpath parallel to stream on left
- Cross stream via two small crossings, then up slope to wider path
- Turn right, then left, out to open green
- Bear left towards corner by gate
- Turn left along footpath just before gate
- Follow path to road

Section 4: 1.75mi (2.8km)
- Turn left along road, then right into Folly Road
- Take right fork where road becomes gravel track
- Follow path through trees, out between fields (maybe cows here), passing entrance to gallops on right
- Turn left at junction onto rutted track, down to B4000
- Turn left along road, and left again onto driveway to campsite.

LONG WALK – HORSES, HORSES, EVERYWHERE
Distance: 8.25mi (12.8km)
Time: 5hr (Easy)
Terrain: Footpaths, tracks (mostly stony), woods, fields, pond, streets, roads (quiet)

Section 1: 1.25mi (2km)
- Exit campsite via main entrance
- Turn right along road (grass verge), past buildings on right to wide stony track

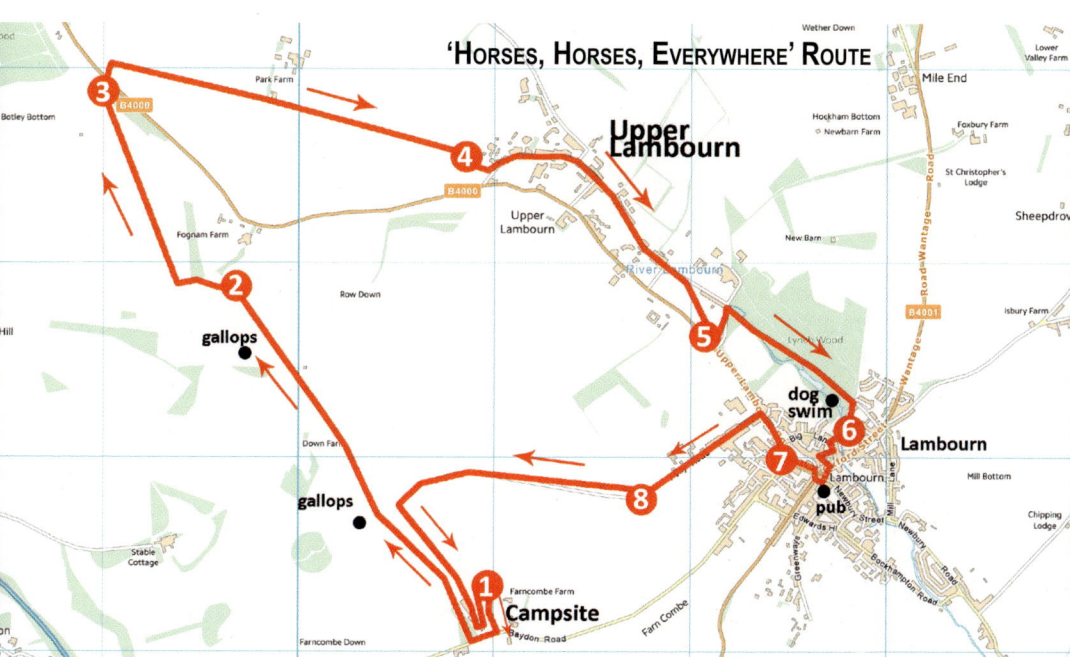

- Turn right along track, signposted
- Follow track, passing gallops in valley on left (you may see the horses training) to junction, and going straight on
- Go straight ahead, along stony track at next junction to gallop entrance

Section 2: 1.25mi (2km)
- Continue straight on across the gallops (take care) onto rutted track
- Follow track round sharp right hand bend, signposted
- Straight on at another four-way junction, signposted, onto grass track, out to B4000

Section 3: 1.25mi (2km)
- Cross road onto wide stony track, bearing left round gate
- Turn right halfway up hill, onto narrow clearly defined path close to telegraph poles (first on right then going across path)
- Straight ahead at junction (telegraph poles now on left), out to road
- Cross road onto road opposite
- Go straight on at bend, onto wide stony track

Section 4: 1mi (1.6km)
- Continue ahead at next bend onto grassy track
- Follow track, still close to telegraph poles, out to another road
- Cross road taking track to right, between hedge on left and grass mound on right, go through gap onto driveway
- Continue along driveway, turning left onto road, passing several large houses on each side (High Street), keeping to path on grass mound on left
- Go straight ahead onto Fulke Walwyn Way, keeping close to white rail and ditch on left, out to Uplands Lane
- Continue ahead at first left, then right bend
- Turn left at T-junction

Section 5: 0.75mi (1.2km)
- Turn right just before left bend, to climb over gate/fence into woods
- Go straight ahead over disused railway, onto narrow path through woods, ignoring those leading off, to wider section
- Take right fork down to pond (an ideal place for dogs to swim and meet other dogs)
- Retrace steps to T-junction
- Turn right up slope, bearing right at next junction, and onto wide path
- Continue straight ahead at next junction
- Follow path round to left, down slope, and out to road

Section 6: 0.5mi (0.8km)
- Turn right along road, Goose Green, with woods on right, over bridge to wide junction
- Turn left, then right along Chapel Lane, under arch to church

Everywhere we walked, we encountered horses.

- Turn left, passing church on right, to small car park
- Bear right across car park and road to The George pub on corner
- Exit pub, retracing steps to across car park to lane, with church now on left
- Follow lane, passing Chapel Lane on right, out to road

Section 7: 0.75mi (1.2km)
- Continue straight ahead along B4000, crossing Big Lane, passing village hall, and crossing the Park on right
- Turn next left onto Folly Road
- Take right fork where road becomes gravel track

Section 8: 1.5mi (2.4km)
- Follow path through trees, out between fields, passing entrance to gallops on right
- Turn left at junction, onto rutted track, down to B4000
- Turn left along road, and left again onto driveway to campsite.

IN THE VICINITY
CYCLING
There are numerous tracks criss-crossing the Downs for cyclists, as well as walkers. Riders need to be cautious because some of them are rutted and very uneven. Many of them are also used by horse riders.

BIRDWATCHING/WILDLIFE
There are plenty of birds and wildlife to spot around Lambourn with its gently rolling hills and clusters of trees. The absence of motorized vehicles on the lanes and tracks creates a stillness and tranquillity conducive to observing wildlife.

Wonderful walks from dog-friendly campsites on a budget

LAMBOURN VALLEY WAY
This 22mi (35km) trail stretches from Uffington Castle on the Berkshire Downs, along the River Lambourn Valley, linking the well known Ridgeway with the Kennet and Avon Canal. It is a particularly enjoyable trail, because it not only passes various gallops on the Downs but also passes through the Berkshire villages of Boxford, Great Shefford, East Garston and Lambourn.

UFFINGTON WHITE HORSE
Just seven miles (11.3km) north of Lambourn, on the slopes of the Berkshire Downs, is the prehistoric figure of the Uffington White Horse. It is an imposing chalk-cut figure of a horse, 360ft (110m) in length, that is visible for miles around, though obviously the aerial view is incredible.

It is an odd looking horse and even though it has been referred to as a horse for several centuries there is still some debate as to what animal it actually is and what it is suppose to signify.

The horse is formed from crushed chalk, filling deep trenches. These have to be regularly cleared of vegetation. This is known as the Scouring of the White Horse and from 1755 was part of a sports festival, with large crowds attending. By 1857, however, the festival eventually died out. Nowadays the Scouring of the White Horse has been revived by the National Trust, with a group of volunteers regularly clearing and re-chalking the figure.

ST MICHAEL'S AND ALL ANGELS CHURCH, LAMBOURN
There has been a church on this site since at least Anglo Saxon times, if not before. It is an imposing building and an important village landmark with a long and interesting history. It is kept locked so visits need to be during services.

EAST GARSTON
This village is 4mi (6.4km) southeast of the campsite. It has a very long history going back to pre-historic times. The church is especially interesting. A chalice used on special occasions dates from 1576, as do the baptisms, deaths and marriage registers. It is thought some of the yew trees in the churchyard are centuries old; maybe as old as 600 years.

SEVEN BURROWS
These Bronze Age burial mounds can be found 4mi (6.4km) northeast of the campsite. Ploughing of the area has hugely damaged them, and only a few mounds are now visible.

ASHDOWN HOUSE
The house was built in 1662 by the 1st Earl Craven as a safe haven for Queen Elizabeth of Bohemia, who he loved. Their story is romantic but also tragic, as Queen Elizabeth never lived in the house. She died before it was finished. In 1956 it was given to the National Trust by the wife of the 4th Earl of Craven. It is now leased as a private residence. Tours are by arrangement only but dogs are not allowed. However, the woodlands surrounding the house are open all year and are an ideal place for four-legged companions.

Suffolk, Sutton Hoo – A Treasure Hunt

OS MAP: EXPLORER 212 WOODBRIDGE & SAXMUNDHAM

Learning about the past can be exciting and gripping; as good as or even better than a Hollywood blockbuster film. In fact, a film was made in 2021 about the discovery of the finds at Sutton Hoo called, appropriately, *The Dig*, and starring Carey Mulligan and Ralph Fiennes. Being British, it is understated, not big and brash like the Indiana Jones films, although it has many of the same ingredients. The theme is the same, making discoveries through archaeological digs, hoping to find 'treasure' with little support from local community, and an outside jeopardy. The forthcoming WW2 very much diminished the ramifications of the find at Sutton Hoo until much later.

As with most films of true events, there is some embellishment of the facts to make the film more appealing. The film of the discovery of artefacts at Sutton Hoo is, by and large, pretty accurate and well worth seeing.

In 1926, the Sutton Hoo estate, which overlooked several mounds, was bought by the recently married Edith and Frank Pretty. When Frank died in 1934 these mounds took on a special significance for Edith, in part due to her experiences of archaeology when travelling abroad. Investigating some of them seemed to be a fitting undertaking. She met Basil Brown, a local amateur archaeologist to discuss this. In the summer of 1938, despite the prospect of World War II, Basil Brown began work on the two smaller mounds, but with little success. The dig stopped during the winter, but resumed again in the spring of 1939, this time on the biggest of the mounds, revealing an amazing 88ft (26.8m) long Saxon ship with an undisturbed burial chamber full of, yet to be discovered treasures, in the centre. Naturally the 'professionals' wanted to take over, but Edith insisted Basil remain on the dig.

With more personnel the work quickly progressed. What they found astounded them; hundreds of precious objects and a rare ceremonial helmet. There was so much, all of

A replica of the huge Saxon boat found at Sutton Hoo, on display in the courtyard of the visitors' complex

exceptional quality, and from unexpected places. On 25th July 1939, a reception at Sutton Hoo was held hosted by Edith Pretty to celebrate the culmination of the dig. Unfortunately the reception was marred by spitfire aeroplanes passing overhead. All the artefacts were donated to the British Museum, and were stored away for safekeeping in a London Underground station until 1945, when they were carefully catalogued and analyzed. In 1983 further excavation of the mounds produced additional artefacts.

A careful study of the artefacts from the dig has established the unparalleled importance of the Sutton Hoo burial and site, resulting in a much better understanding of life during the Anglo-Saxon period. It caused a radical rethink of the period termed 'the Dark Ages'. Visitors can see the amazing treasure buried with an Anglo-Saxon King 1400 years ago in the exhibition at the British Museum.

When Edith Pretty died in 1942 her 12 year old son Robert inherited the estate. He never lived there, instead staying with his aunt in Hampshire. The property was taken over by the War Office and used to house Land Army girls. It was eventually sold, with the Tranmer family being the final occupants. The family gifted it to the National Trust in 1998 who renamed it Tranmer House in recognition of the donation.

When the National Trust acquired the site it started transforming it into a key historical and tourist attraction with guided tours, talks and exhibitions about Anglo-Saxon society. Nowadays a visit to Sutton Hoo is informative, with lots to see, as there are replicas of some of the treasures that were found, as well as a visit to Tranmer House where Edith Pretty lived. The estate is still large and there are many delightful walks, not only around the mounds but also along the river, following in the footsteps of the mourners of the Anglo-Saxon king. It brings home how revered he must have been for them to haul a loaded boat to the burial site.

SUTTON HOO HOLIDAY CAMPSITE

Access to the campsite is through the farmyard, past a large barn into the big rectangular field, with the facilities block on the right, handy for all the pitches, and the reception/information hut directly ahead. Though there is no one to greet you, this does not affect the running of the campsite, which is well organized and efficient. Each new day's arrival is posted on a large whiteboard on the hut with a map and pitch number. With each pitch clearly marked it is easy to find your allocated place. The majority of the pitches are arranged around the perimeter, have electric hook up, water and waste water outlet, and are enclosed by low hedges, all of which creates a feeling of privacy. In the centre of the field is a children's play area and space for games. The facilities block has two toilets and showers for both ladies and gents, as well as a disabled/family room, and a dishwashing area. They are kept spotlessly clean. Should it be necessary to contact the owners, a number is displayed in several locations. The campsite is part of a working farm and the adjoining fields house chickens, which are part of the Sutton Hoo Chicken brand.

PEARLS OF WISDOM 🐕

I loved that our space was surrounded by low hedges, as there was less sudden movement around to startle me. I also loved the field next door; space to chase the frisbee.

The pitches were around the perimeter leaving the central area for games and playing

Also fun was going along the trail to the field between the trees. Places to run and explore. Lots of interesting smells, especially from over the fence with funny creatures waddling about making a noise; my owner said they were chickens. I thought that was some kind of food we sometimes had for a treat. In addition to all of this there was a lovely short walk. It was along the tarmac, but very little traffic so we didn't have to be on lead, and there was a lot of grass at the sides. Walks were good, but too much water and not enough swimming.

RATING ££
PRICING STRUCTURE (SEE CHAPTER 3) – FLAT RATE
PROS:
- Simple easy pricing
- Excellent value during peak season
- Dog walk on site
- Excellent location
- Bus stop near by

CONS:
- Price not available until booking process complete
- Nearby roads very busy
- Lovely pub along busy road

SHORT WALK – WANDERING AROUND THE HOO ESTATE
Distance: 4mi (6.4km)
Time: 2.5hr (Easy)
Terrain: Footpaths, tracks, riverside paths, footbridges, kissing gates, fields, woods, some climbs, roads (quiet)

Section 1: 1mi (1.6km)

- Exit campsite via main entrance, turning left, then right along road (farm access only)
- Follow road round right hand bend, through gap in hedge, onto gravel path of Sutton Hoo complex
- Go straight ahead onto tarmac path between trees round right bend then left bend onto stony track signposted Riverside View Walk
- Continue along downhill path ignoring paths off
- Turn left at junction signposted Valley Walk
- Turn right along farm driveway

Section 2: 1mi (1.6km)

- Keep left at post onto footpath under wooden gazebo
- Continue along grass path with fence on right up onto river bank
- Follow path with river on right through woods over 6 footbridges up steps out to field round left bend (Amazing views of river and Woodbridge on opposite bank)
- Continue along edge of field with hedge on left turning right at corner still along edge of field
- Turn left at next corner onto wide track
- Turn right along wide grass path

Section 3: 1mi (1.6km)

- Follow path keeping close to trees on left
- Continue straight ahead at corner along track across field through gap in hedge to road
- Turn left along road to junction
- Take left fork with grain towers and large parking/turning area on left
- Follow road passing copse on right

Section 4: 1mi (1.6km)

- Turn left at corner of field onto wide sandy path along edge of field with hedge on right
- Go straight on at corner passing Sutton Hoo burial mounds on left
- Turn left at next corner.
- (Gate on left leads into burial mound and viewing tower).

The walk around the Sutton Hoo Estate offers wonderful views of the town of Woodbridge on the opposite bank.

- Turn right through gate follow path through metal gate
- Turn right along path between hedges (before visitors; centre, café etc) past waymarker post out to road
- Go straight ahead passing building on left round left bend out to road
- Turn left then right into campsite entrance

LONG WALK – A RIVERSIDE WALK

Distance 6+mile (9.6+km)
Time: 4.5hr (Easy)
Terrain: Footpaths, tracks, tarmac paths, woods, playing fields, streets, roads (one busy) rail tracks

Section 1: 0.25mi (0.4km)
- Exit campsite via entrance turning left along road to main A1152 with bus stop on corner
- Take bus to Hamblin Road by the Turban Centre in Woodbridge

Section 2: 1mi (1.6km)
- Bear right across turning area to precinct, passing Co-op on right, Boots on left, and out to street The Thoroughfare (information boards on left-hand wall interesting)
- Turn left along road (on the right is the café Christine's Tea Rooms)
- Cross Church Street onto Cumberland Street
- Turn left along road, just past Woodbridge Prep School on right

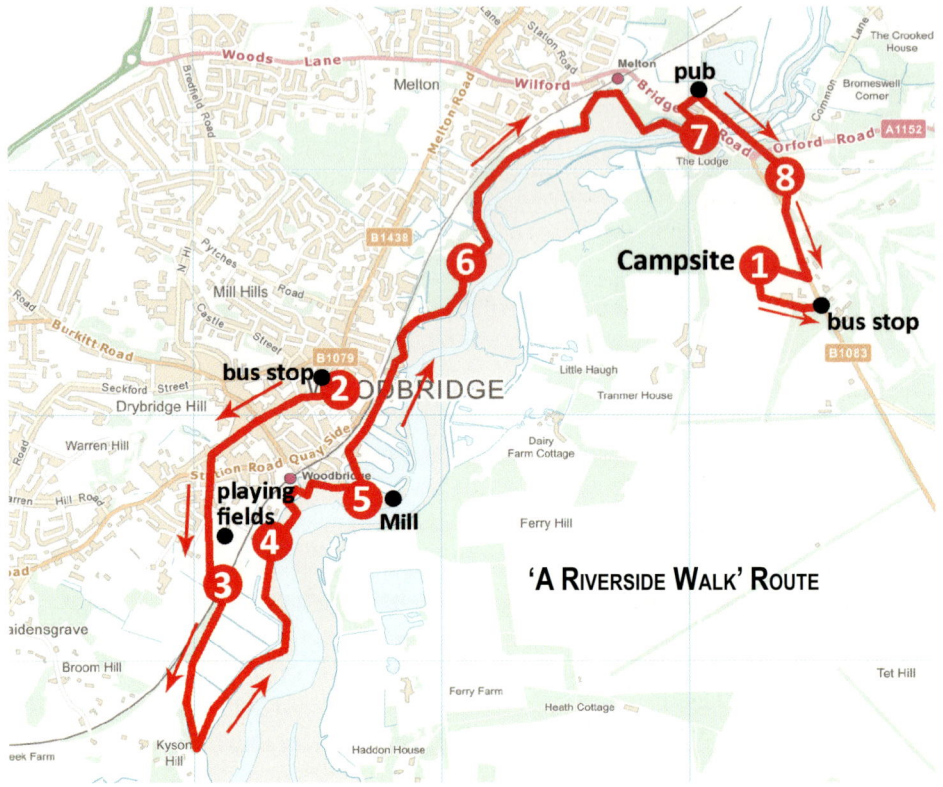

'A RIVERSIDE WALK' ROUTE

- Cross Kingston Road to road opposite via pedestrian crossing to right, passing Morley Avenue to playing fields
- Bear right across field, towards basketball hoop, onto footpath by rail line
- Cross tracks onto stony path between rail line on right and stream on left

Section 3: 1mi (1.6km)
- Follow path to T-junction
- Turn left along tarmac path, with river on right to ramp by yacht club

Section 4: 0.75mi (1.2km)
- Bear left down ramp
- Follow path through park, passing pond for model boats on left, and tea hut on right, to T-junction
- Turn right along tarmac path towards river
- Turn left, back on winding riverside path, with river on right
- Turn right at junction, just past iron steps, to town, then left, passing houseboats on right
- Turn right opposite rail line, left again along narrow path, with water on right and museum on left (a good place to stop for refreshments with a variety of places in the square)

- Continue along path keeping close to water on right
- Turn right at junction by Art Club building to Water Mill

Section 5: 1mi (1.6km)
- Exit Water Mill, retrace steps to Art Club
- Turn right onto stony track between Art Club on right and blue building on left
- Round left bend, towards rail line, then right along narrow path just before it, cross access road onto riverside path
- Go straight ahead with river on right, passing grey Swedish ex-navy ship (now café) on right

Section 6: 1mi (1.6km)
- Continue along riverside path, winding round boat yards, ignoring all paths off to the left, out to A1152

Section 7: 0.25mi (0.4k)
- Turn left to pub on right (Woodbridge Inn Pub, another good refreshment stop)
- Exit pub left to cross bridge
- Continue along road (pavement), taking right fork at roundabout

Section 8: 0.75mi (1.2km)
- Continue along road (busy, but has pavement)
- Turn right at top of hill onto Sutton Hoo access road
- Turn second right into campsite entrance

The riverside path to Woodbridge was easy to follow, with much of interest to see.

Wonderful walks from dog-friendly campsites on a budget

IN THE VICINITY
CYCLING

There are suggestions online of cycle routes around Sutton Hoo. However, the main road into the site is very busy and not pleasant cycling.

FISHING

With so many boats on the river, fishing groups usually use nearby lakes. For more information contact Woodbridge Tourist Information in Woodbridge Station.

BIRDWATCHING

The surrounding countryside is a good place for birdwatching, especially along the footpaths beside the river. There are also some nature reserves not too far away.

WOODBRIDGE

On the opposite bank of the River Deben is the town of Woodbridge. There is a bus from the campsite into the centre of Woodbridge. It is an interesting market town with lots to see and do. Being on the banks of such a large river, all things sailing are important, and there are still some small boat-building enterprises and suppliers for all the boats moored in the harbour. In times gone by, rope-making was also important, and the fighting ships of Sir Francis Drake were built in the town. The riverside walks are fascinating, with so much to see.

WOODBRIDGE TIDE MILL

This mill is on the banks of the River Deben on the outskirts of Woodbridge. There has been a mill on this site since 1170. In 2011, thanks to the volunteers, it was restored together with the adjacent small reservoir and is now a fully working mill. It is open to visitors and produces flour to make bread. It is a large three-storey building, and dogs are allowed in, but only on the ground floor.

WOODBRIDGE MUSEUM

Set back along one side of a courtyard near the mill is the Woodbridge Museum. The displays chronicle the history of the town and surrounding area through the lives of ordinary people, from the Anglo-Saxon era through to the medieval period and the Napoleonic times, when it was a large ship-building centre, right up to the present day.

LONGSHED

On another side of the courtyard is the Longshed; a community space where a variety of events take place. A current project is building a replica Sutton Hoo ship. Dogs on leads are allowed.

BOAT TRIPS

Boat trips with Suffolk River Trips along the river and estuary depart from Malting Quay near the Riverside Bandstand. The 45-60 minute trip, with commentary, is a unique way of viewing the landscape. The trips are very popular, so booking is advisable. Dogs are allowed on all boats.

Walks in South West England
(Cornwall, Devon, Dorset, Wiltshire)

Cornwall – The Heel of Cornwall
OS Map: Explorer 103 The Lizard

Most people know of Cornwall because it is a popular holiday destination. It occupies the most south-westerly part of the UK. The far southwest part of Cornwall could be considered to be shaped like a foot, with Lands End as the toe, pointing out into the Atlantic Ocean, and the Lizard Peninsula as the heel.

The rugged coastline of the Lizard Peninsula with its precipitous inclines and declines is the result of its unique geology. The outcrop of serpentine rock and minerals was formed some 350 million years ago somewhere south of the equator, and is responsible for the distinctive landscape: rugged and dramatic cliffs capped with an undulating plateau. Over the millennia the pummelling seas have carved out the cliffs, caves, harbours and coves. Some of the beautiful sandy beaches, that are only accessible by boat or on foot, are wonderful places on sunny days for sunbathing, picnicking, and swimming.

Many of the small sandy beaches can only be reached by boat or on foot.

Wonderful walks from dog-friendly campsites on a budget

This area is extremely important because it is home to an extraordinary range of habitats: woods, freshwater ponds, and streams, in addition to the stunning cliffs and the breaking waves, providing a home for a vast array of flora and fauna. Wild flowers grow in abundance, especially inland on the plateau; about 600 different kinds, including some very rare ones such as the Cornish heath and Cornish eyebright, that are only found here. Most of the nature reserves on the The Lizard are managed by the National Trust, whose aim is to protect and conserve the unique ecosystem. The Trust arranges guided walks for visitors to learn more about the flora and fauna.

The Lizard Peninsula is amazing, and the South West Coastal Path is the ideal way to discover this. Such a long coastline jutting out into the Atlantic is open to the elements, and exposed to wind, rain and sea squalls. Consequently the region is sparsely populated with only a few isolated hamlets and a couple of small villages.

The village of Lizard is the southernmost settlement in the UK. Apart from the road from the north entering the village, all other roads and lanes lead to the South West Coastal path, especially the one going directly south, which just leads to a car park. A triangular green is the centre of the village but it is rather nondescript as there is a bus terminal on one side with parked cars on the other two sides. As expected several tourist type establishments are scattered around the village but it is a good place to access interesting places situated along the coastal path.

One of these is Lizard Point. This is the southernmost point of the UK. This iconic spot is very popular, so the place is often crowded, and as a result amenities have sprung up to service them. There is a café, a gift shop, ice cream hut and a restaurant. The views are spectacular, but the surrounding seas are extremely hazardous for shipping, especially in bad weather, and are known as the 'Graveyard of Ships'.

Despite being so remote, the Lizard Peninsula has a long history dating back to the Bronze Age, with evidence of mining activity and settlements. For the Romans it was an important trading centre. Unsurprisingly, for many centuries the Lizard Peninsula was vital in defending England from invasion. In fact it was from here that the Spanish Armada was first sighted at 3pm on 29th July 1588. Of course smuggling was a common activity, particularly during the 18th and 19th century. A more common (and legal) livelihood was fishing, though not so much today. Instead, tourism is the main industry, catering to many visitors from all over the world.

TENERIFFE FARM CAMPSITE

This is a large spacious campsite with ample space for tents spread over three fields. There are only 20 grass pitches for tourers, all with electric hook-up. Access is along a narrow cul-de sac, which leads to a NT car park. However, getting there with a large unit is not a problem as there are plenty of passing places. All the facilities and amenities are constructed of wood where possible, though the play area is metal. The reception also houses a small shop, with only basic supplies due to supply issues, plus some NT pamphlets and merchandise. The large toilet block is situated in the small field behind reception and the glamping pods, near the entrance to the campsite, therefore some pitches are quite a distance away. It is modern and clean, and has a large dishwashing

There were plenty of place to exercise the dogs around the site, even though there was no designated area.

section at both ends. Though there is no designated dog walking area, there is plenty of space to walk dogs.

Pearls of wisdom 🐕

Oodles and oodles of space; fields to explore around the edge; even places to chase my frisbee. Then just as we were taking our last stroll we discovered a gate with a grass path the other side. Oh to poke along it and see where it went; no time. Perhaps we will come back. I hope so. Though there were some tarmac lanes, the route across the fields to a swimming place was fab-u-lous; as was the swimming. The people, some in funny rubber clothing with things in their mouths, did not mind us. My son Pippin wanted to join those jumping off a high wall. My owner said NO. The boat ride on the water wasn't so much fun, neither was the café, even though we got treats. I was happy to just swim after the ball.

Rating ££££
Pricing structure (see Chapter 3) – Itemized/Seasonal
Pros:
- Good value for solo traveller.
- Only a small rise during peak season
- No charge for dogs
- Friendly helpful staff

Cons:
- Sharp price increase for couples and families.
- Price not available until booking process complete
- On-site shop only very basic items (and NT stock)

Wonderful walks from dog-friendly campsites on a budget

SHORT WALK – IT'S SWIM TIME FOR DOGS

Distance: 5.25mi (8km)
Time: 3hr (Moderate)
Terrain: Footpaths, tracks, fields, kissing gates, stone stiles, roads (some very busy), bridges, short climbs

Section 1: 1.25mi (2km)

- Exit campsite via main entrance
- Turn right, then immediate left along road, passing house on left (selling cakes)
- Turn right at bend onto wide stony track, passing white house on left, signposted
- Follow track past 'Pradanack Morva' entrance on left, onto grass path.
- Continue straight ahead towards rock outcrop, to second gap in fence at footpath junction
- Turn left at junction, keeping rock outcrop and sea on left
- Follow coastal path, keeping the sea on the left, heading towards big white building ahead (hotel)

'IT'S SWIM TIME FOR DOGS' ROUTE

Dogs swimming at Mullion Cove.

- Continue along path, going steeply downhill, away from sea
- Turn left along flat stony track back towards sea

Section 2: 1.25mi (2km)
- Turn right down steps beside old stone building, and onto Mullion Cove slipway. The slipway is concrete, leading to a pebbly beach and water, enclosed by two large stone breakwaters, and is an ideal place for dogs to swim (dogs allowed all year)
- Exit via slipway, turning left at top
- Continue straight ahead up steps between buildings
- Turn left onto narrow path, climbing up to road (lots of seats to stop and rest)
- Continue straight on, along road, passing hotel on right
- Turn left onto footpath at turning circle, signposted
- Follow stony track with sea still on left, passing houses on right, out to road, turning left down track to beach
- Take either fork (sloping right fork leads to wooden bridge and very stony path down to sandy beach)
- NB: Dogs are not allowed on this beach from 1st July to 31st August
- Exit beach, crossing wooden bridge towards signpost
- Turn right along bridle path, passing steps, to signpost on left
- Follow bridle path up hill

Section 3: 1.25mi (2.km)
- Continue straight on at junction, taking right fork along lane to road.

- Turn right along main road to pub, The Old Inn
- Exit pub, turning left along main road
- Turn right along Laflouder Fields
- Continue along winding road, passing football club on right to T-junction
- Turn right, then first left, along stony track, Trenance Lane, to road
- Go straight on across road to Ghost Hill, passing Chocolate Factory and Craft Centre on right
- Follow road, passing footpath on left and stream, turning right onto narrow grass path between hedge and fence, signposted

Section 4: 1.25mi (2km)
- Continue along the edge of three fields, between hedge and fence, crossing unusual stone stiles between each one, and out to stony lane
- Bear slightly right, over stone stile between gates
- Follow path along edge of field, over stile, out to path across heath
- Continue along path, crossing several stiles out to field
- Go straight ahead across three fields, crossing stiles, out to grass path beside house
- Turn right along path, and out to road
- Turn left along road, then right at junction to campsite entrance

Long Walk – All at sea
Distance: 9.25mi (8km)
Time: 5 hr (Difficult in places)
Terrain: Footpaths, tracks, coastal path, footbridge, fields, kissing gates, roads (some very busy), bridges, several climbs and descents, bus journey

Section 1: 1.5mi (2.4km)
- Exit campsite via main entrance
- Turn right, then immediate left, along road, passing house on left (selling cakes)
- Turn sharp right at bend, onto grass footpath beside house, over stone stile, into field
- Continue ahead, keeping close to hedge on right, crossing three fields over stone stile between them onto heath
- Follow path across heath over stone stile into field
- Go straight on along edge of field between hedge on right fence on left out to lane
- Bear slightly right cross lane onto path opposite
- Follow path through copse and over stile out to field
- Continue along edge of next two fields, with hedge and houses on right, out to road
- Turn left along road, uphill to B3296, passing chocolate factory on left
- Cross road to Trenance Lane opposite, passing small car park on right
- Continue along wide stony lane out to road
- Turn right along road then left into Clifden Close
- Wait at bus stop on left just before football club (the stop is for buses going in both directions, and, for the bus to The Lizard, it is necessary to go out into the middle of the road to get on the bus)

'ALL AT SEA' ROUTE

Section 2: 1.25mi (2km)

- Get off bus at terminal 'The Green' (pub and cafés opposite The Green)
- Retrace the bus route along Beacon Terrace, passing school on left, round left bend.
- Turn right opposite Cross Common Nursery, onto wide stony road signposted Bass Point
- Follow road onto wide track, Lloyds Lane, passing old Lookout Post

One of the many stunning inlets visible from the coastal path.

- Turn right through kissing gate, then right again along path, away from large white building labelled Lloyds Signal Station (this is now a private house), with sea on left and passing the Marconi Wireless Station (open to visitors)

Section 3: 1mi (1.6km)
- Continue along the coastal path, passing Housel Bay Hotel, ignoring all paths going off to the right to Lizard village, lighthouse or Lizard Point, (this is a hot tourist hot spot, and best place along coastal path for meal)

Section 4: 1.75mi (2.8km)
- Exit Lizard Point via path in front of Wavecrest Café, with sea still on left
- Continue along coastal path, taking left fork at footbridge, with right path easiest at wide three-way route at top of hill out to car park

Section 5: 1mi (1.6km)
- Follow gravel track from car park down to beach
- Cross beach, go up steep steps to café
- Exit café turn right to gravel path
- Turn right uphill passing toilets on right, past signpost (coastal route at high tide), to right bend leading to car park at top of hill
- Turn left along wide track, then right along sandy track
- Turn left in 25yd (22.8m), along wide track over footbridge, through gate by notice board

Section 6: 1mi (1.6km)
- Follow path, taking right fork away from road through gate
- Turn right along track, keeping close to fence on right, through kissing gate (possibly cows)
- Continue along path, past building on left, through second gate, and out to wide stony track
- Turn right, following track through gate into airfield

Section 7: 0.75mi (1.2km)
- Turn immediate left, along narrow footpath, through gate, out of airfield onto heath
- Continue straight ahead at junction, over stone wall via stone steps, into field
- Turn right along edge of field between hedge and fence on left, over wall (stone steps) on right, into second field
- Bear left, passing gate on left, round hedge, through gate in corner, onto path
- Continue straight ahead across junction

Section 8: 1mi (1.6km)
- Take right fork along stony track towards farm, ignoring paths off to left
- Follow track through gate into farmyard
- Cross farmyard, turning right opposite car park, along road
- Follow road through field to campsite entrance on right

IN THE VICINITY
BIRDWATCHING
The whole peninsula affords great opportunities for spotting birds, as a variety of seabirds such as gannets and puffins use the cliffs for nesting. The RSPB nature reserve at Lizard Point is a particularly suitable place.

WILD SWIMMING
With so many coves along the coastline there are plenty of places to wild swim. Be sure to check the tide timetables, look out for local safety signs, and take extra care of tides and swells.

SURFING
Just about everywhere in Cornwall it is possible to find somewhere to surf. The Lizard Peninsula is no exception. Polurrian Cove and Church Cove are suitable, but Poldhu Cove is really popular, as the waves usually satisfy the needs of both beginners and experienced surfers.

CYCLING
This is an ideal way to explore all the nooks and crannies scattered across the peninsula. Not necessarily an easy ride, but well worth the effort as it is truly an amazing experience. For those who like more of a challenge there is the newly established West Kernow Way: a 150mi (241km) cycle route around the south tip of Cornwall.

Wonderful walks from dog-friendly campsites on a budget

LIZARD LIGHTHOUSE
Very close to Lizard Point is the lighthouse. The first one was built in 1619 to guide vessels safely through the waters. It did not last long, however, and was rebuilt in 1752, a massive 63ft (19m) high. Since then it has been modified several times, but in 1998 it was automated and lighthouse keepers were no longer required. In the lighthouse engine room is a heritage centre, where it is possible to see some of the old workings, various displays and interactive exhibits. There are also tours of the lighthouse where you can climb the stairs to the top. The view must be astonishing.

LLOYDS SIGNAL STATION
Approximately 1mi (1.6km) southeast of Lizard village is Bass Point, on top of which is a magnificent building overlooking the sea. This is Lloyds Signal Station. It was built by the Fox Shipping Company in 1872 to communicate with passing vessels. This was done by semaphore, using flags from the top floor of the building. In 1883 Lloyds took over the operation until its closure in 1969. It is now a holiday let, and so not open to the public.

KYNANCE COVE
Because there is a car park nearby it is always busy. This is not such a problem at low tide when there is plenty of space. At high tide there is only a narrow strip of sand among the boulders at the base of the cliff, though this is perfect for swimming. To compensate, overlooking the cove is a café and public toilets.

MARCONI CENTRE
Marconi, the Italian wireless inventor, chose the Lizard Peninsula for his experiments because the view was not obstructed by any land mass and it was so remote he did not have to worry about interested visitors. He built two wireless stations. The first is at Bass Point, to send messages to the Isle of Wight. This has been restored in what seems to be a wooden hut on the coastal path. It is an extremely interesting place to visit. Dogs are allowed, but opening times are restricted as it is run by radio enthusiasts. The second one was at Polurrian. From here he sent messages to Newfoundland in Canada crossing a distance of 2100mi (3380km). It is now the Marconi Centre which was built in 2001.

PREDANNACK AIRFIELD
Behind the campsite is this airfield. It was built in May 1941, and was an extremely vital part of the war effort. On 15th September 1945 it put on a 'Battle of Britain' air display for the public. 4000 visitors came. In 1958 it was taken over by the Royal Navy. Nowadays it is used mostly for training practice by Royal Navy helicopters. Low flying helicopters frequently fly over the area, even the campsite.

MULLION
Situated 1mi (1.6km) up the hill from the cove, Mullion is the largest village in the

peninsula, with shops, cafés, restaurants and pubs. The central part of the village, around the church, has very much retained its medieval character, and the roads are very narrow, especially for large vehicles like motorhomes and buses. Access is only possible due to a one way system. It is a delightful place to visit, especially the Old Inn pub where there is the most amazing 'reading' room, and dogs are welcome.

MULLION COVE

About 1mi (1.6km) from the campsite, either via a fairly flat route across the fields, or a spectacular rugged and rocky coastal path, is Mullion cove. It is unusual because it has a harbour financed by Lord Robartes of Lanhydrock in 1895. There is always plenty to see and do here: wild swimming (Pippin wanted to join them jumping off the harbour wall) kayaking, paddle boarding, canoeing, even scuba diving (which Pearl wanted to join in with). With plenty of seats along the top of the harbour wall, and a café, it is a wonderful place to spend time. The dogs enjoyed it because they could go swimming.

BOAT TRIP

These run from Mullion Harbour. Excursions can be booked online or via phone (noticeboard at the harbour embarkation point). The tour guide is a Cornish fisherman who uses his boat during the high season to give guided tours and supplement his income.

CHOCOLATE FACTORY AND CRAFT CENTRE

Situated on the B3296 road to Mullion Cove, the Chocolate Factory incorporates a group of businesses and a coffee shop. It's a wonderful place to spend time looking at various arts and crafts, as well as learning about chocolate and how it is made.

Mullion Cove is very popular.

Devon – Let's Go Down to the Sea
OS MAPS: EXPLORER – OL20 SOUTH DEVON

The county of Devon is unique in that it is the only county in England to have two separate and distinct coastlines: the North Devon coastline overlooking the lower reaches of the Bristol Channel and the Atlantic Ocean, and the South Devon coastline overlooking the English Channel towards France. The main resorts on the south coast are the towns of Paignton and Torquay, but there are also several smaller ones such Dartmouth and Salcombe, and an array of villages. Inland, amongst the landscape of rolling hills, are many other charming towns and villages.

Although Salcombe is one of the sea resorts of South Devon, it's not actually on the coast but on Salcombe Estuary. This tumbles out to the English Channel and sweeps up to Kingsbridge. Unusually, the estuary is not fed by a major river, but by several small streams.

Because the estuary is so remarkable, a magnificent harbour has been created. These days the harbour is a primarily used for recreation, and is the ideal place for anyone who wants to participate in a variety of water activities from wild swimming to sailing. It is astonishing the number and variety of boats in the harbour. Many are anchored to moorings, but numerous vessels can usually be seen cruising about. When we were there, the sail boats manoeuvring across the waters were practising for one of the several regattas that are held in the estuary. The premier event is the Salcombe Town Regatta held in August. Besides the sailing, there are many fun events such as sandcastle building, and occasionally something really spectacular such as a fly-past by the Red Arrows.

The sand bar at the entrance to the estuary prevents larger commercial vessels using the harbour. Even so, Salcombe was a successful port and boat and shipbuilding centre

Sail boats practicing for one of the many regattas which are held throughout the year.

due to its sheltered harbour and the long easily accessed waterfront. There is also a fleet of shell fishing boats; small, about 20 boats, but still active.

The narrow streets of the town wind down the hill which is very steep in places, and along the shoreline. Narrow roads, lanes and alleyways give access to sandy beaches, ferry terminals, and jetties, as well as several independent shops, cafés and restaurants: a warren to be discovered. There is so much to see, and plenty of places to stop for refreshments. The ferry from South Sands into the centre of the town has to be the most unique experience. Embarking necessitates a ride on a sea tractor to the water taxi out in the estuary, then a trip passing the town to Whitesands Pontoon in the centre. You can take your dog – fantastic! A brilliant way to see the town, and quite an adventure.

There is so much to see in Salcombe, not just because of its amazing harbour and fantastic landscape, but also its history. Originally the town was situated inland because of the threat of invaders and pirates from the sea. Later, being so close to the shoreline and English Channel, Salcombe became important in the defence of the country from the French and the Spanish. It was even ferociously fought over during the English Civil War, with the fort being partly demolished when it was eventually captured by the Parliamentarians. It then became a quiet fishing village with a partiality for smuggling.

This changed in 1835 when Salcombe became the centre of the fruit trade. Schooners (sailing ships) with cargo from all over the world docked at Salcombe to unload. This fruit was then transported to cities such as Bristol. Eventually, the fruit trade gradually ceased due to diseased produce. Salcombe reverted to a quiet attractive village and a popular holiday resort. And so it still is, though with plenty to see and do.

HIGHER REW CAMPSITE

Because the huge campsite field ripples across the countryside, the pitches are dotted about in a haphazard way to make efficient use of the tiered level ground available. The dog exercise area is a steep field adjacent to the site. It is a popular site with several caravans permanently sited on the 90 grass pitches, 70 of which have electric hook-up. Water taps are scattered about so there is always one handy. The barns at one end of the field have been uniquely converted into a variety of amenities. Unusually, the toilets are off in one part of the barns and the showers in another part. There is also an extremely useful large laundry/dishwashing area. Undercover in another section of the barns is an intriguing children's play area. On the roof of the barns were many solar panels. The Squire family, who have run the campsite for three generations, are keen to be as eco-friendly as possible, and are continually adapting as new technologies become available.

PEARLS OF WISDOM 🐎

What a lot of green spaces. Can we play in them? Oh dear; no. But wait! On the other side of the hedge was a huge field where we could run and run and run. Mind you, my owner was very slow climbing up to the flat place at the top. It was very, very steep. Not really suitable for chasing balls and frisbees, but a big place, with so much to explore. We even went down to the sea for a swim. It wasn't too far, but again there was a lot of climbing up and sliding down, so we were dry by the time we got back.

The campsite with the steep field behind it and the hangars visible on the horizon.

RATING ££££

PRICING STRUCTURE (SEE CHAPTER 3) – FLAT RATE/VARIABLE/COMPLICATED

PROS:
- Good location
- Spacious
- Good amenities, including undercover play area
- Dog walks on site
- Reasonable charge during low season for small units

CONS:
- Very complicated fee structure
- Expensive if accompanied by a dog/dogs
- Dog walk very steep, only suitable for ball chasing at top
- Charge for showers

SHORT WALK – TO THE SEA THEN UP AND OVER
Distance: 4.5mi (7.24km)
Time: 2.5hr (Moderate)
Terrain: Footpaths, tracks, woods, fields, beach, gates, airfield, roads (quiet)

Section 1: 1.5mi (2.4km)
- Exit campsite via main entrance out to road
- Turn right downhill (steep) to junction beside stream and bench
- Turn right uphill, passing roof of house on right
- Bear left up steps onto narrow path at Skylark/Rivendell, signposted, going slightly uphill
- Go straight on at junction, signposted, onto stony driveway passing incredible white building on left

- Turn right at junction, signposted
- Continue along road onto wide green track, going downhill, narrowing to a stony path that winds down to coast road

Section 2: 1.25 mi (2km)

- Turn right along road (take care, narrow) down to beach, South Sands on left
- Exit beach via road, turning left, passing café and ferry point on left and car park on right, uphill round left bend
- Continue straight ahead at right bend, along cul-de-sac, through gate into Overbecks Garden
- Continue along path, taking left fork, signposted Bolt Head
- Follow road onto wide track, into woods, through gate
- Continue along coastal path through two gates
- Turn right at next junction

'To the Sea then Up and Over' Route

Section 3: 0.75mi (1.2km)

- Follow grass path uphill onto wide grass track, signposted East Soar
- Bear right through gate on right (East Soar marker on gate), then up steps
- Turn left at top, through gate onto wide grass path
- Continue ahead towards buildings, go through gate, straight on, passing house on left, through kissing gate to Walkers Hut Café, where honesty box refreshments are available)
- Bear right, keeping close to wooden fence on right, along track to bend

Section 4: 1mi (1.6km)

- Continue around left bend, passing airfield on right, out to road, passing car park on left
- Turn right along road, passing houses on left
- Turn right through gate at junction onto access road
- Turn sharp left, keeping close to hedge on left, onto stony track
- Continue straight ahead at bend, onto grass track, and through gap in hedge into field
- Go straight ahead along edge of field, keeping close to hedge on left
- Turn right then left, round hedge, signposted 'l', along edge of field, downhill to campsite entrance

The unique ferry from South Sands to centre of Salcombe.

LONG WALK – A VISIT TO SALCOMBE

Distance: 6.5mi (9.6km)
Time: 5hr (very steep hills)
Terrain: Footpaths, tracks, fields, woods, stiles, gates, roads (narrow, steep), streets. Lots of places for refreshments in Salcombe

Section 1: 1mi (1.6km)

- Exit campsite via main entrance out to road
- Turn right downhill (steep), to junction beside stream and bench
- Turn right, uphill, passing roof of house on right, turning left onto stony track, going uphill (steep) and narrowing, out to road
- Cross road up slope (steep), through gate into field
- Continue along edge of field, with fence on right, through kissing gate into another field
- Bear left across field, through gate in left corner, and into third field

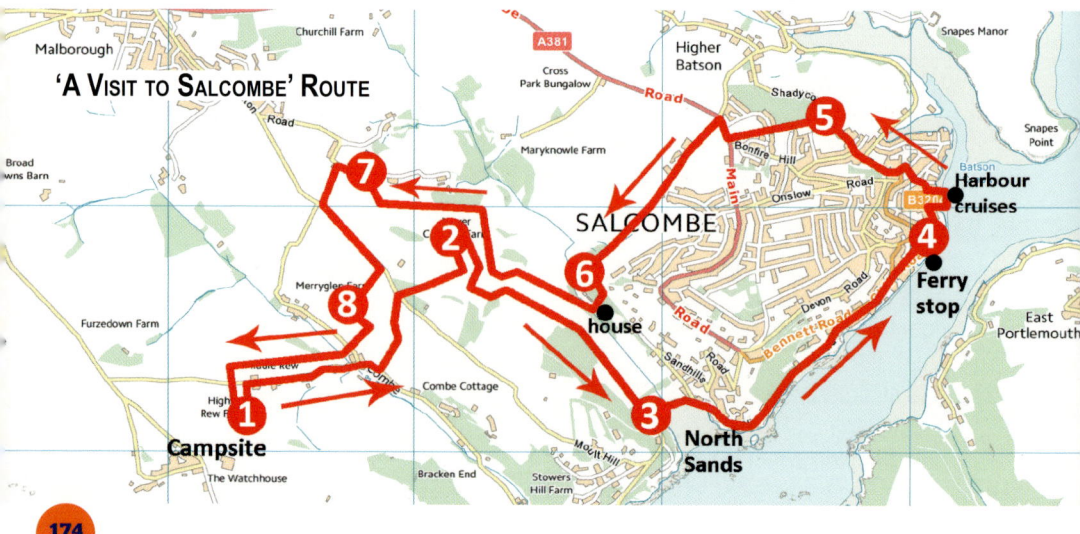

- Continue ahead along edge of field, with hedge on right, round left corner by barbed wire gate, over stile in right corner, onto wide track, signposted bridleway

Section 2: 1mi (1.6km)
- Turn right along track, taking left fork downhill
- Go straight on at next junction, out to road (sea visible ahead)
- Continue ahead towards sea, following wall on right to beach entrance (good place for dog swim)

Section 3: 1mi (1.6km)
- Exit beach where you went in, turning right along road
- Follow road uphill, close to wall on right, ignoring paths off to left, under footbridge, and passing interesting buildings
- Take right fork along narrow 'no entry' road
- Continue along the road as it narrows, passing houses and shops, and ignoring sign on right for pedestrian ferry

Section 4: 0.75mi (1.2km)
- Pass sign on right for pedestrian ferry, turning right into square opposite Victoria Inn, beside Kings Arms, and on to Whitestrand Pontoon to embarkation points for harbour cruise
- Retrace steps to street by Victoria Inn, turning right, passing Kings Arms Hotel on right
- Turn left along road signposted 'Park & Ride'
- Bear right up steep hill, passing Buckley Street on right and long flight of steps on left
- Continue around left bend, passing church on right, taking first turning left, signposted Health Centre (take care, very narrow and no pavement)
- Follow road past car park on right, Coronation Road on left, uphill (very steep), past Shadycombe Court on right

Section 5: 1mi (1.6km)
- Turn left up steps just after Cross Trees Garage, onto narrow path, through gate, passing cemetery on right, and large car park out to A381
- Turn right onto path between hedge and car park fence, then cross road onto cycle path on left verge
- Turn left along wide track, signposted, going downhill
- Turn left at barns, onto narrow path, signposted, out to track by house on right

Section 6: 0.75mi (1.2km)
- Turn right, keeping house on right, and bearing left at front, through gate onto narrow path, signposted Bridle path
- Continue along path to T-junction, turning right along wide track which narrows, twists and bends, out to road, ignoring all paths and stiles leading off

Wonderful walks from **dog-friendly campsites** *on a budget*

A view of Salcombe stretching from the beach up the steep hill.

Section 7: 0.5mi (0.8km)
- Turn left along road, then left again in 30yd (27.4m), onto wide grass track and out to another road
- Turn left along road, then right in 100yd (91m), opposite signpost onto grass track
- Turn left onto narrow stony path, going downhill out to road

Section 8: 0.5mi (0.8km)
- Turn right, passing house on left
- Take left fork, passing bench and stream on left, going uphill (steep) to campsite entrance

IN THE VICINITY
CYCLING
The roads around Salcombe and the campsite are very quiet. They are also very narrow and extremely hilly, even for experienced cyclists. During the holiday season, the influx of people and cars is an additional consideration.

BIRDWATCHING/WILDLIFE
The area is a haven to a host of wildlife, from the seabirds that flock to the harbour and cliffs along the coast, to the field and woodland birds that inhabit the inland rolling landscape. Binoculars are extremely useful. Marine and seashore animals can also be seen from boats or from the coastal path.

FISHING/SAILING
Surrounded by so much water there are plenty of opportunities to hire boats for either fishing or learning to sail.

Ferries/Boat Trips

Because the harbour is so extensive and popular, there are several ferries linking various places, and sightseeing trips around the estuary, Perhaps because there are so many they do not all leave from the same embarkation point. The main ones include:

- Salcombe/East Portlemouth Ferry, which departs from the pier at the aptly named Ferry Street. From here also departs the Salcombe/Kingsbridge Ferry, though this is more of a boat trip. (Dogs are allowed on ferries)
- Boat trips from Whitestrand Pontoon, Whitestrand Quay behind the Kings Arms. (Dogs allowed on all boats)
- South Sands Ferry operates between the Whitestrand Pontoon and South Sands Beach. (Dogs allowed)
- RIB rides (fast speed boat type) depart from the jetty at the end of Normandy Way. (No dogs permitted)
- Whitestrand Boat hire has an office at the side of the car park, but also accepts online bookings. Many different kinds of boats can be hired for a variety of activities. Departure is at Whitestrand Pontoon

East Soar Outdoor Experience

The National Trust farm which houses the East Soar Outdoor Experience is situated on a headland above Salcombe. It mainly offers outdoor activities to groups of disadvantaged children.

Walking Hut

On the premises of East Soar farm experience is this refreshment stop, which offers locally sourced produce including drinks, biscuits, and, on occasion, freshly baked cakes. This is a very isolated spot so the supplies are especially welcome, payment is via an honesty box, so make sure you take cash with you. All kinds of people drop in for a cuppa.

Salcombe Maritime Museum

Housed in a converted chapel at Market Street junction, so easily missed, it has information and exhibits of local shipwrecks and Salcombe's history.

Overbeck's Garden Museum

When scientist and inventor Ottto Overbeck lived here, he acquired an unusual range of objects, as well as creating a striking subtropical garden. It is now a National Trust property with a café on site, which is just as well as it is a steep climb to the entrance. Dogs are not allowed, except on the public footpaths around the perimeter.

Bolt Head Airfield

On the hill above the campsite is this airfield and old radar station, which was used by the RAF during WW2 as a stop off airfield for RAF Exeter. Now there is only a grass strip used by small light aircraft and microlights.

Wonderful walks from dog-friendly campsites on a budget

SOAR MILL COVE

Just over 1mi (1.6km) from the campsite is this secluded beach, only accessible on foot. A fabulous place for dogs to swim all year, but a steep climb up from the campsite, unless taking the route around the edge of the field. There is also a long steady climb up from the beach.

MALBOROUGH

Just 1½mi (2.4km) north of the campsite along a bridleway is this bustling, thriving village with two pubs, a village hall, primary school and a farm shop/post office, Co-op, and petrol station. The church spire can be seen from miles around.

Dorset – A Rural Dorset
OS MAPS: EXPLORER 117 CERNE ABBAS & BERE REGIS

Dorset is probably best known for its amazing Jurassic coastline. Because of the landforms, rocks and outstanding fossils it is a UNESCO World Heritage Site. Also noteworthy is the absence of a motorway passing through the county. But part of the busy A303, London to Cornwall road, does cross a northwest section.

There are also some other rather surprising particulars about the county. First, there are no canals. Second, despite all the different people throughout the ages who have made their home in the county, Dorset does not have a cathedral anywhere. Third, over half the population live in the conurbation of Bournemouth and Poole in the southeast of the county. The remainder of the county is rural with small villages scattered about and just two modest towns: Weymouth, a seaside resort; and Dorchester, the county town.

Between the Wiltshire border and Dorchester the Dorset Downs of rolling chalk hills and small broad valleys stretch across the centre of the county. The dense hedgerows divide the landscape into the quintessential patchwork panorama with clumps of woodland dotted about. The spots of varying colour sprinkled around some of the squares are, on closer inspection, cattle and sheep. Agriculture is important in this area, although not as much as it used to be, as it has been necessary in recent years to diversify. This is exemplified by Brewery Farm campsite, which has developed into a complex establishment.

What is also incredible about the county is the enormous number of listed buildings: in the region of 12,850 which includes Clavell Tower, Corfe Castle and Sherborne Abbey. In addition to this there are over 1500 Scheduled Ancient Monuments, which of course include the chalk figures that have been carved into hillsides, such as the renowned Cerne Abbas Giant. This was gifted to the National Trust in 1920 by the then owners, although access is restricted to preserve the site.

The Cerne Abbas Giant is especially memorable. It is the figure of a huge naked man 180ft (55m) tall) complete with a giant erection and holding a club in his outstretched right hand. There is a path that passes beside the figure, and, although it only offers a view of sections of the figure, it gives a sense of the enormous scale of it.

The best view, like most chalk figures is from above. This proved problematic during WW2 as it could be used by enemy planes as a landmark, and so it was camouflaged. For

The Giant on the hill at Cerne Abbas.

the majority of people the best place to get a good sight of the Cerne Abbas Giant is from a small car park opposite it on the A352.

The age and meaning of the figure is a mystery. Speculation as to its origin has been rife for many decades. Many theories have been proposed over the years ranging from it being a prehistoric carving to it a Celtic god or some kind of fertility symbol. There has even been a suggestion that is a late 1600 satirical representation of Oliver Cromwell. Many historians and archaeologists have studied it. The most recent research attributes the figure to the Saxons; sometime between 700-1100AD. The authenticity of the figure is somewhat irrelevant. Over time it has become an integral part of local folklore and culture attracting thousands of visitors.

For many years it has been the custom on May Day to gather on The Trendle, an iron age enclosure to the right of the Giant's head. This was, in the past, accompanied by a maypole and Morris Dancers, to watch the sunrise and welcome the summer with a barrel of Beltane beer. Since 2021 this tradition has morphed into a festival running for up to five weeks which hosts a variety of events including workshops, walks and talks usually based on a theme.

Because Dorset has such a variety of different landscapes I visited two campsites, to illustrate the diversity of the county and its ability to cater for all sorts of visitors.

Giants Head Campsite

Location, location, location: this is as important for campsites as it is for houses. This campsite's location is amazing. It is extremely well promoted, with a very helpful owner, and lots of clear and precise suggestions about a whole range of activities. Unfortunately the campsite itself does not chime with expectations. Yes, it does have hook-ups, toilets, showers, a dishwashing area, and a laundry. Apart from the laundry, which has a dedicated room at one end of the barn, the other facilities are all squeezed tightly into

The sloping field, leading to a small dog exercise area and a footpath.

the other end. Similarly with the pitches; there were no markings, and the positioning of units appeared chaotic. This was exacerbated by the fact that it was a very sloping field. A number of seasonal caravans appeared squashed up on the flattest places on both sides of the access road, so trying to find a suitably flat place in the remaining sloping field was difficult. The grass was very long, which caused wet legs when dewy in the morning. The £3.00 a night for each dog was a bit steep, though I only paid for one dog because I was a solo traveller and one of my dogs was counted as a person. Location however was fabulous, and the staff were all very friendly.

PEARLS OF WISDOM 🐕

It seemed that we had a special place to run in a very small wooded area at the bottom of the field, but this soon opened back out up into the campsite then into another really big field. We did not have a long poke around here because over the road was a flatter ginormous field with footpaths criss-crossing it; a fabulous place, all the more exciting because every time we went into the field we went a different way. Awesome. The outings were great because with a footpath running through the place there were no roads, except quiet ones in the nearby village, but we did have to avoid some of those whiffy cows and it was hilly in places.

RATING £££
PRICING STRUCTURE (SEE CHAPTER 3) – FLAT RATE/SEASONAL
PROS:
- Excellent location
- Plenty of local dog walking places
- Simple easy pricing

CONS:
- High charge for dogs so extra £ rating
- Cramped amenities block

SHORT WALK – THE GIANT'S HOME

Distance: 3.75mi (9.6km)
Time: 2.5hr (Moderate)
Terrain: Lanes, footpaths, tracks, woods, fields, long climb up and down, gates, kissing gates, roads (quiet), pavements

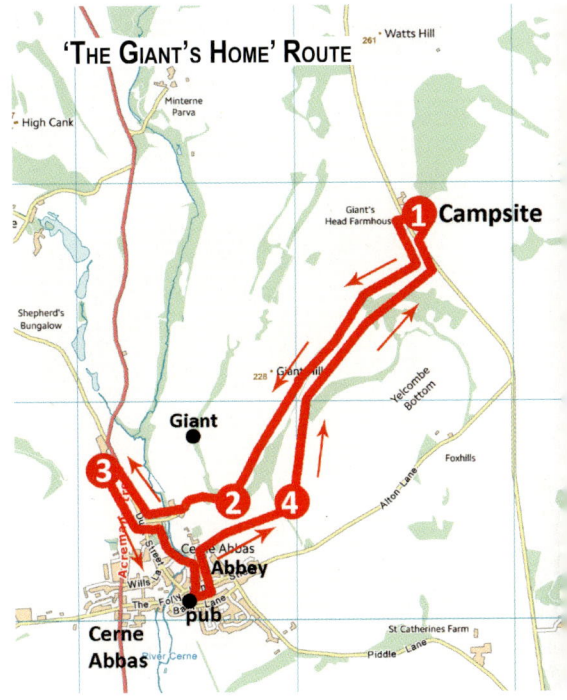

Section 1: 1mi (1.6km)

- Exit campsite via main entrance, crossing road, and through gate opposite into field
- Turn left along edge of field, with hedge on left, round right bend at corner, still keeping close to hedge on left
- Turn sharp left at corner of hedge and go through gate into another field
- Turn sharp right, along track out to field
- Go straight on along edge of field, keeping close to hedge now on right, and through gate on right
- Bear slightly left onto narrow downhill path between hedges
- Take left fork at junction, still going downhill, passing stile in fence on left
- Take right fork at junction

Section 2: 0.75mi (1.2km)

- Follow path up short steep slope, round to right, then round left bend through woods, with fields visible on left, ignoring stile and gate on left
- Take left fork at next junction, go through kissing gate ahead, passing steps on right (these lead to the Giant, but you can't see clearly from there because it's too close to see whole), take path signposted Kettle Bridge
- Follow path out to concrete access road by barn
- Turn left, then right, along wide stony track, go over bridge, passing village hall on left
- Bear right into car park, straight ahead into play area
- Bear right towards top left corner, onto narrow path between fences, passing large gate and green building on right
- Continue along path to kissing gate in fence on left (ideal place to see Giant on hill opposite)

Section 3: 1mi+ (1.6km+)

- Retrace steps to car park entrance, turning left with village hall now on right
- Turn right along path immediately before bridge, with river on left, signposted Village Centre

One of the amazing buildings in the village of Cerne Abbas.

- Turn left at junction over bridge, signposted Village Centre, out to Abbey Street
- Turn right passing church on left (look for stocks) to pub on left corner and pub opposite (The Giant Inn, I had a meal here)
- Exit pub, turn left to village stores and Post Office on corner, and souvenir shop on opposite corner
- Turn right along Duck Street, right again along Mill Lane
- Follow lane between houses, turning right along footpath before bridge, signposted
- Continue along path beside river over stone slab bridge
- Turn right over wooden bridge, along lane out to Abbey Street
- Turn left for abbey ruins and St Augustine's wishing well at top of street
- Turn right through gate into graveyard
- Take left fork through graveyard gate into field
- Bear right across field, taking path closest to wall on right
- Continue ahead up slope, between mound on right and hedge, keeping to path on right through gate into field
- Go straight ahead along edge of field, keeping close to hedge on left, passing football field on right through gate out to T-junction

Section 4: 1mi (1.6km)
- Turn left along wide track, climbing steadily, ignoring all paths leading off
- Continue along track which gets narrower, and steeper through gate at top into field
- Go straight ahead along edge of field with hedge on left, through gate in left corner into another field

- Turn right along edge of field, with hedge now on right, round corner through gate on right out to road
- Cross road to campsite entrance

Long Walk – Wessex Ridgeway
Distance: 6mi (9.6km)
Time: 4hr (Moderate)
Terrain: Footpaths, tracks, woods, fields, lanes, gates, kissing gates, roads (quiet)

Section 1: 1mi (1.6km)
- Exit campsite via dog walk at bottom of field, by trees and dog bin
- Follow path up slope, through copse, passing campsite on right, through kissing gate into field
- Go straight on, along edge of field, with hedge on left
- Bear left at corner, through gap in hedge, onto narrow path into field

- Continue along edge of field, with hedge still on left
- Turn right across field at overgrown area, opposite onto wide stony track
- Turn left along track, passing barn on right, and go through gate onto another wide track

Section 2: 1mi (1.6km)
- Turn right through farmyard out to driveway
- Turn right towards road, turning left along road
- Turn right in 50yd (45.7m), through gate on right into field
- Go straight on along narrow path between hedge and mound on right, out into field
- Go straight ahead along edge of field with hedge still on left, through gate into second field
- Continue ahead along edge of field, still with hedge on left, along narrow path to wide track

Section 3: 0.75mi (1.2km)
- Turn left through gap in hedge, straight across four-way junction onto wide grass track between hedges out to road
- Bear left out to B3143
- Turn right along road to junction, turning left, signposted Henley

Section 4: 1mi (1.6km)
- Follow road straight across four-way junction, passing postbox on right, out to T-junction
- Turn left to pub, The Gaggle of Geese on left (good refreshment stop)
- Exit put to road, turning left, passing postbox and telephone box on left
- Turn left at bend, passing Box Cottage on right, along cul-de-sac to junction, passing Court Farm Business Park and equestrian stables on right

Section 5: 0.75mi (1.2km)
- Take left fork with Knap Farm entrance on left, through barrier, along concrete lane, passing lorry park on left and Knap Farm barns on right, into field
- Go straight on along edge of field, close to hedge on left (climbing), through gate at top
- Bear right along path beside fence on right, go through gate to T-junction

Section 6: 1mi (1.6km)
- Turn along narrow path between trees through gate into field
- Cross field through gate opposite onto wide stony track
- Turn right along track, ignoring paths off, go round bend and through gate

Section 7: 0.5mi (0.8km)
- Turn left onto very narrow path 50yd (45.7m) and on to overgrown field
- Cross field to hedge opposite, turning right along edge of field, with hedge on left
- Bear right across field after long left bend, towards clump of 12 big trees opposite, through gap in hedge, passing clump on left, then out to busy road

Section 8: 0.5mi (0.8km)

- Bear left across road, through gap in hedge into field
- Turn left along edge of field, go through gate in hedge on left, and out to road
- Cross road to campsite entrance

IN THE VICINITY

CYCLING

Cycling routes around the village and the giant are available online. A certain level of fitness is necessary as there are some steep hills.

BIRDWATCHING

Every kind of birdwatcher is catered for in Dorset with both countryside and coastal locations available. There are also guided tours. Check online for details.

CERNE ABBAS

This historic Dorset village is dominated by the chalk Giant, but it is well worth visiting as there is a lot to see. The significant event was the founding of the Benedictine Abbey in 987AD, which also gave the village the Abbas part of its name (it means father, the monastic name for an abbot). The fortunes of the village have waxed and waned over the centuries; beer-making, using local water, helped smooth the transition when Henry VIII sold off the abbey; the lack of a railway contributed to a steady decline; but tourism during the mid-20th century has slowly reversed its fortune. It is now a prosperous village with three pubs, a local brewery, and shops. The layout of the village and several buildings are much the same as in mediaeval times. Even the stocks are still there, in front of the church in Abbey Street.

MINTERNE HOUSE & GARDENS/MINTERNE MAGNA AND MINTERNE PARVA

In Latin 'Magna' means large and 'Parva' means little. Neither settlement is especially large. Minterne Parva is more of a hamlet, with a few cottages and a farm, whilst Minterne Magna is distinguished by the proximity of Minterne House & Gardens. The house has had a long colourful history, most notably its connection with the Churchill family. It still remains a private residence so is not open to the public; however, it is the gardens that set this house apart, especially the rhododendrons of the Himalayan garden, which is open to the visitors and dogs are allowed.

BADGER WATCH

With badgers notoriously difficult to find, Old Henley Farm provides hides from which to observe their comings and goings from dusk until approximately midnight. (Tel 01300 345293)

BUCKLAND NEWTON

The residential part of the village is stretched out along the B3143, whereas some of the other community amenities such as the church and the pub, etc, are located along quieter, narrower roads. The pub is especially notable, with its quirky name, The Gaggle of Geese, it has a shepherd's hut at the back available for hire as well as a small basic campsite (although no EHU).

Dorset – second campsite
BREWERY FARM CAMPSITE

This campsite in Ansty is unusual in that it is part of a quite comprehensive complex. On turning into the entrance there is a long approach to the actual campsite. The first section on the left comprises a small car park, at the rear of which are two shops. One is a Post Office with a small convenience store; the other is a farm shop selling local produce. The next section is the farmhouse and sundry buildings. These too are set back from the driveway. The final section is the campsite field, the entrance to which is through a large gap in the tall hedges. Just inside the entrance on the left is the modern facilities block with the field stretching ahead. There are nine hardstanding pitches dotted about and a large grass area for tents. Large fields border two sides of the site, and these can be used to exercise dogs if the farm's cattle are not grazing in them. In addition to this, the farm also owns the pub across the road, The Fox Inn. The farm has continued the tradition of helping the small rural village of Ansty to remain a practical thriving community. Back in the 18th century, ale was brewed on the farm by the farmer's son Charles Hall, and sold in the pub (hence the farm's name). Over time this became a very successful business. Then in the early 1900s the brewery moved to larger premises in Blandford Forum (tours are available).

Cattle from the farm grazing in a field next to the campsite.

PEARLS OF WISDOM 🐎

Oodles of places to chase my frisbee: the green space nearby if it was empty, the green across the road, and the field at the far end of the campsite. This was also wonderful to explore, so big and heaps of interesting smells. Sometimes there were large bushy animals, cows, I think, mooching about in the field. I didn't want to get too close to them. Neither did my owner, so we found somewhere else to play. Walks galore, but again these cows meant at times it was best to go a different way. Walks were intriguing, even though there seemed to be a lot of hard roads. It was all very quiet so we could roam freely; a bonus.

RATING £££

PRICING STRUCTURE (SEE CHAPTER 3) – FLAT RATE

PROS:

- Good location
- Close to pub and shop
- Simple easy pricing with discount for solo travellers

CONS:

- High charge, but reasonable for peak season
- Cows in many of the fields
- Several roads, but quiet

SHORT WALK – ROUND AND ABOUT

Distance: 5.5mi (8.8km)
Time: 3.5hr (Moderate)
Terrain: Footpaths, tracks, woods, fields, gates, kissing gates, stiles, roads (mostly quiet), lanes, some climbs

Section 1: 1.5mi (2.4km)

- Exit campsite via main entrance, turning right along road
- Turn right onto driveway opposite Aller Lane, go over stile beside gate, onto grass track
- Follow track over stile into field
- Cross field to bottom right corner, to cross stile onto fenced path along edge of

'ROUND AND ABOUT' ROUTE

field, over stile and out to road
- Turn right along road (very quiet) passing Cothayes Farm on left
- Turn right at left bend, through farmyard onto wide grass track between trees
- Bear left onto narrow path, through woods, slight left bend, signposted out to field
- Continue straight ahead, along edge of field, keeping close to hedge on left
- Turn right just before large tree, cross field to gap between trees opposite, and go through gate into field

Section 2: 1.5mi (2.4km)
- Bear left across field through gate into another field
- Cross field, bearing slightly right towards farm
- Go straight ahead, passing gate on left, onto concrete track with farmyard on left
- Continue ahead onto muddy track, with farmyard still on left, back onto concrete driveway, through gate and onto road
- Cross road onto wide muddy track opposite
- Bear left onto narrow footpath (wet due to stream!) between hedges
- Bear right at junction, signposted, fording stream onto stony path, going uphill out to field
- Go straight ahead towards right corner, climbing steadily
- Keeping close to hedge on right, follow round to left, through gap on right into another field
- Bear slightly left, cross field, go through gate, still climbing, into another field
- Bear slightly right, up steep hill (amazing views behind), through gate into another field
- Go straight ahead, climbing gradually onto stony track at top
- Continue straight on, along grass ridge, skirting historic camp on left, go through gate
- Follow narrow stony footpath, passing large wooden cross on left, keeping mound on left
- Turn right before second mound, along wide grassy track, heading towards gate (views on both sides are amazing)
- Keep left at fork, right at second fork, through gate in fence on left, and out to road

Section 3: 1.5mi (2.4km)
- Turn right along road (quiet), passing junction on left
- Turn next right along Cuckoo Lane
- Continue straight ahead at junction, going slightly downhill (busier road)
- Turn right, signposted, opposite Warren Farm, onto wide stony track, going downhill to Rawlsbury Farm turning left along driveway

Section 4: 1mi (1.6mile)
- Follow driveway, passing Peck Cottage on right
- Turn right at bend between hedge and new wooden railing, go through small wooden gate with waymarker
- Turn right at T-junction, then left at next T-junction
- Right over stile into field
- Bear right across field, climb over stile (difficult) into back of campsite

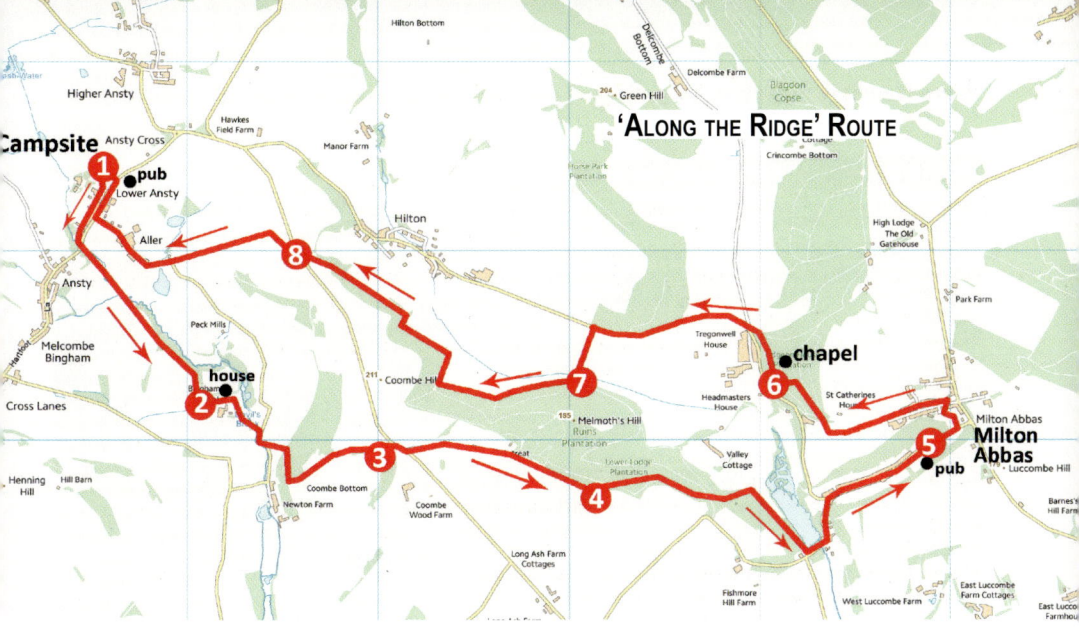

'ALONG THE RIDGE' ROUTE

LONG WALK – ALONG THE RIDGE
Distance: 8mi (12.8km)
Time: 4hr (Moderate)
Terrain: Footpaths, tracks, woods, fields, long climb up and down, gates, kissing gates, roads (quiet), lanes

Section 1:1mi (1.6km)
- Exit campsite via entrance onto road
- Turn right along road, crossing bridge
- Turn left through gate into field
- Go straight ahead along edge of field, with stream on left, go through gate
- Follow narrow path, and through kissing gate into field
- Continue along edge of field, cross footbridge into next field
- Turn left, taking right fork uphill into large field
- Go straight ahead, keeping close to trees on left, through kissing gate in corner onto narrow path going down through woods
- Take right fork, crossing bridge, river still on left, out to private estate
- Turn right along grass avenue leading to gravel drive

Section 2: 1mi (1.6km)
- Follow gravel track round to left, towards church, with wall on left
- Continue straight ahead at bend, passing church on right, cross over bridge and go through kissing gate
- Turn right, cross field, go through fixed kissing gate onto road
- Turn right along road, go through second gate at corner into field
- Continue along edge, going slightly uphill towards trees, go through gate in left corner
- Turn right along grassy path, climbing steadily (long), keeping close to hedge/fence on right (amazing views), and through gate into field

The Post Office and village shop at Milton Abbas.

- Turn right along edge of field fence, still on right, through gate onto road
- Turn right along road

Section 3: 0.75mi (1.2km)
- Turn left onto stony track, passing house on left
- Follow track into woods to T-junction
- Turn left along track onto road, turn left, then left again, at bend onto wide track through barrier into forest

Section 4: 1.mi (1.6km)
- Continue along track, turning right at three-way junction, going down then immediately right, still going down to road
- Turn right through large metal gates to junction
- Turn left along road to Milton Abbas High Street (lots of amazing thatched buildings), continue up to pub

Section 5: 1mi (1.6km)
- Exit pub, turn right, continuing along High Street
- Turn left after village picnic area, onto footpath, up steps round bend to road
- Turn left, then left at signpost to St Catherine's Chapel, along road leading onto wide track
- Continue along track, passing driveway
- Turn immediate right onto footpath, into woods
- Follow path, bearing left, parallel to track on left
- Cross track onto wide path, passing fallen tree on right
- Turn left, going down, passing Chapel on right

Section 6: 1mi (1.6km)
- Follow path to three-way junction
- Take middle path, going down to T-junction
- Turn left, still going down, turn right just before road out to lane
- Turn left to road junction, taking left fork (take care busy road), passing entrance to Milton Abbey School and playing fields on left
- Turn left through barrier onto wide track
- Follow track towards woods, turning right through gate

Section 7: 1.25mi (2km)
- Continue along path through woods, with fields visible through trees on right to T-junction
- Turn right along narrow path, fields still visible on right
- Turn left just before field onto very narrow footpath, going up round to right, then left, passing kissing gate

Section 8: 1mi (1.6km)
- Take right fork, still close to field, climbing steeply through gate into field
- Cross field out to road
- Turn right along road, left into field (no gate), signposted
- Bear right across field, towards buildings, and through gap in hedge
- Turn left along edge of two fields, through gate to road
- Turn right along road, passing between cottages to The Fox pub, and campsite entrance

IN THE VICINITY
CYCLING
The roads around Ansty are quiet, so suitable for cycling, but care needs to be taken as some are quite narrow.

ANSTY
The village name is, in one sense, rather a misnomer. It is more a collection of hamlets; Higher Ansty, Lower Ansty, Little Ansty (also known as Pleck), and Ansty Cross, as well as Ansty itself. On the other hand it is aptly named, as Ansty originally meant 'narrow path' and the road through the village snakes its way through the muddled patchwork of mid-Dorset hills. For centuries it was a quiet backwater, until 1777 when the brewery company was founded. When it was relocated to Blandford in the 1940s the village returned to a peaceful, tranquil place amid the Dorset countryside. The campsite complex is actually located on the outskirts of Lower Ansty.

MILTON ABBAS
The original 'new town' was built in 1780 on the instructions of Lord Milton, Earl of Dorchester, because his view was obstructed by the old village. 36 almost identical thatched cottages of cob were built on either side of a broad street, and painted yellow.

Each had a lawn at the front and a chestnut tree between them. Each cottage was intended for two families. At the same time a church and almshouses were also built. With the villagers relocated, the original village was demolished. Unsurprisingly there have been changes over the years: the cottages are now white, the trees have been removed, only one family lives in each cottage, and some of the cottages are now businesses. There is now a pub, post office and shop, though the names of some of the cottages give a clue as to their previous usage. The Earl of Dorchester's house and adjacent abbey is now a school. The cottages are much the same as when they were built, and often used as an example of rural Dorset. Every two years in July there is a street fair celebrating the traditional arts and crafts of the area.

BULBARROW HILL
This is one of the highest chalk hills of the Dorset Downs overlooking Somerset, Wiltshire and Devon, as well as Dorset. Occupying a ridge is an Iron Age Hillfort, with several barrows which gives the hill its name. The views are incredible.

BINGHAM'S MELCOMBE HOUSE
Little remains of this mediaeval village. To the southeast is the parish church of St Andrew, a few farm buildings, and Bingham's Melcombe House, so-called after Robert Bingham who acquired the property in the 13th century through marriage. It remained in the Bingham family until 1895. It is still a private residence.

HIGHER MELCOMBE/MELCOMBE HORSEY
To the west of Ansty is another deserted medieval village, Melcombe Horsey. All that remains is a 15th century Manor House and estate, Higher Melcombe. This is now a B&B and wedding venue with a farm on the estate.

Wiltshire – Slow Boats West to East
OS MAP: EXPLORER 156 CHIPPENHAM & BRADFORD ON AVON
The Kennet and Avon Canal is a feat of Victorian engineering, linking Bristol to London via the River Avon at Bristol to the River Kennet (upgraded to a canal) at Newbury, then on to the River Thames and so into London. The Canal provided a quick and easy way to transport goods between Bristol and London.

The journey by horse and cart took more than three days and also included expensive tolls. The sea route, down the Bristol Channel, around Cornwall and along the English Channel up to the Thames Estuary, was not an option, as it was more hazardous with the possibility of Atlantic storms and even attack from enemy ships, mainly French. A waterway between the two cities was suggested as far back as 1558. In the 1600s a survey was even carried out. The plan did not materialize, partly because of political changes but also because of opposition by farmers and traders. (Nothing much changes – sounds much like the 21st century!)

Work eventually began in 1718, upgrading the River Kennet at its junction with the River Thames, but it wasn't until 1794 that work finally began on the actual canal. There

The engineering masterpiece; 16 locks forming a series of steps up an incline.

were many delays, some financial, some due to the complexity of the project, so the canal was not fully open to through traffic until 1810. The long wait proved viable, as it provided a cheaper, faster, and definitely a safer method of travel.

This project may have taken a long time to complete, but sections of it were operable several years before. The canal was built in three sections. Work on the eastern section, Newbury to Devizes, took just three years, 1796-1799. The western section, Bath to Foxhanger, took six years, 1801-1807. The middle section joining these was the most difficult, and was the last to be built, as the elevation of the final two miles was a colossal 237ft (72m). This was resolved with a series of locks; 29 in total in three groups. The first series of seven locks around Foxhanger were spread over ¾ mi (1.2km). The next 16 are very close to each other, and form a series of steps up the incline. How this is achieved is an engineering masterpiece, and is rightly today designated a scheduled ancient monument. The final six locks cover the three-quarters of a mile into Devizes.

For about 30 years the canal was 'the' way to transport goods to and from London, 24 hours a day, as the canal was lit by gas. The coming of the railways in 1841 changed all that. Despite their best efforts, traffic along the canal soon declined, and it gradually fell into disrepair, until it eventually closed in 1948. Communities along the canal objected to its closure, so during the 1950s campaigned against this. In 1962, with the formation of The Kennet and Avon Canal Trust, restoration began to return the canal to its former through navigation facility, but now as a public amenity.

Restoration of the canal, especially the 29 locks at Caen Hill also took a long time. Again, like the original build, it was done in sections. Due to an enormous amount of work done by volunteers, many of the locks were refurbished and operational during the 1980s. In 1990, a 17 mile section between Newbury and Reading was officially opened, but it was not until 2003 that the restoration of the whole canal was complete. Even so, upgrading and maintenance is a continual process.

Today, the canal again provides a living for a variety of people, as well as a place for those living full-time in their boats. It may be a heritage tourism destination, but the sliver of water that meanders through some amazing landscape gives pleasure to thousands of people. More information about the canal is available at the Kennet and Avon Museum on Devizes Wharf.

THREE MAGPIES PUB CAMPSITE

Through the pub car park and round the side reveals quite a large flat field, stretching off into the distance, and separated by a delightful row of bushes. One side has several electrical hook-up points ideal for tourers (it was suggested room for only eight, but it looked large enough to accommodate more). The other field was set aside for off grid campers and tents. The hardstanding section appeared wedged into the gravel area at the top end of the two fields, so units were parked in a rather haphazard fashion. The facilities block was a large Portakabin, but much better than many I have encountered. There is no reception; staff in the pub deal with checking in. Of course having a pub so handy is a bonus, especially as the food is good, so it is best to book a table.

PEARLS OF WISDOM 🐾

No specific place for me to exercise here but it didn't matter as just a frisbee throw down a quiet road was an whopping field to explore, with lots of engrossing smells. It was a really fab place. My son Pippin had plenty of space to run (his favourite pace) and lots of pals to meet. Like all youngsters he had fun playing with them; as for me, saying hi was sufficient. A bonus, this field led to other fields and paths; oodles and oodles of exploring and investigating to do. Shame about the water; a canal I think my owner said. No swimming; boo! But the path beside was so intriguing, especially the large wooden objects tied up to the sides. I wanted to nose around one but this was not possible

The Three Magpies Pub, with pitches behind it accessed via the car park on the left.

RATING ££
PRICING STRUCTURE (SEE CHAPTER 3) – FLAT RATE
PROS:
- Good location
- Pub on site
- Simple easy pricing
- Plenty of places to walk dogs
- Bus stop nearby

CONS:
- Squashed hardstanding pitches
- Portakabin amenities

SHORT WALK – NEAR THE CANAL

Distance: 5.75mi (9.2km)
Time: 2.5hr (Easy)
Terrain: Tracks: (grass, stony tarmac), quiet roads, lanes, fields, gates, kissing gates, towpath, busy road (verge/pavement)

Section 1: 1.75mi (2.8km)

- Exit via A365, turning right along road (pavement)
- Turn second left along road, passing equestrian centre on left and house to junction, signposted Rowde
- Turn left, signposted Bridleway, onto wide stony track that narrows
- Continue straight ahead at bend, onto wide grass track

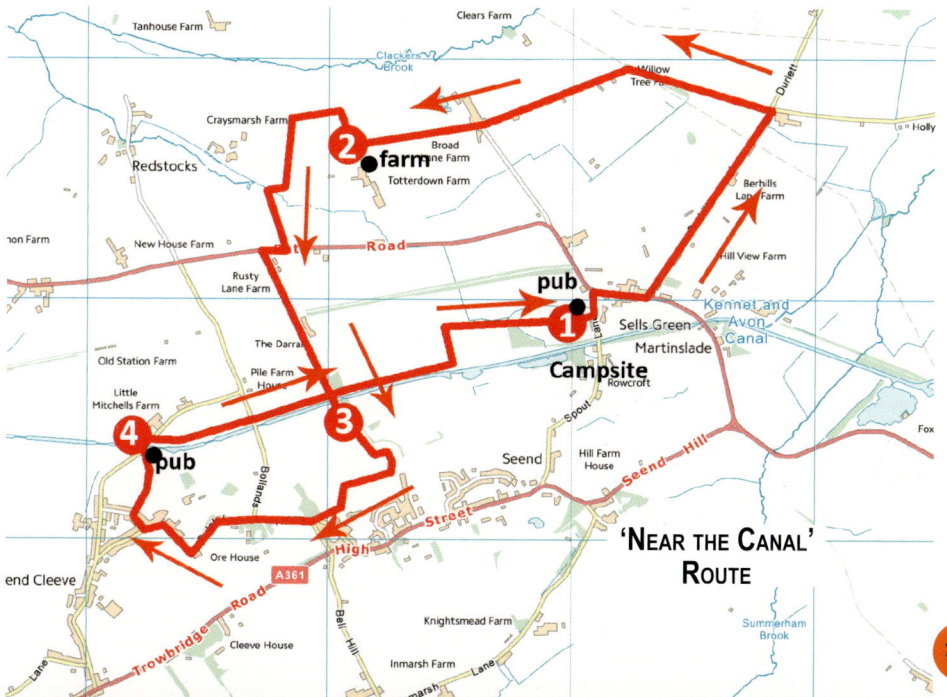

'NEAR THE CANAL' ROUTE

Amazing views of the canal from the outskirts of Seend village.

- Bear right at next bend, onto grass path, close to hedge on right
- Follow winding path through farmyard, passing coach yard on left, then out to road
- Turn left, then sharp right, and through gates by notice board of business park
- Bear slightly right onto wide track, passing two gates on right, through gate onto wide track, keeping close to hedge on right
- Follow track through another gate into farmyard (very muddy)

Section 2: 1.25mi (2km)
- Turn right along track, away from muddy farmyard, go through gate, turning immediate left (muddy)
- Go straight ahead at bend, through gate onto lovely wide grass track between hedges, through another gate
- Turn left into field, then immediate right, along edge of two sides of field, through the gate in right corner, onto grass area
- Turn right, then immediate left, along wide grass path, through gate out to A365 (very busy)
- Turn right (narrow grass verge opposite), turn left along driveway, signposted, opposite
- Keeping close to hedge on right, follow green path, ignoring sign for horses, through gate
- Bear right across track onto grass path between hedge on right and wooden fence on left, go through three gates and out to canal

Section 3: 1.25mi (2km)
- Go straight ahead across swing bridge onto narrow path

- Continue along path becoming stony track, uphill (steep)
- Turn right at top (Seend Village is straight on) onto narrow path, signposted Bolland Hill (amazing views)
- Follow winding path out to minor road, turning right onto busier road
- Turn right, passing reservoir on right
- Go straight on at bend along Belcher Road
- Follow road passing houses to second bend
- Turn right between pillars of Ferrum House, onto driveway, keeping left at junction
- Continue along tarmac lane out to road
- Turn left to pub (great for refreshments beside canal)

Section 4: 1.5mi (2.4km)
- Exit pub via road, turning left to cross bridge
- Turn immediate left down slope, left again to towpath, left along towpath under bridge
- Follow towpath past swing bridge, to second bridge
- Turn left, through kissing gate, into field
- Cross field through gap in hedge opposite
- Turn right along path, go through gap in hedge ahead
- Cross field, go through kissing gate in right corner out to road
- Turn left to pub and campsite

LONG WALK – CANAL STEPS
Distance: 5.5mi (8.8km)
Time: 4hr (Easy)
Terrain: Bus ride, footpaths, towpaths, tracks, woods, gates, road, streets

Section 1: 0.25mi (0.4km)
- Exit campsite via reception
- Turn left along road towards pub, to A361
- Turn right along A361, crossing road to bus stop opposite
- Catch bus to Devizes (bus timetable available at campsite reception)

Section 2: 0.75mi (1.2km)
- Get off bus at terminal Devizes Market Place
  (Devizes is an interesting town with lots to see before walk. Obtain a street map to plan route returning to Market Place)
- Turn right along road towards Greggs, passing WH Smith and café (welcomes dogs, good place to stop for a drink and plan town route)
- Turn left into Shambles Market Hall
- Go straight ahead to exit at opposite end
- Continue on to A361, bearing right, to cross at crossing
- Turn left along road, passing church on right
- Take first right onto New Park Road

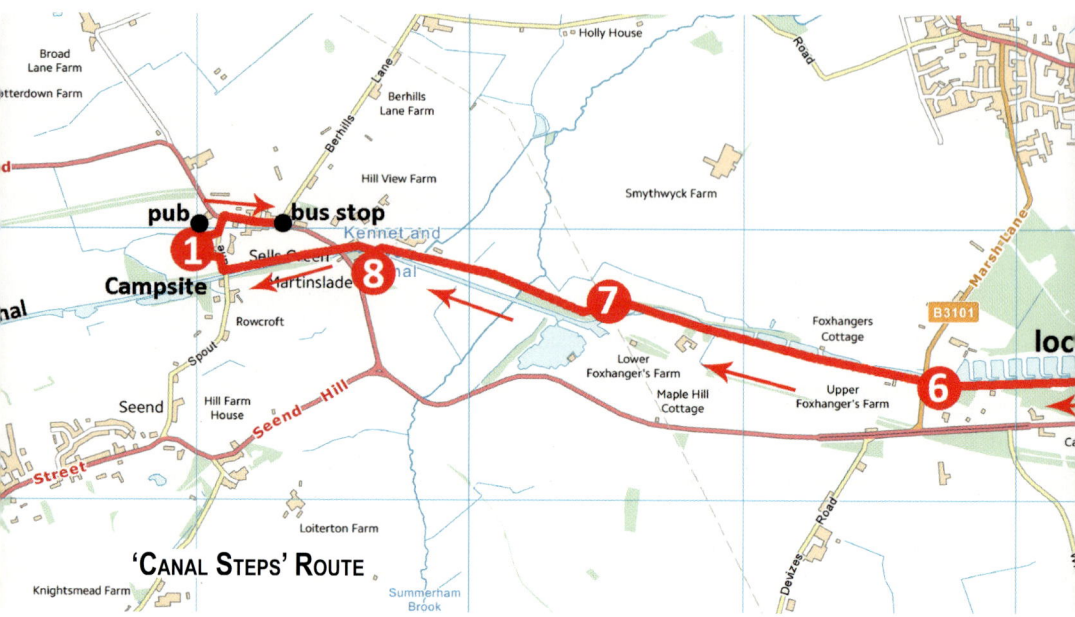

'CANAL STEPS' ROUTE

- Follow road to double mini roundabout
- Take second exit on left, still on New Park Road
- Continue along road, passing Victoria Road on right, to bridge over canal with large double gates at other end
- Continue straight ahead, go right round gates, onto wide track between trees, turning left at junction

Section 3: 1mi (1.6km)
- Cross green, going through kissing gate into wood
- Turn left along footpath, with fence visible through trees on left
- Follow path as it winds up and down, through trees, to junction at top of slope
- Turn left through kissing gate, then immediate right, along footpath into cemetery
- Turn left along concrete path
- Turn right at next concrete path, right again, then left, through large gates, onto road by bridge
- Cross road, bearing right down path onto towpath, with canal on left (Kennet & Avon Canal Museum is on other side of bridge, and a café)
- Follow towpath to Northgate Street

Section 4: 1mi (1.6km)
- Turn left, along road, and over bridge (for Wadworth Brewery Visitor Centre, continue along road, over roundabout, and right at next roundabout onto A361. Centre is 30yd (27m) on left.)
- Turn left, down slope, then sharp right, onto towpath
- Continue along path under bridge, with canal now on right, to Lock 46

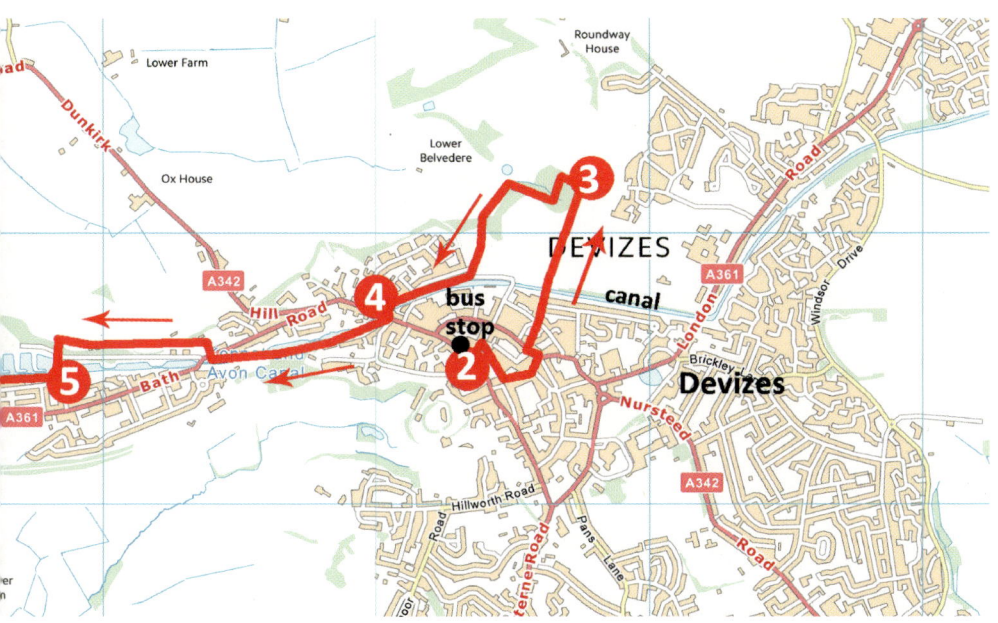

- Turn right across footbridge
- Follow footpath round to left, with canal now on left and road on right
- Continue along path, passing Lock 45 on left

There's always plenty to see along the towpath.

- Cross small car park to path opposite, through wildlife garden and gate to Caen Café (another good place to stop for a drink)
- Exit café, turning left, across footbridge at Lock 44
- Turn right onto towpath, with canal on right

Section 5: 0.75mi (1.2km)
- Follow towpath past series of locks to Lock 28
- Continue along towpath, under bridge, with canal still on right, with lots of boats tied up

Section 6: 0.75mi (1.2km)
- Follow towpath, passing Foxhanger campsite on left, to Lock 23 passing campsite and village shop junction
- Go straight ahead, up slope to bridge
- Turn right, across bridge, then left back onto towpath, with canal now on left

Section 7: 0.5mi (0.8km)
- Continue along towpath, passing marina on right
- Keep left under A365 at bridge 148

Section 8: 0.5mi (0.8km)
- Continue along towpath under bridge 149
- Turn immediate right, round gate, to road
- Turn left along road to campsite entrance

IN THE VICINITY
DEVIZES CAMPING AND CARAVANNING CLUB SITE
An alternative campsite for this area, located right next to the Three Magpies Pub. The walks described can be adapted to start from this site. Details are listed in Appendix ii.

CYCLING
There are several quiet roads, and cycling is permitted along the towpath. Suggested routes can be found online.

FISHING
Although there is an abundance of fish in the canal, and fishing is allowed from the towpath, large sections are leased to various angling clubs. Check online for details.

WILDLIFE
Conservation of wildlife is an important part of the upgrade and maintenance of the canal, and there are many different species of birds to spot as well as a variety of flora and fauna to see. Some of the surrounding areas have been designated Sites of Special Scientific Interest.

KENNET AND AVON MUSEUM
(Open 10am-3pm Tues, Weds, Sat, Sun – cash only)
This is housed in a warehouse on Devizes Wharf and has a huge amount of information about the canal. They open only part of the week, and apparently only take cash in the shop and café.

KENAVON VENTURE
During the summer a group of volunteers run trips in a traditional narrowboat along parts of the canal, allowing members of the public a taste of canal life. Check out the website for details and special events. Dogs are allowed at the discretion of the skipper.

WHARF THEATRE
The theatre is housed in an industrial building on Devizes Wharfe, and has an extensive programme.

DEVIZES
This Wiltshire market town has a lot to offer visitors. One of the best ways to explore and learn about it is to follow the town trail. Leaflets are obtainable from Kennet and Avon Museum or the Wiltshire Museum on Long Street, just off Market Place. As the name suggests, there is information about the county, including the iconic Stonehenge, as well as the development of Devizes itself. The trail includes various buildings such St John the Baptist Church and castle. There are also shops, cafés, pubs and an indoor market in the Shambles, just off Market Place, and an outdoor one every Thursday in Market Place.

WADWORTH BREWERY VISITORS CENTRE
This is situated in Northgate Street, not far from the canal, and remains an important part of the town's economy. Although it is known locally for its beer, of equal acclaim are the shire horses that are still used to deliver the beer to pubs in the town and up to a 5mi (8km) radius of it. Check online for tours of both brewery and stables. Dogs are allowed in the visitors' centre, but not on the tour or in the stables.

ROWDE
Just 2mi (3.2km) northeast of the campsite is the village of Rowde, which is lucky to have a number of local amenities including two pubs, a farm shop and café overlooking Roundway Hill.

SEEND
This Wiltshire village is situated 300ft (90m) above sea level on a hill top, with the A361 Devizes to Trowbridge Road passing through on its narrow streets. At one time, with the canal and the railway passing nearby, it was a busy hub and expanded to accommodate them. Now it is a quiet village, with the Barge Inn in prime position beside the canal to offer a respite with a view.

Walks in Scotland
(Fife, Lothian, Skye)

The Countryside Code for Scotland is different from the rest of the UK. (See Appendix i). Generally it is summarized as the 'right to roam', suggesting it is possible to go anywhere one pleases. Perhaps this is why the OS Maps only mark the long distance trails and not footpaths, as there are no officially approved ones. In reality there are huge swathes of land which are not accessible to the general public. Either they are fenced off, in which case landowners are obliged to allow easy access to any feature which is significant in some way, or, as is frequently the case in many areas of the Highlands, the terrain is so challenging there is only one hiking route to the local landmarks. Most of these routes are generally only discovered when visiting the area. This makes it very difficult to plan in advance, particularly walks that are circular and those which do not involve clambering up hills and mountains. Of course the compensation is the stunning scenery, especially in the Highlands.

Fife – The Once Home of the Kings
OS MAPS: EXPLORER 371 ST ANDREWS & EAST FIFE
Fife is one of Scotland's oldest regions, squeezed between the Firth of Forth and the Firth of Tay, with the peninsula's eastern border spilling out into the North Sea. The western border of Fife butts up against the Scottish counties of Perth & Kinross and Clackmannanshire, straddling hill and mountain ranges. The names of these vary as to the source. This, no doubt, is due to the Fife's long and important history, with different generations and communities giving them a particular moniker, many of which have remained in use if not familiar to everyone. The Cleish Hills stretch into the north-western part of Fife, whilst the Lomond Hills, or the Paps of Fife as they are known locally, sweep across the more central to southern area of the county. This makes large parts of the county difficult to access from the rest of Scotland, as it often necessitates crossing a body of water.

Despite being quite small and somewhat remote from the rest of Scotland, it was an important place. Before the arrival of the Romans in the UK, and for many decades after, it was one of the seven great Pict Kingdoms of Scotland, though, during this period it was known as Fib. Even today it is often referred to as the Kingdom of Fife.

Because Fife was more southerly it became the centre of royal and political life during the reign of King Malcolm III (1058 to 1093 CE), with Dunfermline being the principal residence and the capital of Scotland. His wife, Margaret, sponsored Dunfermline Abbey, and so it became the final resting place of the royal elite, replacing Iona. Many of the

The northern border with the Firth of Tay.

kings and queens of Scotland are buried there, including Robert I (1306 to1329) whom many Scots consider a hero (Robert the Bruce) defending Scotland against the invading English. This tradition ceased in 1371 with the Stuart royal family, who preferred the city of Falkland, also in Fife. It was more convenient for hunting and other such sports, so they built a palace there, which then became the favourite place of the Scottish royal family. So it is that Fife is the ancestral home of Scottish royalty, and there is evidence of this throughout the county with castles, cathedrals and historic places to be found scattered about.

Being home to the capital of Scotland for so long, Fife has been at the heart of Scottish history. The first Scottish university was founded in 1410 at St Andrews, a town on the northeast coast. Just three years later it was formally constituted. Then in 1432 James I confirmed the charter and succeeding kings gave their support to it. The university has continued to thrive, adapting to the changing times and so maintaining its reputation. At the start of the 21st century Prince William decided to study there for his degree.

In addition to this, Fife is known all over the world as the home of golf. The Old Course at St Andrews is thought to be the oldest golf course in the world, with a document from 1552 mentioning 'playing at golf'. In fact, there are seven golf courses in and around the city, called, respectively: Old, New, Jubilee, Eden, Strathtyrum, Balgove, and the Castle, and there are more than 50 golf courses in Scotland.

In the 19th century, Fife became the centre of Victorian technology, with a huge surge in coal mining in the southern part of the county on the banks of the Firth of Forth. With bridges now able to span large areas of water, and the coming of the railways, goods became easy and cheap to transport. Villages and small towns suddenly grew with the influx of workers. Coal mining and heavy industry stopped almost completely by the end of the 20th century, however, and now the area is the home of 21st century technology with various tech companies located along the Firth of Forth.

Wonderful walks from dog-friendly campsites on a budget

Nowadays, in the northern part of the county, agriculture is important, mostly arable. There is some fishing, but not as much as there once was. With easier access, due to the bridges, and the abolition of tolls in 2008, tourism is becoming more important, and there is plenty for everyone to see and admire in this often overlooked area of Scotland, the Kingdom of Fife.

LARICK CAMPSITE

This is a medium-sized campsite of 32 pitches, 18 of which have electric hook-up and two of which are hardstanding. Adjacent is Larick Leisure Centre, which is useful for rainy days, and a café. All three of these are unusually managed by a Community Trust. Because it is a new enterprise at the moment it is a bit stark, but changes are regularly made to improve the complex, with some of them just needing time to bed in (such as the recently planted hedges and bushes). The amenities block of the campsite is very new and modern, housing comprehensive facilities including a useful drying room, reception, and the toilets and showers. The location of the campsite makes it an ideal place to spend time. Besides all the walks there are lots of other things to do, and the pub and Co-op supermarket are just 10 minutes walk away. The campsite wardens are very friendly and extremely helpful, happy to answer any questions.

The campsite next to amenities block on the left and the Larick Centre on the right.

PEARLS OF WISDOM

My tail is wagging so hard my whole body is shaking, and Pippin is rushing about all over the place because there is so much room for him. A quick bound and we are through the gate into a large green open space; ideal for chasing frisbees or balls. Another few bounds and there is a beach and the sea! Yippee! Swim time. Oh! No swimming; no water just mud – shame. Never mind, a few more bounds further on is a huge forest. So much to do and explore there, as well as meeting other four-legged companions. Every time we go through the gate it is fun, fun, fun time; different fun every time. Even going with my owner to the café is fun; Pippin and I have a special entrance AND a special table. Everyone makes a fuss of us; it's great.

RATING £££
PRICING STRUCTURE (SEE CHAPTER 3) – FLAT RATE
PROS:
- Good value for peak season.
- No charge for dogs
- Plenty of places to walk dogs
- Space to throw frisbee and ball
- Café on site
- Near bus stops
- Really helpful wardens

CONS:
- Price not available until booking process complete
- Slightly above my benchmark, but so much to do

SHORT WALK – THE LARICK AND THE LIGHTHOUSES

Distance: 4mi (6.4km)
Time: 2hr (Easy)
Terrain: Coastal paths, footpaths, footbridges, tracks, fields, open green spaces, gates, roads (quiet), lots of places for dogs to swim

Section 1: 1mi (1.6km)
- Exit via gate in right corner of campsite, out to green
- Bear left to recycling area and car park
- Bear left across green, with static vans on left, towards bin, crossing footbridge on left

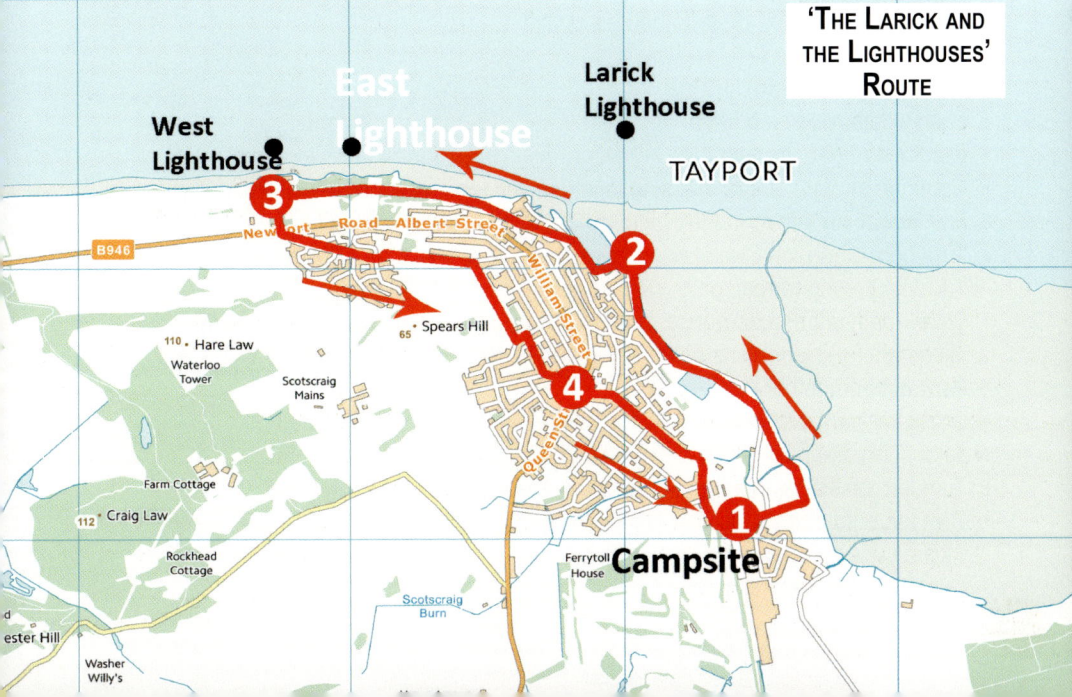

The 3rd lighthouse, the Larick, after which the campsite and community centre are named, is still standing in Tayport harbour.

- Turn right, go through zigzag barrier into caravan park, following footpath parallel to sea on right, and with caravans on left, go through gap out to small car park and playing fields on left
- Continue ahead, down steps, onto pavement, close to sea wall on right
- Turn right through gap just after left bend
- Follow narrow path along top of sea, passing houses on left, up steps, turning right along concrete path, close to houses on left

Section 2: 1mi (1.6km)
- Follow path round left bend, onto pavement, with marina on right
- Continue ahead, turning right at harbour wall around marina
- Continue straight ahead, passing toilets on left, and through gap in fence onto green
- Follow wall on left, round left bend out to road
- Turn right along Inn Street, passing slipways on right
- Turn right along tarmac path, with stone wall on right just after slipway
- Follow path left around house, onto red stony path, going uphill
- Take right fork, signposted with green arrow, out to grass space
- Bear right out to car park
- Cross car park, onto tarmac road, going downhill, with sea on right
- Take right fork, following path, with sea and two lighthouses on right
- Turn left, up steps, then right onto tarmac path (disused railway)
- Turn left onto narrow footpath between hedge on left and fence on right, away from sea with second lighthouse visible behind
- Continue ahead, up steps, and go through gate to road

Section 3: 1mi (1.6km)

- Turn left, then right at roundabout, along Scotscraig Drive, across both entrances of Scotts Crescent and Hamilton Ave, onto narrow path, passing bin on left
- Turn right at T-junction onto wide track, passing field on right, and out to road
- Continue ahead, turning right at corner of field, onto path with field still on right
- Follow path parallel to sea on left, passing footpath off left, down steps and out to road
- Turn left, then right along Provost Rd, left again at T-junction, and out to B945 with memorial on left and garage on right

Section 4: 1mi (1.6km)

- Turn right then left along Maitland Street to roundabout
- Take second exit along Mill Lane
- Bear right across green to car park
- Cross car park, keeping close to buildings on right, onto stony track leading to narrow path beside wooden fence, and out to green space
- Cross green space, bearing slightly right, out to Nelson Street
- Turn left into Shanwell Road to campsite entrance

LONG WALK – TREES AND BEACHES

Distance: 8.25mi (13.2km)
Time: 4.5hr (Easy)
Terrain: Coastal paths, footpaths, footbridges, tracks, fields, woods, beach, open green spaces, gates, roads (quiet)

An entrance to the fabulous Tentsmuir Forest, which the dogs loved.

Section 1: 1mi (1.6km)
- Exit campsite via main entrance, turning right along road
- Turn left onto tarmac path through golf course (watch out for golf balls)
- Go straight on, passing buildings on right, through small gate to the left of a large wooden gate, onto wide track, passing buildings and house on right
- Follow narrow winding path, go through gate into forest

Section 2: 1mi (1.6km)
- Bear left along wide track between trees, then through gate onto red stony track with fence on right
- Straight on at bench, passing gate to nature reserve on right (some hides situated there), continue to hide and bench at junction
- Turn first left along stony track to T-junction
- Turn right, then left again, passing car park on right
-

Section 3: 0.75mi (1.2km)
- Follow track round left bend, then round right bend, signposted Tentsmuir Forest
- Continue along winding track back into forest, turning sharp left at Fetterdale, signposted Tentsmuir Forest

Section 4: 1mi (1.6km)
- Take left fork, signposted, then left fork again, passing barrier to signpost at T-junction
- Turn left, signposted Tentsmuir Point, then take right fork

Section 5: 1.25mi (2km)
- Continue on winding path through trees (be aware of cyclists), ignoring other paths, straight across two junctions, signposted Tentsmuir Point, to very wide junction

Section 6: 1.25mi (2km)
- Turn left, signposted Tayport 3mi (4.8km), onto coastal path, passing 'March Stone'
- Turn right up slope, through gate ahead into nature reserve, then up to junction by bench
- Turn left along grass path, turning right at left bend, continue along narrow path down to beach

Section 7: 1mi (1.6km)
- Turn left, along beach, to fence across beach
- Turn left, up to footpath, then right through gate and back down onto beach
- Continue along beach, with black stone blocks on right, to beach covered with black stones
- Turn left, up onto narrow footpath, turning right along path
- Follow path, passing mound on left, to footpath parallel to beach, and sea on your right, down to beach of black stones
- Turn left onto sandy beach, passing huge stone blocks on right
- Keep left, winding around mud flats and reed beds, onto footpath, to junction signposted Tayport 1mi (1.6km)

Section 8: 1mi (1.6km)
- Bearing right, continue along beach, keeping close to dunes on left, onto wide stony track passing two bins on left, onto tarmac access road, through gate and over bridge
- Bear right across road (bus stop), onto grass path
- Turn right at junction, then left onto footpath
- Go straight ahead, onto wide grass path at bend, through recycling area
- Bear left across green, and through gate into campsite

IN THE VICINITY
FISHING
Fishing is very popular in Tayport. Check at reception for further details as to permits and local clubs.

CYCLING
With quiet roads and some dedicated cycle paths there are plenty of routes to discover. Information can be found online

Wonderful walks from dog-friendly campsites on a budget

GOLF

As the home of golf is Scotland, needless to say there is a golf club next to the campsite. Just 10mi (16km) south of Tayport is the world famous St Andrew's Golf Club. Visitors are welcome. Check online for further details and information.

BIRDWATCHING/WILDLIFE

Because Fife has a variety of habitats, there are many different birds to see, especially in The National Nature Reserve in Tentsmuir Forest. Seals can often be seen in the bay, on a rising tide.

HERITAGE TRAIL

The 4mi (6.5km) heritage trail around the town provides information about both the town and the parish, as well as the surrounding countryside. Details of the route are available from the Larick Community Centre next to the campsite.

LIGHTHOUSES

There are, in fact, three lighthouses which have played an important role in guiding shipping up the estuary. Two of them are on the banks of the estuary. The first to be built, in the early 1800s, was the Low Lighthouse (or the East Lighthouse as it is sometimes referred to). The other one is the High (or West) Lighthouse, which was built in 1832 to operate in conjunction with the East Lighthouse. There is a footpath to both these lighthouses from a nearby car park. Then, in 1848, a third lighthouse was built in the river, which rendered the East Lighthouse redundant. This third lighthouse also has two names: either the Larick or the Pile Lighthouse, as the 52ft (16m) timber frame sits on top of a series of piles driven deep into the muddy riverbed, so it can only be accessed by boat. It was abandoned in 1960, but still stands proud in the estuary, clearly visible from Tayport, home to gulls, and inspected occasionally by inquisitive dolphins.

BUSES

There are several buses that run from the town, some of which go right past the campsite entrance. Details of times and destinations are available at reception or online.

BOAT TRIPS

Just recently operational are boat trips from Tayport. The campsite reception has further details and information.

DUNDEE

On the other bank of the River Tay is Dundee. There is a regular bus from Tayport.

LEUCHARS

5mi (8km) south of Tayport is this charming town. It too can be reached by bus.

The incredible road bridge across the Firth of Forth.

West Lothian - In the shadow of Edinburgh
OSMAPS: EXPLORER 349

Stretching along the southern banks of the Firth of Forth, on each side of the capital Edinburgh and north of the Lammermuir Hills, is a region of the Scottish lowlands known as the Lothians. This is one of the most populated areas of Scotland, due partly to the presence of the capital Edinburgh.

The roots of the Lothians go back many, many centuries, so far, in fact, that the origin of its name forms part of the myths and legends of the region, so there are many versions. One suggests the name is derived from King Lot, a friend, ally, possibly even brother-in-law of King Arthur. However it acquired its name, in the 7th century the Lothians were subjugated to the ancient kingdom of Northumbria. By the 10th century, however, the River Tweed was established as the Anglo-Scottish border, so they were incorporated into the Kingdom of Scotland. As frequently happened in this area over the centuries, there was much to-ing and fro-ing of English and Scots across the River Tweed, so the 'Scottishness' is somewhat diluted. Right from earliest times it had a significant population who adopted the English language and culture, so Gaelic was never dominant.

Surprisingly, even as early as 1305, the Lothians were divided into three regions or, because they were controlled by a sheriff, 'shires':

- East Lothian stretches across to the North Sea and is the most scenic with sand hills, cliffs etc. It is also known as Scotland's Golf Coast because of the number of golf courses.
- Midlothian was the coal mining centre during the 19th and early 20th century.

Wonderful walks from dog-friendly campsites on a budget

- West Lothian is the smallest of the Lothians, and it was here that the world's first oil industry was situated. Nowadays, of more importance, the electronic and technological industries are dominant.

West Lothian was once a very rural county, and history records many different settlers spent time here because of its central location, some leaving evidence of their visit such as hill forts, some not. The discovery of coal, iron, shale and oil during the Industrial Revolution totally changed the county. The building of the Forth Rail Bridge in 1890, and the Forth Road Bridge in 1964, failed to halt the decline of heavy industry, which finally ceased by the late 20th century, to be replaced by modern technologies.

The county is heavily urbanized, partly due to its position between Edinburgh and Glasgow, making it a convenient commuter location for both cities. But also, in the area itself, there are significant employment opportunities. Despite this, it still has a rural feel. There is still significant farming, mostly in the north and west of the county, and between the towns and cities. Tourism is also important with several public country parks and nature reserves established.

The largest of these is Beecraigs Country Park, covering 915 acres (370ha), just outside Linlithgow. There is a visitors' centre where you can find information about leisure and recreational opportunities, Ranger services, and a café. The staff are most helpful and accommodating. In the park itself there is a loch, and miles and miles of forest trails. Interestingly, Beecraigs Country Park was used as a location for the TV programme *The Outlander*, since when it has become a 'must visit' place for fans.

BEECRAIGS CAMPSITE
This campsite is unusual in that it is run by the local authority (West Lothian) as part

The campsite is on the edge of the woods of Beecraigs Country Park. It is just through the barrier and into the woods.

of Beecraigs Country Park. In 1974 the council bought Beecraigs Loch when it was decommissioned as a reservoir for the nearby town of Linlithgow, along with the surrounding land. On the outskirts of the Country Park near the Visitor Centre is the large campsite. It is very spacious with 27 hardstanding pitches, all with electric hook-up, and divided into five small circular sections, each named after a tree. Between each section are large gently sloping lawns which create an atmosphere of space and privacy. The amenities block is centrally located so not too far from any pitch. It is comprehensive and very modern, with designated toilets for men and women but large unisex shower rooms. Access is via a code. Adjacent to the campsite is the visitors' centre, the check in point where there is also a shop and a café. Unfortunately dogs are not allowed in the building. This is offset by the fabulous surrounding woods.

PEARLS OF WISDOM 🐾

We were very lucky; just a bound and we were past the barrier out onto a wide black hard path, that in two wags of the tail led into the woods. This way, that way; on and on and on. Mostly the paths were this hard black stuff, but on either side it was greenish, brownish, wet and squelchy, with oodles of sticks. Oh so much to explore! Lots and lots of streams; too shallow for a swim, but also a huge lake, or loch, as they called it. Many, many places for a swim, but these funny creatures skimming along the top didn't like us, especially the big white one. My owner suddenly called us to hurry out. We lost the ball! Not to worry; plenty in the bag.

RATING ££
PRICING STRUCTURE (SEE CHAPTER 3) – COMPLICATED
PROS:
- Friendly, helpful staff
- Café on site
- Amazing amenities
- Fabulous walking; woods adjacent

CONS:
- Booking process very, very complicated
- Pricing only available when booking
- Dogs not allowed in buildings
- Only one easy route to Linlithgow

SHORT WALK – ZIGZAGGING THROUGH THE WOODS
Distance: 4.25mi (6.8km)
Time: 2.5hr (Easy)
Terrain: Footpaths, tracks, woods, some climbs, roads (quiet)

Section 1: 1.25mi (2km)
- Exit campsite at vehicle exit barrier
- Continue ahead along road, taking right fork towards house

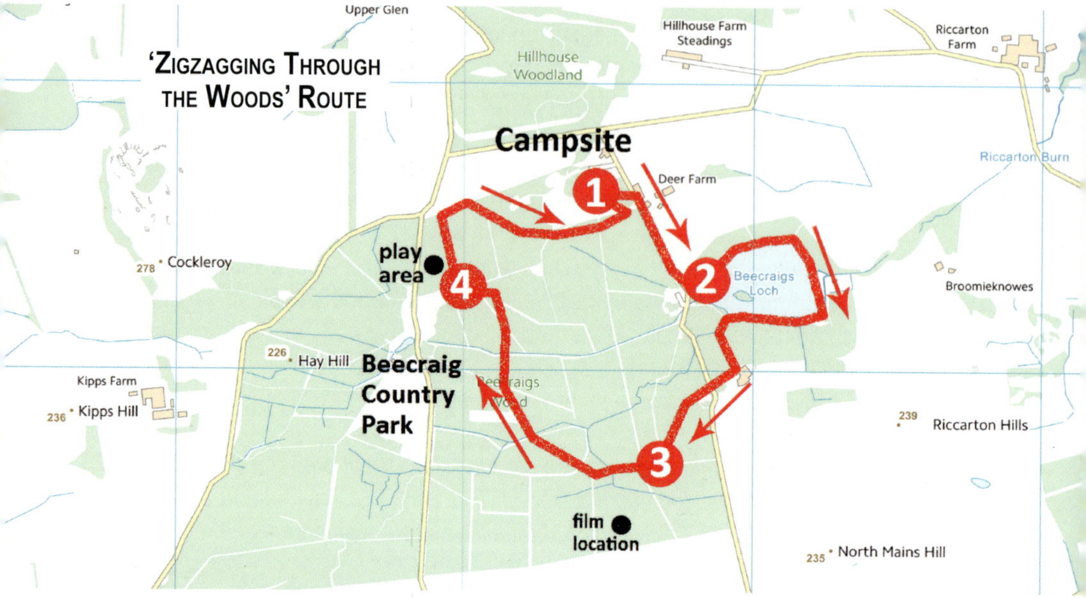

Wonderful walks from dog-friendly campsites on a budget

'ZIGZAGGING THROUGH THE WOODS' ROUTE

Upper Glen

Hillhouse Woodland

Hillhouse Farm Steadings

Riccarton Farm

Riccarton Burn

Campsite

Deer Farm

278 · Cockleroy

play area

Beecraigs Loch

Broomieknowes

1

2

4

3

226 · Hay Hill

Beecraig Country Park

Beecraigs Wood

239 · Riccarton Hills

Kipps Farm

236 · Kipps Hill

film location

235 · North Mains Hill

The loch in the woods of Beecraigs Country Park.

- Turn right along path, signposted Beecraigs Loch, going downhill parallel to road on left (look for trees growing in middle of path), go through gate and out to road
- Cross through gate opposite, turning left onto path, then left again and over wooden walkway
- Follow path around loch, taking right fork, turning right around loch, down steps and along path

Section 2: 1mi (1.6km)
- Turn left immediately after bridge, down steps onto path, with stream on left
- Follow path over footbridge, uphill, parallel to road
- Turn right by post with orange circle, through gap in wall, across road onto path opposite
- Continue ahead over footbridge, up a short very steep climb to T-junction

Section 3: 1mi (1.6km)
- Turn left along track taking right fork
- Follow path beside stream on left climbing steadily through gap in wall to signpost
- Turn right, signposted Balvormie Play Area, to T-junction
- Turn left along track, then right at open space with felled trees, crossing stream via stepping stones, onto earth track
- Continue ahead and out to tarmac path by signpost

Section 4: 1mi (1.6km)
- Turn left, then right, passing play area on left
- Follow path round right bend with stone wall on left, round another right bend, and onto track with fence on left
- Continue along track, bearing left at junction, out to barrier, to access road
- Turn left, passing barrier, back into campsite

LONG WALK – MARY QUEEN OF SCOTS BIRTHPLACE
Distance: 7.25mi (11.6km)
Time: 2.5hr (Easy)
Terrain: Footpaths, tracks, fields, green open spaces, lanes, roads (some busy), pavements, rail tracks, towpath

Section 1: 0.5mi (0.8km)
- Exit campsite via visitors' centre
- Take tarmac path opposite play area gate, towards picnic tables, turning right onto grass path just before bench
- Follow grass path with visitors' centre on right, passing noticeboards about rocks on right (amazing views), through gate out to road
- Cross through gate opposite, following path signposted Linlithgow, round right bend, up slope, round left bend parallel to road on left, to junction, signposted
- Turn right along stony track

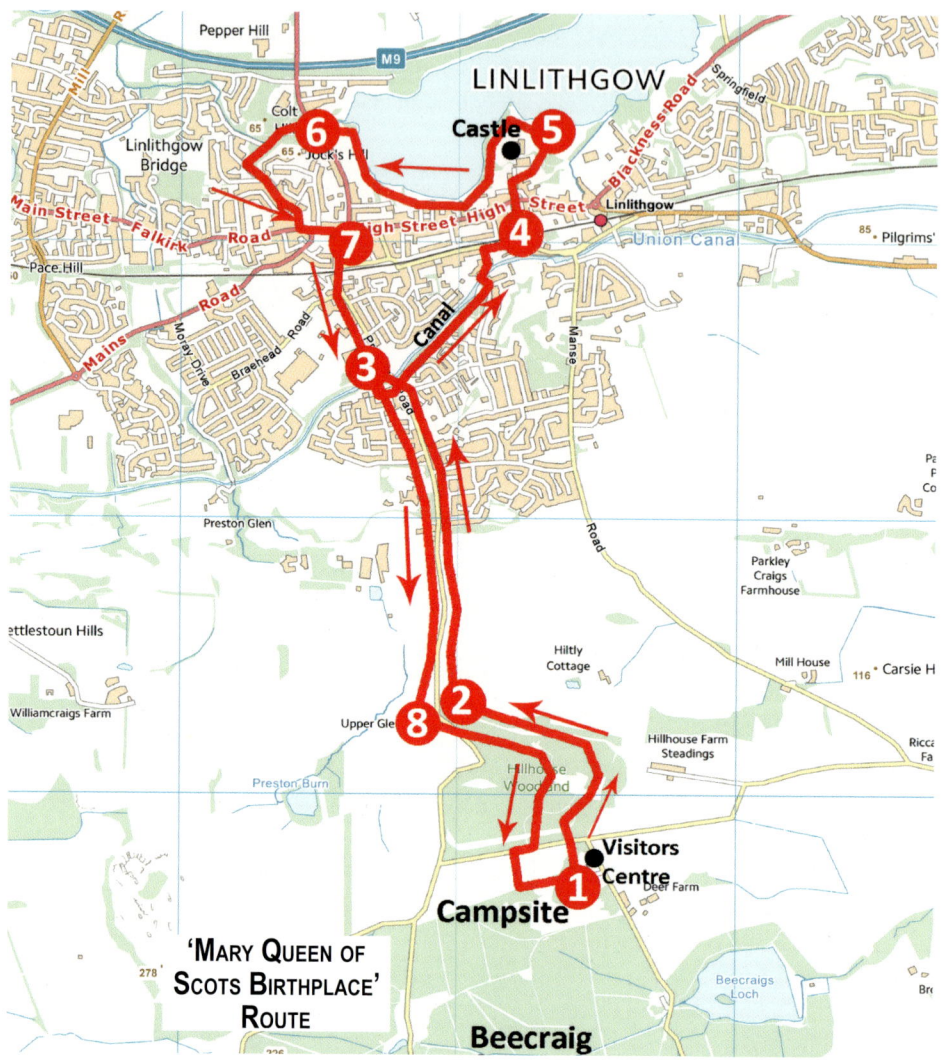

'MARY QUEEN OF SCOTS BIRTHPLACE' ROUTE

Section 2: 0.5mi (0.8km)
- Continue along stony track, gradually going downhill, round left bend, passing open space on left with amazing views (take care with dogs: open space leads to cliffs!), through gate
- Bear left through another two gates, round right bend, with road on right

Section 3: 1 mi (1.6km)
- Follow path downhill, parallel to road, through gate and out to road
- Continue straight ahead along pavement, crossing road when no pavement, go over canal bridge
- Turn left along canal access path, down to towpath

The ruins of the Palace where Mary Queen of Scots was born.

Section 4: 1.25mi (2km)

- Turn sharp left under bridge
- Continue along towpath, bearing left, up road at next bridge
- Turn left with canal on right, left again, down to main road
- Turn right along Strawberry Bank with rail-line on left
- Turn left under tunnel, round left bend, through open doorway in wall on right, down steps, out to High Street
- Turn right along High Street, then left into Kirkgate (good place for refreshments, multiple choices)
- Continue up Kirkgate, through arch into Linlithgow Palace grounds (birth place of Mary Queen of Scots)
- Turn right in front of Palace, then left across grass to loch-side path

Section 5: 1mi (1.6km)

- Turn left along path, passing Palace on left and loch on right
- Follow path around loch, passing buildings on left, and boating pontoon on right, with field (sheep) on left, over footbridge
- Take left fork, passing signpost on right, out to road
-

Section 6: 0.75mi (1.2km)

- Cross road, bearing left into Mill Lade
- Continue along road, taking left fork onto earth path, into copse, keeping close to wooden fence on left

- Take left fork, with wooden fence still on left, out to road
- Turn left along road, out to main road, Falkirk Road, with church on right
- Turn left, crossing road at pedestrian lights, turning left, and then right into Preston Road

Section 7: 1.25mi (2km)
- Continue along Preston Road, under railway bridge, over canal, uphill, crossing road at Canal Centre signpost, onto pavement on opposite side
- Turn right, continue along road, with low wall on right, through gate, onto stony track
- Follow track uphill between stone wall on right and fence on left, go through gate

Section 8: 1mi (1.6km)
- Continue round left bend into Country Park, through another gate, and round right bend
- Follow stony track, passing open space with views, round left bend, through metal zigzag barrier, out to road
- Cross road, bearing right and turning left in 39 paces, go through gate onto grass path between fences
- Turn left at T-junction, passing campsite on right, to signpost
- Turn right down to access road barrier and campsite entrance

IN THE VICINITY

BEECRAIGS VISITORS' CENTRE
At the entrance to the country park is a large visitors' centre. Those using the campsite check in here, and other visitors can find information about the park and the range of activates on offer, as well as have refreshments in the café. NB Dogs are not allowed into either the visitors' centre or the café.

FISHING
This is possible at both the loch in Beecraigs Country Park and Linlithgow Loch. Further information can be obtained at the visitors' centre or online.

CYCLING
There are a multitude of trails in the 900+ acres of Beecraigs Country Park, suitable for cyclists of varying abilities. Details, maps and leaflets are available from the visitors' centre.

BIRDWATCHING
Dotted throughout the country park are dedicated hides from which to watch the huge variety of birds.

LINLITHGOW
Just 2mi (3.2km) from the campsite is the town of Linlithgow, an interesting and delightful market town. It is an easy and pleasant walk, as there is a separate dedicated footpath to and from the town beside the main road.,

Linlithgow is most notable for the Palace where Mary Queen of Scots was born, and, next to it, the medieval church of St Michael's where she was baptized, as well as the amazing Loch they overlook. There is plenty to see in the town: the museum on High Street; the canal centre in Manse Road; and a regular market every fourth Saturday of the month. All the main places of interest are included in the Heritage Trail which can be downloaded or obtained from Linlithgow Museum or Beecraigs Visitor Centre.

Isle of Skye – The mystery of Skye

OS Maps: Explorer 411 Skye – Cullin Hills

The Isle of Skye – just the name conjures up the prospect of something special and fires the imagination. This is confirmed by *National Geographic* magazine whose readers voted it the fourth best island in the world. Why this should be the case is open to debate. Perhaps it is its history; the dispute over the land with English landowners; the battles between the clans; the unsuccessful Stuart rebellions against the unacceptable German on the English throne, with Flora MacDonald rowing Bonnie Prince Charlie to Skye to rendezvous with a French ship that would take him away to safety, and pursued by the English army. All very romantic sounding.

It could be the geography and the epic landscape that appeal. With so many

The peninsulas of Skye look like fingers pointing out into the sea.

peninsulas jutting out into the sea, and the immensely jagged coastline, it means the sea is never further than 5mi (8km) from anywhere on the island, its impact is all pervasive, providing the perfect location for all kinds of water sports, boat trips, or just walking along a beach. Then there are the Cuillin Hills that separate the long narrow peninsulas of the north from those in the south. At 3257ft (993m) above sea level, and with several munroes to be climbed, the island offers a challenge to the most experienced of hill walkers, as well as some incredible scenery.

Perhaps it is the location, being part of the mysterious-sounding Inner Hebrides group of islands. Being the largest (50mi/80km north to south), the most northerly, and yet the nearest of the islands to the mainland, it appeals to the adventurous spirit of exploring a wilderness. Until recently it could only be reached by ferry; a 45 minute trip from Mallaig to Armadale on Skye – an adventure in itself.

While ferries still sail to Skye and the other islands of the Inner Hebrides, since 1995 it has been possible to use the Skye Bridge from Kyle of Lochalsh to Kyleakin on Skye, and since December 2004 it has been toll free. Somehow this dilutes the experience. Nothing much seems to change from the road on the mainland to the one on Skye. Everything looks so 'normal' and it seems so much easier to explore the island travelling up the main A road to the north of Skye.

Very subtly, however, the landscape changes and all the roads leading off are quite different; narrower (usually single track), twisting and turning, climbing up and down, so slowly the magnificent landscape is revealed. Odd houses perched high up the hills, with seemingly no road access; were they crofts (the small farms that are found all over Scotland)? The rugged peaks are mostly devoid of trees; these all disappeared centuries ago and have never recovered due to the farming of native cattle

The campsite is informally arranged over several seemingly large disconnected grass or gravel areas.

and the introduction of sheep. This is slowly changing, due to the plans to increase the biodiversity of the island.

It might be a small island, but there are so many places to visit: the spectacular scenery that changes hue and colour according to the weather; the beaches of black sand; the charming little towns and villages, and the castles and museums. Despite being easier to reach there is still an air of mystery and magic that is unique to the Isle of Skye.

GLENBRITTLE CAMPSITE

This campsite is located at a place that feels like the ends of the earth, and yet there are hardstanding pitches, electric hook-ups and a modern amenities block with even a laundry. In addition to all this there is also a café and a small shop. Getting to the site is straightforward but adventurous. There is only one long single track road (with quite a few pot holes) winding through the glen, so it is necessary to proceed slowly and steadily making full use of the numerous signposted passing places en route. The campsite itself is informally arranged over several seemingly disconnected grass or gravel areas. This informality even carries over to the booking system: non-electric pitches are assigned on a first come, first served basis, though it is best to book for hook-up. All the amenities are at one side of the campsite, so quite far from some pitches. Also there is no phone signal, though there are small pockets of hotspots (EE) which is useful, or WiFi. There is no facility on site for recycling empty glass bottles, so it is essential to take them away with you. Bear in mind that being so remote has implications on the cost of many items for sale. The views, especially on clear days, are incredible, and the beach is a bonus.

PEARLS OF WISDOM 🐕

Finally we arrived; out over a footbridge, and wow, a beach! But, odd, it feels like the usual yellow stuff my owner calls sand, but this is black: the whole beach is black! Feels the same as the yellow stuff and the water smelt the same, so some swim time. (We went a few times to the beach, but it was so windy because of a storm my owner was hesitant, muttering about currents. I thought those were things I could eat. Peculiar.) Next to the café was a big field. This was great for chasing balls and frisbees, unless there were sheep. These pesky sheep get everywhere. Stupid animals, they look at us but we ignore them so they run away, often right where we are heading – daft! The walks were okay, mostly there and back again ones. The ground was very wet.

RATING £££
PRICING STRUCTURE (SEE CHAPTER 3) – ITEMIZED
PROS:
- Good value for solo travellers
- No charge for dogs
- Space to throw frisbee and ball (if no sheep)
- Café on site (fresh warm bread available for breakfast)

Wonderful walks from dog-friendly campsites on a budget

- Beach allows dogs all year

Cons:
- Pricey for multiple occupants (special family price)
- EHU expensive due to remote location
- Café had limited menu due to remote location (not good for gluten free)
- Limited easy walks, but plenty of hiking and hill walking trails

Short Walk – And so to the Woods

Distance: 2.25mi (3.6km)
Time: 3hr (Moderate)
Terrain: Footpaths, tracks, fields woods, some climbs, roads (mostly quiet), possibly sheep

Section 1: 0.75mi (1.2km)
- Exit campsite via kissing gate at rear of campsite, passing café on right, into field
- Go straight on along edge of field with fence on right, through gate onto wide track, with farmhouse on right, turning left through another gate
- Follow track round right bend, then left and right again, taking care to watch for sheep
- Go straight across junction through gate out to tarmac road

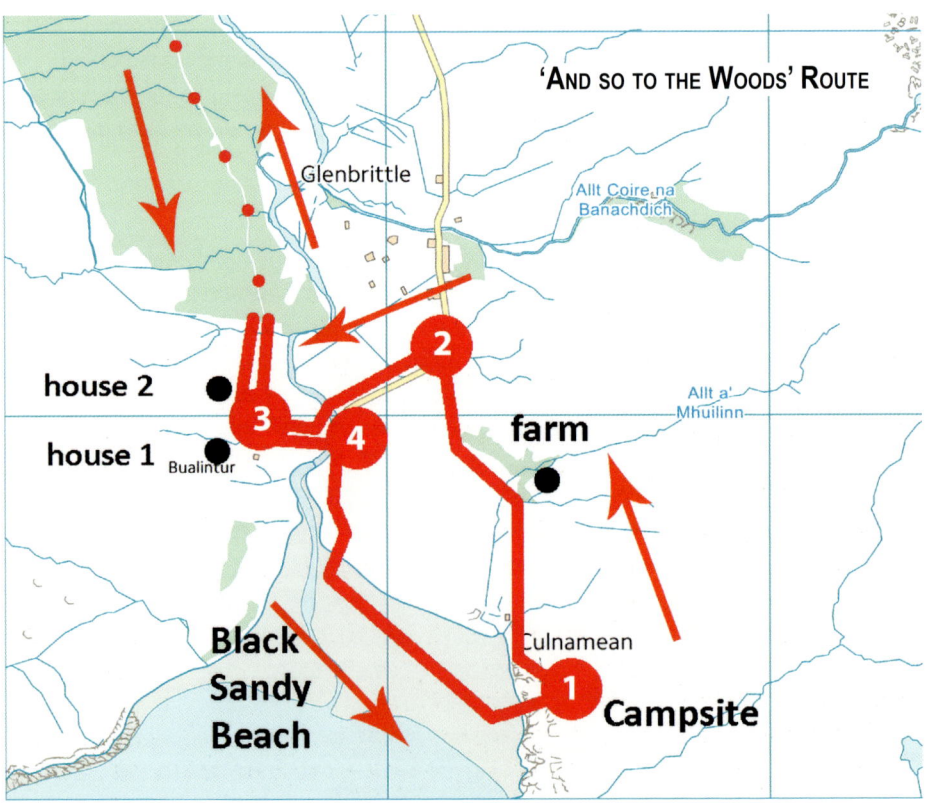

The beach of black sand with the two houses on the right, clinging to the mountainside, and with no access road.

Section 2: 0.5mi (0.8km)

- Turn left along road, go over cattle grid, through kissing gate at bend
- Follow path over footbridge, straight across junction, and through gate
- Continue along narrow path, then uphill, towards house, to T-junction
- Turn right, passing house on left, along path (very wet) through gate into woods (the views here are amazing especially of the campsite)

Section 3: (depends)

- (Use your judgement here, depending on conditions) The path through the woods is a wide track. It does not look well used. According to the map it runs parallel to the river on the right, eventually swinging round to the right to ford the river back onto the road. I didn't complete this, as I surmised the ford would be impassable due to the recent heavy rains, and it is several miles before the path is accessible again from the road. I turned around and retraced my steps to the footbridge and kissing gate out to the road. It looked very interesting to explore especially as a walking route to the Fairy Pools, but not in a storm.

Section 4: 1mi (1.6km)

- Exit kissing gate onto road, turning right towards campsite
- Follow road, turning right just before parking area, onto narrow path
- Continue downhill, along path, keeping close to fence on right, go through gate onto beach
- Turn left along beach, taking fifth exit off to left, through gate
- Continue ahead across footbridge into campsite

LONG WALK – HUNTING FOR VIKINGS

Distance: 10mi (16km)
Time: 4.5hr (Moderate)
Terrain: Rocky footpaths, wide stony tracks, steady gentle climb then descent, stepping stones across streams (some wide), amazing views (take a picnic to have en route), watch out for sheep

This is a 'there and back again' walk. I did not go all the way to the Viking canal. I stopped after about 5mi (8km) at one of the highest points on the trail and admired the view before retracing my steps back to the campsite.

Section 1: 2.5mi (4km)

- Exit campsite via footpath, passing toilet block on right, through kissing gate
- Bear slightly right, going uphill along rocky path, towards green storage tanks
- Bear right again, along path passing storage tanks on right, still climbing steadily

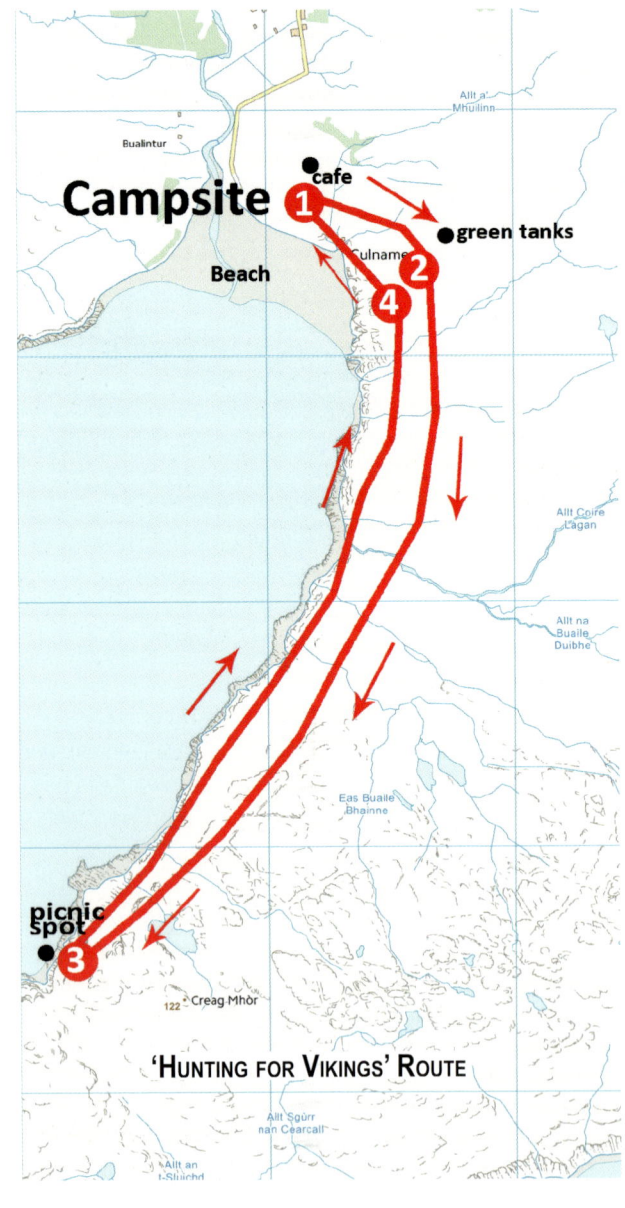

'HUNTING FOR VIKINGS' ROUTE

- Turn right at T-junction onto wide stony track

Section 2: 2.5mi (4km)
- Follow track parallel to sea on right, crossing streams via stepping stones, and passing waterfalls on left. *(It is an easy path to navigate and for walking, even though it goes very slowly uphill. Make sure footwear is appropriate as it is very wet in places.)*
- Go up a long steep climb, with views out across the Atlantic
- At top is a good place for rest and picnic (take care with dogs: steep drop on right of path)

Section 3: 2.5mi (4km)
- Retrace steps downhill, if not going on to find Viking canal
- Follow the track back down crossing streams

Admiring the view on the return leg of the walk.

Section 4: 2.5mi (4km)

- Take left fork behind storage tanks, then left again down narrow path towards toilet block, through gate into campsite

IN THE VICINITY
FISHING

With the sea so close and so many lochs, fishing of all kinds is very popular on Skye. An abundance of information as to where it is possible to fish, what can be caught, guided tours to the best rivers, boating excursions, etc, is available online.

CYCLING

This is an ideal way to explore the stunning landscape that is Skye, and there is plenty of choice with over 50 cycle routes to choose from, although many of them very hilly. The roads are mostly quiet, except during July and August when traffic increases significantly due to the influx of tourists. Information about these routes can be found online.

WILD SWIMMING

The Isle of Syke is unique in offering the whole range of wild swimming, from dips in the sea to the many rock pools scattered about. Wild swimming may be the ultimate adventure but remember to stay safe. Details of places to wild swim can be found online.

BIRDWATCHING

There is an abundance of birds of all kinds to see on Skye, including various eagles. However, it can be difficult to find them as they tend to shun busy places such as built up areas and tourist hotspots.

CLIMBING

Skye is the ideal location with numerous opportunities for rock climbing.

FAIRY POOLS

In the foothills of the Black Cuillins, about 3mi (4.8km) from the campsite in Glenbrittle is the car park for this attraction. The dramatic waterfalls and mirror like pools are about 1mi (1.6km) into the foothills. Because it is so popular with visitors the route is straightforward and easy to follow, but does require some effort as it winds its way into the mountains. It has only recently become known as The Fairy Pools. Why is unclear and it certainly does not have anything to do with fairies. In fact, it is the site of the last clan battle in 1601, between the MacDonalds of Sleat and MacLeods Of Dunvegan.

The road to the Fairy Pools is quite straightforward but is narrow, and can be busy at times. According to the OS map there is a path through the woods to the car park.

CARBOST/WATERFALLS/TALISKER DISTILLERY

At the top of Glenbrittle on the banks of Loch Harport is the fascinating village of Carbost. Besides the nearby waterfalls on Carbost Burn is Talisker Distillery, the oldest working distillery in Skye. There are regular tours of the distillery. Check online for details. Also in Carbost is the Oyster Shed, which specializes in sea food.

COIRE LAGAN

This scenic loch is surrounded by the jagged mountain peaks of the Black Cuillins. It is 2.5mi (4km) from the campsite into the foothills of the mountains. Initially the path is easy to navigate, but does becomes a bit of a scramble in places.

DUNVEGAN/DUNVEGAN CASTLE

This large village situated on the banks of Loch Dunvegan is also the site of Dunvegan Castle, the ancestral home of the Clan MacLeod. Boats leave regularly from the castle pier for the seal colony, and may also pass near dolphins and porpoises if fortunate, maybe even minke whales.

Appendix i
Countryside codes

UK Government: Rights of Way and Open Access Land
PUBLIC RIGHTS OF WAY
You can walk on all public rights of way.

Some public rights of way are also open to horseriders, cyclists and motorists. You can use –

- Footpaths – for walking, running, mobility scooters and powered wheelchairs
- Bridleways – for walking, horseriding, bicycles, mobility scooters and powered wheelchairs
- Restricted byways – for any transport without a motor and mobility scooters and powered wheelchairs
- Byways open to all traffic – for any kind of transport, including cars (but mainly used by walkers, cyclists and horseriders)

Rights of way in England, Wales, and Northern Ireland
Public rights of way are marked with signs or coloured arrows: for example, yellow for footpaths; blue for bridleways

You can find the route of public rights of way –

- On Ordnance Survey and other maps
- On some council websites

RIGHT TO ROAM
You can access some land across England without having to use paths: this land is known as 'open access land' or just 'access land.'

Access land includes privately-owned mountains, moors, heaths and downs, common land registered with the local council, and some land around the England Coast Path. Your right to access this land is called the 'right to roam,' or 'freedom to roam.'

WHAT YOU CAN AND CAN'T DO
You can use access land for walking, running, watching wildlife and climbing. There are certain activities you can't usually do on open access land, including –

- Horseriding
- Cycling
- Camping
- Taking animals other than dogs on to the land

- Driving a vehicle (except mobility scooters and powered wheelchairs)
- Water sports

    But you can use access land for horseriding and cycling if –
- The landowner allows it
- Public bridleways or byways cross the land – horseriders and cyclists can ride along these
- There are local traditions, or rights, of access

DOGS ON OPEN ACCESS LAND

You must keep your dog on a lead of no more than two metres long on open access land –
- Between 1 March and 31 July – to protect ground-nesting birds
- At all times around livestock

    On land next to the England Coast Path you must keep your dog under close control. There may be other local or seasonal restrictions, but these don't apply to public rights of way or assistance dogs.

EXCEPTED LAND

On access land some areas remain private ('excepted land'), and you **don't** have the right to access these areas, even if they appear on a map of open access land.
    Excepted land includes –
- Houses, buildings and the land they're on (such as courtyards)
- Land used to grow crops
- Building sites and land that's being developed
- Parks and gardens
- Golf courses and racecourses
- Railways and tramways
- Working quarries

    Use public rights of way to cross excepted land.

PRIVATE LAND

You may be able to access private land if the landowner has agreed to let the public use it: for example, for walking, cycling or horseriding (sometimes known as giving 'permissive access'). Look for signs.

Scotland: Outdoors Access Code 2003

Everyone has a statutory right of access to all land and inland waters, unless specifically excluded. These access rights are for outdoor recreation, and for crossing land and water.
    There are some obvious common-sense restrictions, including –
- Private houses and gardens
- Farm buildings and yards

- Farmland that has been planted or has crops growing
- School land and sports or playing fields when in use
- Golf courses (but you can cross a golf course provided you don't interfere with any rounds)
- Airfields, railways, telecommunication sites, military bases and installations, working quarries and construction sites, and visitor attractions or other places that charge for entry

ON OR IN WATER
- The access rights apply to non-motorised crafts only, and open water swimming
- Respect anglers and their desire for peace
- Take care when entering or exiting water so as not to damage the environment
- Avoid areas of commercial fishing unless you have spoken to the landowner
- Access rights extend to swimming (subject to any local bylaws)

IN WOODLAND
- Never light fires during dry periods in woodlands or on peaty ground
- Never cut down or damage trees
- Pay attention to signs, and follow any advice from the forester or land manager

ON FARMS
- Access rights do not usually apply to farmyards. However, if a right of way or core path goes through a farmyard, you can follow this at any time
- Use a gate or stile where one has been provided. Do not climb over walls or hedges unless there is no alternative
- Leave gates as you find them, even if they are open
- Keep away from fields of farm animals or growing crops
- Do not take your dog into fields containing growing crops, calves, lambs, or other young animals

HILLS AND MOUNTAINS
- Avoid areas where red stag stalking is taking place. This is usually between July and October. and notices will give full details of restricted areas
- The same applies to grouse shooting
- Do not let your dog roam near ground-nesting birds, or worry sheep or cattle
- Take responsible care when walking in hills and mountains so as not to damage the environment or disturb wildlife

WILD CAMPING
Scotland's generous outdoor access rights extend to wild camping, except where there are seasonal camping restrictions such as on the shores of the east side of Loch Lomond
- Wild camping should be lightweight, done in small numbers, and only for two or three nights in any one place

- Always responsibly consider where you are camping, and try to avoid causing problems for local people and land managers by not camping in enclosed fields of crops, or near farm animals
- Take extra care to avoid disturbing deer stalking or grouse shooting. If you wish to camp close to a house or building, seek the owner's permission

LEAVE NO TRACE
- Take away all your litter
- Remove all evidence of your tent pitch, and of any open fire
- Do not cause pollution

Country Code
www.gov.uk/government/publications/the-countryside-code/the-countryside-code

RESPECT OTHER PEOPLE
Please respect the local community and other people using the outdoors. Remember your actions can affect both lives and livelihoods.

CONSIDER THE LOCAL COMMUNITY, AND OTHERS ENJOYING THE OUTDOORS
Respect the needs of local people and visitors alike: for example, don't block gateways, driveways or other paths with your vehicle.

When riding a bike or driving a vehicle, slow down or stop for horses, walkers and farm animals, and give them plenty of room. By law, cyclists must give way to walkers and horseriders on bridleways.

Co-operate with people at work in the countryside: for example, keep out of the way when farm animals are being herded or moved, and follow directions from the farmer.

Busy traffic on small country roads can be unpleasant and dangerous to local people, visitors and wildlife: slow down and, where possible, leave your vehicle at home; consider sharing lifts and using alternatives such as public transport or cycling. For public transport information, phone Traveline on 0871 200 22 33 or visit www.traveline.info.

LEAVE GATES AND PROPERTY AS YOU FIND THEM, AND FOLLOW PATHS, UNLESS WIDER ACCESS IS AVAILABLE
A farmer will normally close gates to keep in farm animals, but may sometimes leave them open so the animals can reach food and water. Leave gates as you find them, or follow instructions on signs. When in a group, make sure the last person knows how to leave the gates.

Follow paths unless wider access is available, such as on open country or registered common land (known as 'open access land').

If you think a sign is illegal or misleading, such as a 'Private – No Entry' sign on a public path, advise the local authority.

Leave machinery and farm animals alone – don't interfere with animals even if you think they're in distress. Try to alert the farmer instead.

Wonderful walks from dog-friendly campsites on a budget

Use gates, stiles or gaps in field boundaries if you can – climbing over walls, hedges and fences can damage them, and increase the risk of farm animals escaping. Our heritage matters to all of us: be careful not to disturb ruins and historic sites.

PROTECT THE NATURAL ENVIRONMENT
We all have a responsibility to protect the countryside, now and for future generations, so make sure you don't harm animals, birds, plants or trees, and try to leave no trace of your visit. When out with your dog, make sure he is not a danger or nuisance to farm animals, horses, wildlife or other people.

LEAVE NO TRACE OF YOUR VISIT, AND TAKE HOME YOUR LITTER
Protecting the natural environment means taking special care not to damage, destroy or remove features such as rocks, plants and trees. These provide homes and food for wildlife, and add to everybody's enjoyment of the countryside.

Litter and leftover food doesn't just spoil the beauty of the countryside; it can be dangerous to wildlife and farm animals – so take it home with you. Dropping litter and dumping rubbish are criminal offences.

Fires can be as devastating to wildlife and habitats as they are to people and property, so be careful with naked flames and cigarettes/pipes at any time of the year. Sometimes, controlled fires are used to manage vegetation, particularly on heaths and moors between 1 October and 15 April, but if a fire appears to be unattended report it by calling 999.

KEEP DOGS UNDER EFFECTIVE CONTROL
When you take your dog into the outdoors, always ensure he does not disturb wildlife, farm animals, horses or other people by –
- Keeping him on a lead, or
- Keeping him in view at all times, being aware of what he's doing, and confident that he will return to you promptly on cue
- Ensure he does not stray off the path or area where you have a right of access

Special dog rules may apply in particular situations, so always look out for local signs: for example –
- Dogs may be banned from certain areas that people use, or there may be restrictions, bylaws or control orders limiting where they can go
- The access rights that normally apply to open country and registered common land (known as 'open access' land) require dogs to be kept on a short lead between 1 March and 31 July, to help protect ground-nesting birds, and all year round near farm animals
- At the coast, there may also be local restrictions that require dogs to be kept on a short lead during bird breeding season, and to prevent disturbance to flocks of resting and feeding birds during other times of year

It's always good practice (and a legal requirement on 'open access' land) to keep your dog on a lead around farm animals and horses, for your own safety and the welfare of the animals. A farmer may shoot a dog who is attacking or chasing farm animals without being liable to compensate the dog's owner.

However, if cattle or horses chase you and your dog, it may be safer to let your dog off the lead. Your dog will likely be much safer if you let him run away from a farm animal without impedance from you – and so will you.

ENJOY THE OUTDOORS

Even when going out locally, it's best to get the latest information about where and when you can go. For example, your rights to go onto some areas of open access land and coastal land may be restricted in particular places at particular times. Find out as much as you can about where you are going, plan ahead, and follow advice and local signs.

PLAN AHEAD AND BE PREPARED

You'll get more from your visit if you refer to up-to-date maps or guidebooks and websites before you set off. Visit Natural England on GOV.UK, or contact local information centres or libraries for a list of outdoor recreation groups offering advice on specialist activities.

You're responsible for your own safety and for others in your care – especially children – so be prepared for natural hazards, changes in weather, and other events. Wild animals, farm animals and horses can behave unpredictably if you get too close, especially if they're with their young, so give them plenty of space.

Check weather forecasts before you leave. Conditions can change rapidly, especially on mountains and along the coast, so turn back if in doubt. When visiting the coast, check tide times on EasyTide: don't risk being cut off by rising tides, and take care on slippery rocks and seaweed.

Part of the appeal of the countryside is that you can get away from it all. You may not see anyone for hours, and there are many places without good mobile phone signals, so let someone know where you're going and when you expect to return.

FOLLOW ADVICE AND LOCAL SIGNS

England has about 190,000km (118,060 miles) of public rights of way, providing many opportunities to enjoy the natural environment. Get to know the signs and symbols used in the countryside to show paths and open countryside. See the Countryside Code leaflet for some of the symbols you may come across.

KENNEL CLUB COUNTRYSIDE CODE

Wherever you go, following these steps will help keep your dog safe, protect the environment, and demonstrate that you are a responsible dog owner.
- Control your dog so that he does not scare or disturb farm animals or wildlife
- When using the new access rights over open country and common land, you must keep your dog on a short lead between 1 March and 31 July – and all year round near

farm animals – and you may not be able to take your dog at all on some areas or at some times. Please follow/abide by any official signs.

- You do not have to put your dog on a lead on public paths, as long as he is under close control. As a general rule, though, keep your dog on a lead if unsure about how reliably he will do as you ask. By law, farmers are entitled to destroy a dog who injures or worries their animals

- If cattle or horses chase you and your dog, it may be safer to let your dog off the lead. Your dog will likely be much safer if you let him run away from a farm animal without impedance from you – and so will you

- Take particular care that your dog doesn't scare sheep and lambs, or wander where he might disturb birds nesting on the ground and other wildlife: eggs and young will soon die without protection from their parents

- Everyone knows how unpleasant dog poo is, and a health hazard to boot, so always clean up after your dog and dispose of the poo responsibly – bag it and bin it (don't leave it hanging from a branch ...). Make sure your dog is regularly wormed to protect him, other animals, and people

Appendix ii
Campsite details

This chapter provides all you need to know about each campsite featured in the book, addresses, contact details etc, with a focus on the fee charged per night at each of these sites, as this is one of the criteria by which they have been selected for this book. As I mentioned in Chapter 3 this can be very complicated.

The price range given is as of summer 2024 for a pitch with EHU (electric hook-up) and toilets and showers on site, per night. Where appropriate I will include prices for:

- a solo traveller, weekday in low season
- a couple for the August bank holiday
- dogs (only mentioned if there is a charge)

Please be aware that due to the increased popularity of motorhoming in recent years, many of the more reasonably priced sites get fully booked very quickly, especially at weekends and during school holidays. Prices were correct at time of writing, and provide a good way of comparing the sites. Of course, all details are subject to change and prices are likely to increase year on year, so be sure to check with the respective sites before booking. I haven't included detailed directions for the sites here (as in the previous two books in this series), as SatNavs are so readily available and more reliable these days.

Wales

CAMARTHENSHIRE
Pembrey Country Park Caravan & Camping
Pembrey, Llanelli, Camarthenshire, SA16 0EJ
tel: 01554 742435 email: infopembrey@carmarthenshire.gov.uk
website: https://www.pembreycountrypark.wales/campsite
Open: Mar-Oct

CHARGES
Unit + 2 adults + EHU
- Off Peak: £26.50
- Peak: £30.00 (Peak 22nd Mar-2nd Sept)

Opinion: Good value, even though peak season is most of the year.

Wonderful walks from dog-friendly campsites on a budget

GWYNEDD
Llech Camping & Touring Site
Llechollwyn, Ynys, Talsarnau LL47 6TH
tel: 01766 781082 email: llechcamping@gmail.com
website: www.llechcamping.co.uk
Open: Mar-Sep

CHARGES
Unit + 2 adults + EHU
- £30.00 (Mar-Jun & Sep)
- £35.00 (Jul-Aug)

Opinion: Simple pricing structure. Reasonable charge. Only seven EHU pitches so booking essential.

MONMOUTHSHIRE
Parc Bryn Bach Campsite
Merthyr Road, Tredegar, Blaenau NP22 3AY
tel: 01495 355 920 email: helloparcbrynbach@aneurinleisure.org.uk
website: www.parcbrynbach.co.ukstaycation/#caravan
Open: Mar-Dec

CHARGES
Unit + 2 adults + EHU
- £30.00 (flat rate)

Opinion: Lots of activities, but poor customer care. Limited places to walk dogs off lead.

North-East
LINCOLNSHIRE
Marshland Alpacas CS (C&CC)
Oxmarsh Lane, Newholland   DN19 7EL
tel: 01469 530266/07919 263446 email: marshlandalpacascamping@gmail.com
website: https://www.marshlandalpacascamping.com
Open: All year

CHARGES
Unit + 2 adults + EHU (Grass)
- £22.00 (Sun-Thur)
- £24.00 (Fri-Sat)
- Showers £1.00

Opinion: Excellent value for money, especially in high season. Opportunity to feed alpacas.

NORTH YORKSHIRE
White Swan Inn
Newton Upon Rawcliffe, Pickering YO18 8QA
tel: 01751 472505   email: contactus@whiteswannewton.com
website: https://whiteswannewton.com
Open Mar-Oct

CHARGES
- Unit + Solo traveller £12.00
- Two people £24.00
- Three people £36.00
- Electricity metered
- Dogs free

Opinion: Good value for the single person; not bad for two people, but expensive for a family of four or more.

NORTHUMBERLAND
Highburn House Country Holiday Park
Burnhouse Road, Wooler NE71 6EE
tel: 01668 281344   email: relax@highburn-house.co.uk
website: http://www.highburn-house.co.uk
Open Mar-Nov

CHARGES
Unit + EHU
- Solo £23.00
- Couple £26.00

Opinion: Good value for bank holidays and July/August.

North-West
CHESHIRE
Lady Heyes Touring Park
Kingsley Road, Frodsham   WA6 6SU
tel: 01928 788557   email: enquiries@ladyheyespark.com
website: https://www.ladyheyespark.com
Open: All year

CHARGES
Unit + 2 adults + 2 children + 1 dog
- £21.50 (Oct-Mar)
- £28.00 (Apr-Sep)

- 2nd dog £1.00 per night

Opinion: Good value for bank holidays and July/August.

CUMBRIA
High Laning Caravan & Camping Site
Dent, Sedbergh LA10 5QJ
tel: 015396 25239 email: info@highlaning.com
website: www.highlaning.com
Open: All year

CHARGES
Unit + 4 people + EHU
- £29.50
- Dogs £2.00 each per night

Opinion: Good value especially during bank holidays and July/August (though extra for dogs).

LANCASHIRE
Rivington Brewery Campsite CS
Home Farm, Horrobin Lane, Rivington PR6 9HE
tel: 07859 248779 email: camping@rivingtonbrewing.co.uk
website: https://www.rivingtonbrewing.co.ukstaywithus
Open: Mar-Jan

CHARGES
Unit + 4 people + EHU (5 pitches as CL site)
- £20.00 (Sun-Thur)
- £25.00 (Fri-Sat)

Opinion: Good value especially weekends, bank holidays and July/August.

CENTRAL HEREFORDSHIRE
Poston Mill Park
Golden Valley, Peterchurch, Hereford HR2 0SF
tel: 01981 550225 email: poston@morris-leisure.co.uk
website: https://www.morris-leisure.co.ukcaravan-parks/poston-mill-touring-park.htm
Open: All year

CHARGES (Not including any discounts or fees)
- Solo traveller low season £31.10
- Couple bank holiday £34.60.

- Dogs £1.50 each per night

Opinion: Very complicated fee structure with various offers and discounts throughout the year, so some good deals are possible for both solo travellers and couples.

NOTTINGHAMSHIRE
Clumber Park Caravan and Motorhome Club Site
Lime Tree Ave, Worksop S80 3AE
tel: 01909 484758 / 01342 327 490   email: None
website: caravanclub.co.uk (then look for Clumber Park)
Open: All year

CHARGES
Solo traveller low season:
- £20.40 (club members)
- £35.40 (non-members)
Couple bank holiday
- £37.40 (club members)
- £52.40 (non-members

Opinion: Good value for solo travellers on cheapest pitches. Reasonable for couples on cheapest pitches in high season. Really expensive for families especially on premium pitches and for non-members in high season.

OXFORDSHIRE
Mount Farm Park Campsite
Batchelors Lane, Ratley OX15 6DW
tel: 07730 013544 / 01295 670518   email: bookings@mountfarmpark.co.uk
website: https://www.mountfarmpark.co.uk
Open: All year

CHARGES
Unit + 2 adults + EHU
- £25.00

Opinion: Excellent value, especially for weekends, bank holidays, July/August.

South-East
BEDFORDSHIRE
Rose & Crown Campsite
89 High Street, Ridgmont MK43 0TY
tel: 01525 280245 email: yexleycatering@gmail.com
website:www.roseandcrown-ridgmont.co.ukcontact Open: Mar-Oct

Wonderful walks from dog-friendly campsites on a budget

CHARGES
Unit + 2 adults + EHU
- £25.00

Opinion: Very good value, especially during weekends and high season.

BERKSHIRE
Farncombe Farm Campsite
Baydon Rd, Lambourn RG17 7BN
tel: 01488 71833 / 07836 657357 email: info@farncombefarm.co.uk
website: https://farncombefarm.co.uk
Open: All year

CHARGES
Unit + 2 adults + EHU
- £28.00

Opinion: Excellent value for money. Helpful owners who will show you around their farm 'safaris' and arrange to see a racing stable.

SUFFOLK
Sutton Hoo Holidays Campsite
Castle Farm, Sutton Hoo, Woodbridge IP12 3DJ
tel: 07484 244864 email: None (phone to book or via other websites)
website: None
Open: All year

CHARGES
- Unit + 2 adults + EHU £28.00

Opinion: Excellent value especially during high season.

South-West
CORNWALL
Teneriffe Farm Campsite NT
Predannack, Mullion, Heston TR12 7EZ
tel: 01326 240293 email: teneriffefarmcampsite@nationaltrust.org.uk
website: https://www.nationaltrust.org.uk/holidays/cornwall/teneriffe-farm-campsite
Open: Mar-Nov

CHARGES
- Solo traveller, low season £24.00
- Couple, bank holiday £38.50

Opinion: Because fees are itemized it favours solo travellers, but expensive for groups and families. Complicated fee structure. Final cost only available upon completion of booking enquiry.

DEVON
Higher Rew Caravan and Camping Park
Higher Rew Farm, Malborough, Kingsbridge TQ7 3BW
tel: 01548 842681 email: enquiries@higherrew.co.uk
website: www.higherrew.co.uk
Open: Apr-Oct

CHARGES
Unit + 2 adults + EHU
- Low Season £23.00 + £6.00 (EHU)
- High Season £32.00 + £6.00 (EHU)
- Dogs £1.00 each low season
- Dogs £3.00 each high season

Opinion: Reasonable charge for low and mid season. High season charges rather expensive. The additional charges for dogs (especially two or more) during high season make it an expensive summer outing.

DORSET
Giants Head Caravan and Camping Park
Old Sherborne Road, Cerne Abbas, Dorset DT2 7TR
tel: 01300 341242 email: holidays@giantshead.co.uk
website: https://www.giantshead.co.uk
Open: Apr-Oct

CHARGES
Unit + 2 adults + EHU
- Low season £25.00
- Peak season £30.00
- Dogs £3.00 each

Opinion: Lovely location with lovely walks; fair value. High charge for dogs makes it rather expensive

Brewery Farm Campsite
Ansty, Dorchester DT2 7PN
tel: 01258 881660 / 07900 510916 email: enquiries@breweryfarmstay.co.uk
website: https://www.breweryfarmdorset.com
Open: All year

CHARGES
- Solo traveller, low season £24.00
- Couple, bank holiday £35.00

Opinion: Discount for solo travellers, so good value during high season, but only fair value for a couple.

WILTSHIRE

Devizes C&C Club Site
Sprout Lane, Nr Sneed, Melksham SN12 6RN
tel: 01380 8288398 email: Only through the club website
website: https://www.campingandcaravanningclub.co.uk – select Devizes campsite
Open: All year
NB: An alternative to the Three Magpies Pub campsite, being situated right next to it. The walks described start from the other campsite, but can be adapted to go from here.

CHARGES
- Solo traveller low season £18.35 (members) / £26.60 (non-members)
- Couple bank holiday £40.65 (members) / £52.60 (non-members

Opinion: Good value for solo travellers on cheapest pitches. Pricey for couples on all pitches in high season. Really expensive for families and non-members.

The Three Magpies Pub Campsite
Sells Green, Seend SN12 6RN
tel: 01380 8288398 email: thethreemagpies@outlook.com
website: www.threemagpies.co.ukaccommodation
Open: Apr-Oct

CHARGES
Unit + 2 adults + EHU
- £25.50

Opinion: Excellent value for money all season for both solo traveller and couples.

Scotland
FIFE
Larick Campsite
Shanwell Road, Tayport DD6 9EA
tel: 07859952172 email: booking@larickcampsite.org.uk
website: https://larickcampsite.org.uk
Open: Mar-Dec

CHARGES
Unit + 2 people + EHU
- £31.50

Opinion: Good value during high season. Rather expensive in low season.

LOTHIAN
Beecraigs Country Park Caravan & Camping
The Visitor Centre, Linlithgow EH49 6PL
tel: 01506 284516 email: mail@beecraigs.com
website: https://www.westlothian.gov.uk/beecraigs
Open: All year

CHARGES
Unit + 2 adults + EHU
- Low Season £25.95
- High Season £32.45

Opinion: Complicated booking system. Offers available. A local authority run site. Excellent value during low season. Reasonable value during high season.

SKYE
Glenbrittle Campsite & Café
Carbost IV47 8TA
tel: 01478 640404 email: glenbrittle@dunvegancastle.com
website: https://www.dunvegancastle.comglenbrittle/campsite
Open: Apr–Oct

CHARGES
Itemized
- 1 adult £13.00 + EHU £11.00 = £24.00
- 2 adults £26.00 + EHU £11.00 = £37.00

Opinion: Excellent value for solo traveller all season. Rather expensive for a couple.

Index

Also available:

The first book in this series takes you around the country, exploring some fantastic dog-friendly campsites, and providing detailed instructions for two walks from each location.
The walks are designed to help you and your dog discover the diversity of the British landscape.
Use this book to plan a tour, or simply for an adventurous weekend getaway.

PAPERBACK • 152x225MM • 248 PAGES • 100 COLOUR IMAGES • 45 MAPS • ISBN 9781787220458

Also from Hubble & Hattie...

Written by a qualified veterinarian, this is a comprehensive text that is highly relevant (even indispensable) to every dog and cat carer. Bursting with up-to-date information on all important areas of animal health, the information in this book will help maintain good health, or offer help and support during an illness.

PAPERBACK • 24x20CM • 224 PAGES • 58 PICTURES
• ISBN: 978-1-787114-15-9